D1589118

JOHN KNOX

Other Books by this Author

The Days of Duchess Anne:
Life in the Household of the Duchess of Hamilton, 1656–1716

Mary of Guise

Virgins and Viragos: a history of women in Scotland 1080–1980

Queen of Scots

Bonnie Prince Charlie

Henrietta Maria: The Intrepid Queen

Elizabeth I

Mary I

The Winter Queen

JOHN KNOX

Rosalind K. Marshall

First published in 2000 by
Birlinn Limited
8 Canongate Venture
5 New Street
Edinburgh
EH8 8BH

http://birlinn.co.uk

ISBN 1 84158 091 0

The publishers acknowledge subsidy from The Scottish Arts Council
towards the publication of this volume.

British Library Cataloguing-in-Publication Data
A catalogue record for this book is available
from the British Library

Typeset by Palimpsest Book Production Limited,
Polmont, Stirlingshire
Printed and bound in Finland
by WS Bookwell

for my friends
Margaret Hilton and Elfriede Kaspar,
who shared my travels in the footsteps of John Knox

Contents

List of Illustrations

Acknowledgements

I SHOULD LIKE TO THANK Hugh Andrew, at that time of Canongate Books and now of Birlinn Ltd, who presented me with an irresistible challenge by suggesting that I write this book. The Very Reverend Dr Duncan Shaw and Dr Athol Murray, former Keeper of the Records of Scotland, obligingly read the text and gave me their helpful comments. Dr Murray drew my attention to the unpublished letter of Mary, Queen of Scots in the National Archives of Scotland which I quote in Chapter 14. The Kaspar family entertained me in Frankfurt with their customary generous hospitality, Inge Meyer took Elfriede and me round the old city of Geneva and Marianne Tsioli kindly showed me three non-contemporary portraits of Knox in the Bibliothèque Publique Universitaire of Geneva. Angus Armstrong sent me useful information about Geneva in the sixteenth century and the Reverend Alan Hughes explained the history of the churches in Berwick-upon-Tweed.

The owners who willingly permitted the reproduction of their paintings and photographs are acknowledged in the captions to the illustrations, and I would also thank the helpful staff of the various institutions I consulted, particularly Niki Pollock of Glasgow University Library; Deborah Hunter, Helen Watson and Susanna Kerr of the National Galleries of Scotland; Jane Thomas, Lesley Ferguson and Michelle Walker at the National Monuments Record of Scotland; Andrew Martin of the National Museums of Scotland Library, James Kilvington of the National Portrait Gallery, London and Martha Caspers of the Stadt Frankfurt am Main Historisches Museum. I am grateful to them all.

Rosalind K. Marshall
August 2000
Edinburgh

Introduction

O N THURSDAY 4 SEPTEMBER 1561, a small, sturdy man in black marched determinedly into the Palace of Holyroodhouse at the foot of Edinburgh's Canongate. He was in his late forties, with thick dark hair, a ruddy complexion and a shortish beard flecked with grey. Beneath heavy eyebrows, his dark blue eyes were keen and piercing and he bore himself with an air of authority. John Knox, respected Protestant minister of St Giles Church, had been summoned to the royal presence.[1]

She was waiting for him in the great north tower of her palace, the recently returned Queen. Less than three weeks before, on a foggy August morning, she had sailed into Leith in her stately white galley. A monarch at six days old, a bride at fifteen and a widow at seventeen, Mary, Queen of Scots had spent much of her life in France, but now she was back, a Roman Catholic ruling a Protestant realm, hearing Mass in her chapel royal and, so this man believed, threatening by her very presence all that he had been working for in recent years.

He climbed up the stairs of the tower, entered her second floor apartments and there she was, this eighteen-year-old girl, unusually tall and statuesque, like his old adversary, Mary of Guise, her dead mother. She had the dark auburn hair and brown eyes of her father's family, the royal Stewarts, and a famously fair complexion, set off by the mourning clothes she still wore for her French husband, King François II. Near her stood her half-brother, Lord James Stewart, Knox's ally and friend. But for the fact that he was illegitimate, Lord James would have been King of Scots for, like Mary, he was the child of James V and he was twelve years older than she was. Further off, at the end of the chamber, were two of the ladies of the royal household. Otherwise, Queen and preacher were alone.

The encounter between Knox and Mary, Queen of Scots that day was the first of four such confrontations, and the almost legendary tale of the preacher storming at the young monarch and reducing her to tears has done much to influence the public perception of both of them. They are two of the most colourful figures in Scottish history, and two of the most controversial. It is well known that Mary aroused violent feelings in her own lifetime and bitter debate ever since, but Knox was also the subject of furious partisanship and has subsequently undergone astonishing variations in reputation.

For centuries he was revered by Scottish Protestants as the father of the Reformed Church. Nineteenth-century historians wrote of him with deference and respect. According to Thomas Carlyle he was 'the one Scotchman to whom all others, his country and the world, owe a debt'.[2] Thomas McCrie, himself a minister, wrote a famous biography of Knox, praising him as eloquent, scholarly, active and energetic, fervent, pious, loved by his friends and with an integrity above suspicion,[3] while David Laing, who edited Knox's works, wrote in 1864, 'Well may Scotland be proud of such a man as Knox. His character rises superior to detraction, and will ever stand forth, worthy of admiration'.[4]

This has not proved to be the case. During the increasingly secular twentieth century, Knox's reputation plummeted and in the public mind he has become a caricature of himself, at worst a sinister bigot, at best a bad-tempered spoilsport who was nasty to Mary, Queen of Scots, hated people having fun, and ruined the Arts in Scotland by his narrow, Calvinist views. Feminists have fallen with cries of horror upon his outspoken criticism of female monarchs and historians have diminished his importance, suggesting that he has occupied a central place in Scottish ecclesiastical history only because the subjective version of events, which he gave in his *History of the Reformation,* is one of the principal sources for the period.

So does Knox deserve to become an obscure, forgotten figure, or was he indeed one of the most influential men in Scottish history? What was he really like, this ordinary Scot who had no qualms about haranguing a Queen and earned for himself, for several centuries at least, an extraordinary reputation? The Millennium seems an appropriate time to look for the truth.

Inset

Broughty Castle
Perth
St Andrews
Falkland
Stirling
Firth of Forth
Dunbar
Linlithgow
Edinburgh Haddington

Inset

Berwick-upon-Tweed
Norham
Alnwick
Crossraguel
Newcastle

Amersham
London
Rochester

Frankfurt

Dieppe
Rouen

Paris

Basel

Nantes

Zurich

La Rochelle

Geneva
Lyon

JOHN KNOX'S EUROPE

The Priest

THE MARKET TOWN OF Haddington stands on the banks of the River Tyne in the pleasant, fertile countryside of East Lothian. Close to the river is St Mary's, the largest parish church in Scotland. The long, grey and red sandstone Gothic building has a square tower ninety feet high which, in the early sixteenth century, was almost certainly surmounted by a crown steeple. A little way from the east end of the church, a stone bridge crosses the Tyne, and on the far side a narrow street called Giffordgate leads to the right, along the river bank. John Knox is believed to have been born in a house in that street, in about 1514. Like so much else in his early life, the date is uncertain.

Tantalisingly little is known of his first thirty years. Historians have argued and speculated about his date of birth, his birthplace, his education and his subsequent career. He himself said many years later that he came from Giffordgate. His father, William Knox, was a merchant or a craftsman in Haddington. His mother's first name is not known, but she seems to have been one of the Sinclairs of Northrig, perhaps with a sister married to George Ker of Samuelston, three miles south of the town. Knox once mentioned that his father and both his grandfathers had served in the forces of the Earls of Bothwell, who lived a few miles away at Hailes Castle. Some of these relatives had died under the Earls' standards, he said, but he gave no details.[1]

During the years he spent as a small boy in the house in Giffordgate with his parents and his brother William, Knox must often have glanced across the narrow, swift-flowing river to the east end of St Mary's, heard its bells and watched the many visitors who came to pray there. When he was old enough he was presumably sent to learn to read and write at the local song school, he would certainly have attended services in the church and he might even have sung in the choir. The great pillared nave and the many altars would have been very familiar to him. St Mary's must have been an important element in his life, giving a pattern and a sense of security, for he lost both his parents at an early age.

We do not know when or how William Knox and his wife died, and we can only assume that relatives came to the rescue of their two small sons. Whoever took them in had reasonable resources, for William was eventually able to set up in business as a successful merchant and it was decided that John should become a priest. When he was about ten John would have gone to Haddington Grammar School to study the Latin vital for an ecclesiastical career, and he must have done well, for he was then sent to university. There was not yet a university in Edinburgh, and so he had to go further afield. Haddington lay within the diocese of St Andrews, and it was to St Andrews University that he went, becoming a student of theology in St Salvator's College.[2]

Knox would have been about fifteen when he left home, sailed across the River Forth to Fife and travelled east through a rural landscape, past fields divided into long rigs, past stone, turf and wattle houses with unglazed windows, woods, mill streams and all too often dilapidated churches to Scotland's ancient ecclesiastical capital. St Andrews might be small by modern standards, but it was one of only six Scottish towns with a population of over 2000, a disproportionately high number of whom were churchmen. Far from being a place of remote and cloistered calm, it was constantly crowded as thousands of pilgrims flocked each year to the cathedral, and the castle was the residence of James Beaton, Archbishop of St Andrews and former Lord Chancellor of Scotland. About a year before Knox's arrival, in 1528, a young man named Patrick Hamilton had been burned at the stake for heresy, just outside the archway leading in to St Salvator's College, and, if Knox had not encountered Protestantism before, he must surely have heard all about it now from his fellow students.

A century and a half earlier, persecuted followers of the English reformer, John Wycliffe, fled north and settled in Kyle, Ayrshire. Ever since then, there had been sporadic but increasing criticism of the Roman Catholic Church. In part, this took the form of theological argument. Did the bread and wine really become Christ's physical body and blood at the Mass? Could people confidently assure their future in the next world by endowing Masses, going on pilgrimages and purchasing papal indulgences? Was there any point in venerating the supposed relics of saints? Must all services be in Latin, with the priest as the necessary intermediary between God and man? There was also serious criticism of the behaviour of ecclesiastics, for everyone had heard about the illegitimate sons of kings and noblemen, given positions in the Church simply as a means of providing them with financial support. Most people had first-hand knowledge of uneducated monks and nuns living in idleness, parish priests who never preached and church dignitaries with luxurious residences, bastard children and worldly preoccupations.[3]

Wycliffe had openly attacked these abuses, issuing pamphlets in English instead of Latin, urging people to read the Bible for themselves and even arguing that wicked rulers, by their sins, forfeited their right to rule. His followers were scathingly known as Lollards, from a Dutch word meaning 'mumblers', and the church authorities did their best to stamp out the movement, in Scotland as well as in England. A Lollard named James Resby was burned as a heretic in Perth in 1407, and in 1433 Paul Crawar, a Bohemian studying at St Andrews University, was arrested and burned at the stake because he was a follower of John Huss, a Bohemian reformer influenced by Wycliffe. Even so, Lollardy persisted in the west of Scotland and several Lollards narrowly escaped execution in 1494.[4]

Twenty-three years after that, Martin Luther, a German priest, pinned to the church door at Wittenberg his famous ninety-five theses, criticising the abuses of the Roman Catholic Church, and Lutheranism spread rapidly throughout Germany and beyond. Printed pamphlets criticising the Church were smuggled into Scotland from the Low Countries, on ships sailing to Leith, Dundee and other east coast ports and soon Scots were able to obtain copies of William Tyndale's English translation of the Bible, published on the continent.[5]

Patrick Hamilton had been a member of a younger branch of the powerful Hamilton family and was a distant relative of King James V. He had first encountered Lutheran doctrines while studying in Paris and Louvain, and had later sought out Martin Luther, Philip Melancthon and other leading reformers, openly discussing his controversial views when he returned to Scotland. However influential his connections, the Roman Catholic Church was not going to tolerate his activities, and he was suddenly arrested, tried and burned at the stake on 29 February 1528. Far from quenching heresy, however, his death made him a martyr and Protestant doctrines spread rapidly, especially at St Andrews University.[6]

Knox was not one of those who adopted the new religion. It is almost certain that he studied theology with the internationally famous scholar John Mair, a native of East Lothian, graduate of Cambridge and Paris, and much-admired Professor at the Sorbonne. Although Mair was a leading exponent of the old-fashioned scholastic theology with its all too often complicated and arid arguments, he held surprisingly up-to-date views on contemporary affairs. He criticised the abuses of the church and the idle pomp of many of the ecclesiastics living in Rome and he even turned his attention to recently discovered America, arguing that people there had the right to depose any colonial ruler who abused his position. Monarchs were chosen by God, he said, but ultimately their authority derived from the people they governed. In a society which saw the world in strictly hierarchical terms, these were startling views indeed.[7]

If Knox was excited by these new ideas, he showed no sign of deviating from his chosen career, but he could not have failed to observe the abuses of the Church which were just as prevalent in his own small country as they were elsewhere. Wealth and power lay not only with the monarch and the nobility but with the Scottish Church. Indeed, by the 1560s the Church's yearly revenues would be in the region of £400,000 compared with the crown's income of around £40,000 per annum.

There was nothing wrong with a well-endowed and fully-staffed ecclesiastical organisation, of course, but it was obvious to every one that the money was not being used in the way in which the donors intended. Most of it went to religious houses, cathedrals and universities rather than being used locally. As a result the parish churches were all too often dilapidated and the vicars poorly paid, while monks idled away their time in their own comfortable chambers. The heads of the monasteries and abbeys were frequently laymen, the sons of noblemen, given the office of commendator to sustain them financially. No fewer than six of King James V's illegitimate sons would become commendators of abbeys and, to make matters worse, such men were often able to pass their benefices from one generation of their family to the next. Moreover, although Canon Law forbade the sale of ecclesiastical lands, more and more churchmen were feuing their property to ambitious laymen.[8]

A number of leading Roman Catholics were anxious to improve matters from within the church, but in the face of strong vested interests it was no easy task. It was, however, perfectly possible to acknowledge the Church's failings without espousing the reformed doctrines and Knox may have looked at the problem from this point of view during his university days. His relatives had given him the opportunity of making his way in the world by sending him to St Andrews and there is little doubt that he was a diligent and successful student. He was not going to risk his future by becoming involved with a vocal and rebellious minority group. According to Theodore Beza, the friend and successor of the famous reformer John Calvin, Knox had a distinguished academic career.[9] No written evidence of it has survived, and there is no record of his graduation, but when he left the University he became a priest and in later life was always known as 'Mr Knox', the implication being that he had a degree.

He was not, however, appointed to a parish. Scotland was a small country with a population of some 300,000. There were probably about 3,000 priests, too many for the available parishes. Like other newly ordained men, he had to look elsewhere for a means of earning his living. His activities during the late 1530s are unknown, but by 1540 he had managed to find a position as a notary apostolic in East Lothian. This meant that he had become a country lawyer. He may or may not have had some legal training. John Weddell, several times Rector of St Andrews University and later a judge, probably taught law as well as arts at St Andrews. As he was also the official of Lothian responsible for the training of notaries, he may have found Knox the position.[10]

Notaries apostolic were actually appointed on papal authority and represented their clients in the church courts. Much of their work, however, was done in private houses, drawing up title deeds, marriage contracts and wills, and sorting out minor financial disputes. By nature an energetic man with a keen sense of responsibility for others, Knox at this time must have learned to listen to people's troubles and settle their quarrels with a firm hand. He did not do this work in Haddington itself, but he was based at Samuelston, very likely living with his mother's relatives, the Kers.

On 13 December 1540, Knox enters the written records at last. He appeared that day at Haddington market cross on behalf of James

Ker of Samuelston and two years later he and Ker were umpires in a minor financial dispute. In 1543 he was acting for Ker's niece, Elizabeth Home, Lady Hamilton of Samuelston, the divorced wife of James, 1st Earl of Arran. When he next features in the records, he was definitely living in Ker's house, and was apparently acting as tutor to a boy named William Brounefield, and possibly to Ker's own sons as well. Like so many other aspects of Knox's early life, the timing of his career change is hidden from us. There is no personal correspondence, no notebook or memorandum, no hint in his later writings to tell us when exactly he abandoned the law in favour of teaching. The reason for this shift is obvious, however. He had become a Protestant.[11]

He does not seem to have undergone a sudden conversion, or if he did he never mentions it. It is more probable that, disgusted with what he saw of the corruption of the church, he spent long hours studying the Bible, particularly the Old Testament, and managed to obtain copies of some of the new Protestant tracts, not just Lutheran writings but some of those produced by the Swiss reformers. He may have wrestled with his conscience for some time. Indeed, he would later sympathise deeply with those who experienced dreadful doubts about adopting the reformed religion. Some time in 1543 his decision was finally made, not least because it was suddenly safe to admit to being a Protestant.

In December of the previous year, King James V had died. Throughout his reign he had remained firm in his allegiance to the Pope and the Roman Catholic Church. Even when his uncle, Henry VIII of England, had broken with Rome and urged him to do likewise, he had refused. Instead, James strengthened Scotland's traditional alliance with Roman Catholic France by marrying Princess Madeleine, daughter of the French king. When she died, he replaced her with a tall, handsome, aristocratic French widow, Mary of Guise. Relations between Scotland and England were by now deteriorating rapidly, and in November 1542 James V's army was defeated by Henry's at the Battle of Solway Moss. Distraught, he took to his bed and died soon afterwards, leaving a six-day-old daughter Mary, to become Queen of Scots. James Hamilton, 2nd Earl of Arran, was appointed Regent, to rule the country for her.[12] The Lord Governor, as Arran was known, was not only head of the powerful House of Hamilton. Because there were no close royal relatives, he was also heir to the throne. Should the infant Queen die, he would become King. Personal ambition was always the principal concern of this shifty, indecisive descendant of a Stewart princess, but for once considerations of national safety had priority over everything else. Fearing that an English army would invade Scotland, Arran and his fellow noblemen made peace with England, agreeing that Mary, Queen of Scots should marry Henry VIII's son, Prince Edward. Suddenly, the Lord Governor was encouraging the spread of Protestantism.[13]

Against the background of those events, Knox gave up his notarial appointment, started teaching William Brounfield's son and went to hear a Protestant preacher who was visiting the area. Anxious to convince Henry VIII that his conversion was sincere, Arran was encouraging the distribution of the Bible in English and he appointed two Protestant chaplains to preach throughout the country. One of them was Thomas Guillaume, formerly Prior of the Black Friars of Inverness. Originally a native of East Lothian, he was sent there by the Lord Governor. After hearing him, Knox decided that he 'was of solid judgment, reasonable letters (as for that age) and of a prompt and good utterance: his doctrine was wholesome without great vehemency against superstition' (meaning Roman Catholic practices).

Not long after Guillaume's visit to East Lothian, Arran's other chaplain, John Rough, arrived and Knox went to hear him too. He liked him even better, for although Rough was 'not so learned', he was 'more simple and more vehement against all impiety'. By now, Knox had moved from Samuelston to Longniddry, a few miles away, to become tutor to the sons of Sir Hugh Douglas. Sir Hugh had his own private chapel, and the local people came to listen when Knox catechised the boys and instructed them in the Bible. He was a priest no longer, but a Protestant teacher, and if he had any lingering doubts these were soon dispelled when he encountered a third travelling preacher, George Wishart.

Out of the pulpit, Wishart was not a particularly impressive man, tall, thin and fastidious rather than robust and forceful. When he began to speak, however, his audience listened with rapt attention, for he was a truly charismatic preacher. Wishart was about the same age as Knox. Born around 1513, in Angus, he had been forced to leave Scotland in 1538 when the Church charged him with heresy, and he had continued his studies on the continent. Travelling to England, he settled at Corpus Christi College, Cambridge but he was soon in trouble once more with the authorities. He decided that he would be safer in Scotland and returned in 1543, preached to large crowds in Dundee and Montrose, visited Ayrshire, and moved to Lothian after two attempts were made on his life. It was then that Knox encountered him and was deeply impressed. Knox swiftly became a member of the little band of friends and admirers who guarded Wishart as he travelled from one safe house to the next. It was usually Knox who carried a large, two-handed sword before Wishart, to frighten off his enemies.[14]

This precaution was all the more necessary because Protestantism was no longer being encouraged by the authorities. Soon after Wishart's return to Scotland, the Regent Arran had reverted to Roman Catholicism. In a way, this was hardly surprising, for Arran was notorious for changing his mind. If he was with you before dinner, one contemporary observed, he would be against you after it. Not everyone at Court had agreed with his desire to marry Mary, Queen of Scots to Henry VIII's son. The young Queen's mother, Mary of Guise, was bitterly opposed to the arrangement. She could not contemplate her daughter becoming the wife of an English heretic. If she had been made regent, the treaty would never have been signed, but at the time of her husband's death she had been in no position to oust Arran. She had been lying in Linlithgow Palace, recovering from the birth of her child. Unable to seize power, she had been forced to go along with Arran's arrangements, but she was determined to change them.

Equally against the English match was Arran's dynamic cousin, Cardinal David Beaton. In his one surviving portrait, Beaton is seen in his scarlet robes, with neatly trimmed beard and moustache, the very epitome of the worldly, sophisticated prince of the Church. French-educated, he had combined a diplomatic career with his ecclesiastical offices. He became a cardinal in 1538, succeeded his uncle, James Beaton, as Archbishop of St Andrews the following year, and in 1543 was appointed Chancellor of Scotland. Mary of Guise and he were rivals for power, but, as an energetic proponent of the French alliance, he persuaded Arran that Scotland must break the marriage treaty with England and return to the traditional friendship with France. Arran meekly gave in and, on Beaton's insistence, did public penance for having supported the Protestants.

Henry VIII was furious. He launched the series of devastating invasions of Scotland known as 'The Rough Wooing'. 'Put all to fire and the sword', he ordered his commander, the Earl of Hertford. 'Burn Edinburgh town, so razed and defaced when you have sacked and gotten what you can of it, as there may remain forever a perpetual memory of the vengeance of God lightened upon the Scots for their falsehood and disobedience.' During the next four years, his men set fire to the Abbey of Holyrood where James V lay buried, destroyed crops at harvest time, and burned the Border abbeys of Melrose, Jedburgh and Dryburgh. Protestant England had become the enemy once more, Roman Catholic France the friend.[15]

In the week after Christmas 1545, Wishart almost despaired. He had returned with high hopes of a Protestant revolution, but now it seemed that the people, once so eager to hear him preach the new religion, were about to abandon it and return to their old faith. He went to Haddington in the early days of January 1546 and members of the congregation arranged for him to preach in St Mary's. There was a good audience for his first sermon, but when he preached again in the afternoon, the numbers had fallen dramatically. The Earl of Bothwell, the local landowner, had taken French bribes and, when he heard about Wishart's presence, he ordered his tenants to stay away.

Wishart spent that night at Lethington Tower (now Lennoxlove) and rode back down the hill to St Mary's the following day, again to find a sparse congregation. That afternoon, he received a letter from Protestants in the west excusing themselves from coming to a meeting in Edinburgh. Deeply upset, he called Knox over and told him about it, saying sadly that he 'wearied of the world', for he saw that 'men began to weary of God'. Knox was dismayed. He knew that Wishart usually liked to spend the time before a sermon in quiet contemplation, by himself, removed from worldly concerns. Taking the letter from Wishart, he said 'Sir, the time of sermon approaches' and he went away, leaving his friend to pace up and down behind the high altar, beneath the great pointed east window of the church.

That afternoon, Wishart preached his final sermon, warning his congregation that a fearful fate awaited them if they ignored the word of God. In those familiar surroundings, known to him since childhood, Knox listened as his admired mentor described how Haddington would be plagued by fire and the sword and occupied by foreigners if they did not mend their ways. There was an atmosphere of deep foreboding in the church, and when Wishart came down from the pulpit, he went over and said goodbye to his followers.

John Cockburn, the Laird of Ormiston, had invited Wishart to spend the night at his house, as he often did. Knox lifted up the big, two-handled sword and prepared to accompany him as usual, but Wishart stopped him. 'Nay,' he said, 'return you to your bairns', meaning Knox's pupils, and he added ominously, 'and God bless you. One is sufficient for a sacrifice.' Knox protested, of course, but Wishart was adamant, and Knox always treated him with reverence and respect. Reluctantly, he relinquished the sword and returned to

Longniddry, while Wishart set off for Ormiston on foot, with two or three companions. The ground was so hard with a heavy frost that it would have been dangerous to ride.

Knox reached Sir Hugh Douglas's house safely. Wishart arrived at Ormiston, had supper, and then sang Psalm 51 with his companions: 'Have mercy on me now, good Lord.' They went to bed after that, but they were roused before midnight by a loud banging and shouting outside. The Laird got up and went to the door, to find the Earl of Bothwell there, demanding that he hand over Wishart. The Laird refused indignantly, but Bothwell said that the Regent Arran and Cardinal Beaton were on their way to Ormiston with all their men. If the Laird handed Wishart over then he guaranteed that the preacher would be unharmed. Thoroughly alarmed, the Laird consulted Wishart, who said simply, 'Open the yetts [gates]. The blessed will of my God be done.'

At that, Ormiston allowed Bothwell to come in with some of his gentlemen, and Wishart said to the Earl, 'I praise my God that so honourable a man as ye, my Lord, receives me this night in the presence of these noble men, for now, I am assured, that for your honour's sake, ye will suffer nothing to be done unto me besides the order of law.'

Bothwell answered, 'I shall not only preserve your body from all violence that shall be purposed against you without order of law, but also I promise, here in the presence of these gentlemen, that neither shall the Governor nor Cardinal have their will of you, but I shall retain you in my own hands, and in my own place.'

With that, Bothwell took Wishart away, first to Edinburgh and then back to his own castle at Hailes. Cardinal Beaton was, however, determined to get this notorious heretic into his custody and the result was that Bothwell, ignoring the promises he had made, handed over his prisoner. The Cardinal promptly took Wishart to St Andrews, where he imprisoned him in his own castle. John Knox would have heard the terrible news at Longniddry. When he wrote his famous *History of the Reformation* many years later, he described his friend's arrest in considerable detail, but he ended his account with Wishart being taken to St Andrews. At that point, his pen faltered, and instead of describing what happened next, he simply appended to his text the description of events given in Foxe's *Book of Martyrs*.[16]

On 1 March 1546 Wishart was tried by an ecclesiastical court in St Andrews Cathedral. Cardinal Beaton presided. The preacher denied that he was a heretic, saying that he had taught only what was in the scriptures. His protests were to no avail. The Cardinal pronounced the death sentence, and Wishart was taken back to his prison. The captain of the castle gave him some supper and then prepared him for his ordeal. Wishart was dressed in a buckram coat, the pockets and sleeves stuffed with small bags of gunpowder so that when he was tied to the stake and the fire reached him, the flames would blaze up more fiercely and hasten his end. His hands were tied behind his back, a noose was placed round his neck, and an iron chain was fastened round his waist. He was then led outside, to the east part of the castle. Fearing a last minute attempt to rescue him, the Cardinal had ordered his castle guns to be trained on the place of execution.

Wishart knelt down to pray, and made his final speech, urging the bystanders not to turn against the true religion because he was about to suffer for it. They must continue to learn the Word of God which he had taught them, 'For this cause I was sent, that I should suffer this fire for Christ's sake. Consider and behold my visage, ye shall not see me change my colour. This grim fire I fear not.' Forgiving those who had condemned him, he turned to the hangman who was waiting close by. He forgave him too. He was then strung up on a gibbet, cut down, still alive, and tied to the stake, where he died in the flames. Cardinal Beaton and the Archbishop of Glasgow watched with satisfaction from the east blockhouse of the castle.

Appalled by George Wishart's death and hunted by the church authorities ever since the night of Wishart's arrest, Knox had been forced into hiding. Still in East Lothian, he was moving constantly from one safe house to the next. Meanwhile, Protestants in Fife were vowing vengeance on Cardinal Beaton and, in the early hours of Saturday 29 May 1546, they gathered in the Priory churchyard near St Andrews Castle. They knew that at about 5 o'clock in the morning, when daylight came, the castle gates would be opened so that building materials could be brought in. Aware that he had many enemies, Beaton was strengthening his already formidable fortress. The conspirators waited and watched, and sure enough down came the drawbridge.

William Kirkcaldy of Grange, son of a Fife laird, immediately went over to the porter who guarded the entrance. Was the Cardinal awake, Kirkcaldy asked. He was not, said the porter. As he spoke, Kirkcaldy's companions pushed past. Alarmed, the porter shouted to the castle guards to raise the drawbridge again, but it was too late. John Leslie, brother of George, 4th Earl of Rothes was halfway over and he leaped down into the castle while his companions hit the porter over the head, took his keys and threw him into the moat. Hearing the commotion, more than a hundred workmen came running down from the walls and rushed through a small wicket gate to safety. Kirkcaldy stood guard at the privy postern gate, while his companions ran through the narrow passages of the castle until they reached Beaton's quarters. By this time, the Cardinal had been roused by the noise. Crossing his bedchamber, he shouted from his window, demanding to know what was happening. An unknown voice replied that John Leslie's nephew Norman, Master of Rothes, had taken the castle.

Realising that his enemies were upon him, Beaton fled towards the postern gate but, seeing that the outside passage was guarded by the intruders, he ran back to his chamber, snatched up his sword and ordered his servant to barricade the door. Kirkcaldy and the others were just behind him. They tried to force the heavy door, but it was too strong for them. Someone brought a brazier full of burning coals. They would smoke out the Cardinal. Sure enough, no sooner had the smoke seeped into the room than there was the sound of furniture being moved, and the door swung open.

Inside, they saw Beaton sink down on to a chair. He had dropped his sword, and was making no attempt to defend himself. 'I am a priest!' he cried. 'I am a priest! Ye will not slay me!' Ignoring his pleas, John Leslie and Peter Carmichael of Balmedie struck furiously at him with their daggers until James Melville of Carnbee dragged them back. They must not kill Beaton in anger, he told them. They were carrying out God's judgement, and they must act with greater gravity. So saying, he pointed his sword at Beaton and declared, 'Repent thee of thy former wicked life, but especially of the shedding of the blood of that notable instrument of God, Master George Wishart, which albeit the flame of fire consumed before men, yet cries it a vengeance upon thee, and we from God are sent to revenge it.'

With that, he ran his sword several times through the Cardinal's body, and Beaton fell dying.

'I am a priest, I am a priest!' he moaned, and then, 'Fie, fie, all is gone.'[17]

2

The Galley Slave

WHEN THE CITIZENS OF St Andrews saw the panic-stricken workmen streaming out of the castle, they realised that something was badly wrong. Word spread swiftly and, led by the provost, three or four hundred people ran down to stand at the edge of the moat, gazing anxiously across. 'What have ye done with my Lord Cardinal?' the provost shouted. 'Where is my Lord Cardinal? Have ye slain my Lord Cardinal? Let us see my Lord Cardinal!' The conspirators in the castle took a pair of sheets, tied them to one arm and one leg of the dead man, and hung him over the wall for all to see. The murderers then barricaded themselves in.

The whole country was shocked by the assassination, and eight days later Arran, Mary of Guise and the Privy Council met at Stirling to decide how the death of Scotland's primate and Lord Chancellor should be avenged. It was decided that Arran would have to assemble an army and besiege the castle. This he did, but his efforts were less than successful. He did not have enough men and he was reluctant to mount an all-out attack, for Beaton had been holding hostage Arran's eight-year-old son, Lord James Hamilton, and the boy was still inside. The Lord Governor was likewise unwilling to call on French help, for he secretly harboured hopes of marrying his son to Mary, Queen of Scots and he did not want the little Queen to fall into French hands.

The siege dragged on. Arran had thought that he could starve out the Castilians, as the murderers came to be called, but they managed to get supplies by sea and dispatch messengers to London, begging Henry VIII to send an army to help them. Arran decided to play for time and negotiate a truce. Conscious that their own situation was desperate, the Castilians indicated their willingness to talk, and it was eventually agreed that they could stay where they were until Arran got them papal absolution for their crime. When that arrived, they were to hand the castle over to the Lord Governor, who would allow them to go free and unpunished. In the meantime, the Castilians would continue to hold Lord James Hamilton as a pledge for his father's good faith. Arran had no intention of keeping his promises, and the Cardinal's murderers knew it, but an uneasy calm descended. The Castilians were allowed to come and go from the castle as they pleased, and so were their Protestant friends. More than 120 supporters eventually joined them inside its walls.[1]

The first anniversary of Wishart's death passed, and on 28 January 1547 Henry VIII died. His young son succeeded to the throne as Edward VI, with his uncle the Protestant Earl of Hertford, now Duke of Somerset, ruling as Lord Protector. Known to his colleagues as a big, handsome, affable man with liberal views, it was nonetheless he who had led the expeditions into Scotland during the Rough Wooing and he was still determined to keep the Scots to their promise that Mary, Queen of Scots should marry Edward. When the emissaries from the Castilians arrived in London, he received them in a friendly fashion. They gathered with relief that another English army would soon be marching into Scotland.[2]

In a state of bitter grief and apprehension, Knox was now speaking of leaving the country. He told friends that he was thinking of seeking refuge in Germany, where he could live and study until more peaceful times returned. Horrified, they urged him to stay. With his energy and his strong convictions, he was one of their best hopes for the future. Sir Hugh Douglas of Longniddry and John Cockburn of Ormiston hastily devised an alternative plan. Why did he not take their sons and go to St Andrews Castle, as other Protestants were doing? They would be safe there, and they could continue their studies together until the English army arrived. Knox was doubtful, but in March 1547 word came that François I of France had died. His son, Henri II, was well disposed towards Mary of Guise and her daughter and would presumably intervene on their behalf. Knox decided to accept his friends' advice and at Easter 1547 he rode to St Andrews with his pupils, Francis and George Douglas and young John Cockburn.

Safely installed in the castle, they resumed their lessons. Knox taught the boys grammar, the classics and theology, taking up his examination of his favourite gospel, the Book of John, where he had left off just before Wishart's arrest. He held his lessons in the chapel. Soon, many of the Castilians were coming to listen. Possibly Arran's son took part. Certainly John Rough, previously Arran's chaplain, was amongst this informal audience, and so was Henry Balnaves of Halhill, a graduate of St Andrews, judge and former ambassador. Much impressed by what they heard, both men urged Knox to become a preacher. He refused. He could not do it, he said, unless God called him to the task.

His reluctance may seem to us uncharacteristic, in view of what is generally known of his later career, but it was a reflection of the seriousness with which he regarded the role of preacher. There were practical considerations too. No longer a priest within the shelter of the established Church, he would have a high-profile role at a time of national crisis and the dangers were all too apparent. Supposing the English army did not come in time, he could be captured, handed over to the Church authorities and sent to the stake. Apart from such fears for the future, he was worried about his own capabilities. The supremely self-confident, unassailable Knox of later legend was in reality a sensitive man, at that stage tormented by uncertainty. Rough and Balnaves might think that he could be useful, but would others accept him, a renegade priest, as their minister? All else apart, how could he ever measure up to his revered master, George Wishart?

Having identified a promising colleague, Balnaves and Rough were not about to accept his refusal. Protestant preachers were few and far between, with the result that Rough was dreadfully overworked and desperate for someone to share his burden. He was becoming increasingly involved in public disputes with the Roman Catholic authorities in St Andrews and he was well aware that he was no scholar. He had recently been plagued by difficult questions from John Annand, Principal of St Leonard's College and, to his relief, Knox had always been ready to supply the answers he needed. Knox was the obvious person to take up the debate with these troublesome priests.

Rough and Balnaves sought the advice of Sir David Lindsay of the Mount, who was currently staying in St Andrews. Scotland's chief herald, the author of *A Satire of the Three Estates*, a scathing attack on the abuses of the Roman Catholic Church and an experienced diplomat, Lindsay would know how best to persuade Knox. They discussed tactics together and decided that he should be asked again, in public, with no chance to refuse. A few days later, Rough preached a sermon in the castle. Knox was there, of course. Rough addressed the question of how preachers were chosen, underlining the power of the congregation, however small in number it might be, to select a suitable candidate. It would be very dangerous, he warned, for the chosen candidate to decline. Rough then looked directly at Knox. 'Brother', he said, 'ye shall not be offended, albeit that I speak unto you that which I have in charge, even from all those that are here present, which is this. In the name of God and of his son Jesus Christ, and in the name of these that presently calls you by my mouth, I charge you that ye refuse not this holy vocation . . .' Knox must have regard for the glory of God, the increase of Christ's kingdom and indeed Rough's own need for assistance and take up this office, otherwise he would suffer God's heavy displeasure. Turning back to the rest of the congregation, Rough emphasised the fact that he was speaking for all of them. They had asked him to put the request to Knox. 'Was not this your charge to me?', he demanded. 'And do you not approve this vocation?' 'It was, and we approve it', they shouted at once. All eyes were on Knox. Overwrought, he burst into tears and fled back to his chamber.[3]

For several days he kept to himself, and those who did see him noted his troubled expression. He was usually gregarious, but now 'no man saw any sign of mirth' about him. In the end, it was John Annand who forced him to a decision. Annand was to preach in St Andrews Parish Church, and would undoubtedly take up the cudgels against John Rough once more. Knox decided that he must be there to hear what was said and sure enough Annand, in characteristically combative manner, claimed that there was no point at all in debating, because the Roman Catholic Church was infallible.

Enraged, Knox stood up and offered to prove, either in debate or in writing, that the Catholic Church had degenerated drastically from its original state of purity. The congregation protested that if the argument were to continue in writing, they would have no opportunity of learning Knox's views. Were he willing to preach publicly, however, then they could all come and hear him. He must do it, they shouted, and this time he agreed. He would deliver his first public sermon in the parish church the following Sunday.[4]

His doubts dissolved, he made a fiery and eloquent address that day, based on a text from the Book of Daniel. He was very obviously no stumbling newcomer to public speaking. His verbal fluency, directness and savage humour made him an immediate success and, with his theological training and his exhaustive knowledge of the Bible, he was more than a match for Annand. Citing innumerable scriptural examples, he condemned the corruption of the Roman Catholic ecclesiastical system, which would have people believe that they would be saved if they resorted to pilgrimages, pardons and a multitude of other devices, all of man's own invention. The Scriptures, by way of contrast, taught that man is justified by faith alone. The Pope was therefore antichrist, Knox said, and the teachings of Rome, far from being infallible, were entirely erroneous.

The Protestants who heard him were both enthralled and alarmed. Some told each other delightedly that, while previous preachers had lopped off the branches of papistry, this man struck at the root. Others commented gloomily, 'Master George Wishart spake never so plainly, and yet he was burnt: even so will he [Knox] be'. The Roman Catholic authorities were furious at Knox's temerity, and John Winram, Subprior of St Andrews, summoned both Knox and Rough to appear at a convention of Grey and Black Friars.

This gave further opportunity for public debate. A list of the two men's allegedly heretical beliefs was read out, and they were questioned, first by Winram, who was in reality not unsympathetic to reformed opinions, and then by one of the Grey Friars. Knox soon managed to entangle Friar Alexander Arbuckle in his own arguments, and turned the occasion into a minor triumph. Winram hastily gave orders that there were to be no further disputations and it was announced that all the learned men in both the University and the Priory of St Andrews should take turns at preaching in the parish church on Sundays. There were so many of them that this would deprive Knox of the opportunity of being heard again. Undeterred, he bowed to popular demand and preached instead on weekdays, to an increasingly large congregation. Tired of the convoluted arguments of his opponents, the citizens preferred to listen to his bold, forthright condemnations of the old church and its abuses.[5]

Meanwhile, the general situation remained unresolved. In accordance with the terms of the truce he had signed with the Castilians, the Lord Governor had applied to the Pope for absolution for the murderers of Cardinal Beaton. The necessary document came that spring, but it was found to contain the words, 'We remit the crime that cannot be remitted'. That was unacceptable to the Protestants. Telling each other that the Pope's remissions meant nothing to them anyway, they refused to surrender the castle, in the confident hope that an English army was coming to their assistance. On 29 June 1547, a fleet was at last sighted sailing into the Firth of Forth, but the Castilians' rejoicing soon turned to dismay when they realised that the vessels were galleys flying the French flag. Mary of Guise had been sending urgent pleas for help to Henri II and, seizing the initiative, he had dispatched one of his leading admirals, Leon Strozzi, Prior of Capua, with twenty-one galleys and a military force to besiege St Andrews Castle.[6]

The day after their arrival, the galleys opened fire, and Knox and his companions watched as the French guns blew slates from the houses in St Andrews but failed to do any damage to the castle itself. Encouraged, the Castilians fired back, almost sinking one of the galleys which had come in closer than the rest. Some of the soldiers and several galley slaves on board were killed. Alarmed, Strozzi decided to withdraw, and sailed north into the mouth of the River Tay to anchor off Dundee. When they saw the galleys depart, the Castilians rejoiced. They had driven off the enemy and, they told each other, 'England will rescue us.' Knox was less sanguine. 'Ye shall not see them,' he said grimly, 'but ye shall be delivered in your enemy's hands and shall be carried to a strange country.'

The Lord Governor was in the Borders, waiting near Langholm to confront the expected English army of invasion. On hearing that the French fleet had arrived, he set off to march back to Fife. Once Strozzi knew that Arran was on his way, he sailed to St Andrews once more and landed his soldiers in the city on 24 July 1547. That night, they dragged their cannon through the streets and positioned them on top of the Priory Church and St Salvator's College. At four o'clock on the morning of 30 July they opened fire. The east blockhouse of the castle came crashing down. The south wall was demolished. Men were killed in one of the narrow passages. The French cannon went on battering Cardinal Beaton's once impregnable fortress until a violent storm caused them to pause at about ten o'clock.

Inside the castle, the defenders were in a state of disarray. They could plainly see that the enemy would be able to force their way through the breach in the walls. Their own position was hopeless. There was no chance now of waiting for their English allies. They would have to surrender. They knew that if they gave themselves up to the Lord Governor, Knox and the other leading Protestants would be burned for heresy. They therefore decided to negotiate with Leon Strozzi instead, and sent William Kirkcaldy of Grange to him. Strozzi was ready enough to discuss their surrender. It was true that he could take the castle now, but he would suffer casualties in the process and so it would be better to come to terms.[7]

According to Knox's later account, Strozzi agreed to spare the lives of the Castilians. He would transport them to France, he said, and once there they would be free to join the French king's army, or travel to any country of their choice, other than Scotland. Agreement was reached and the Protestants were herded on to the galleys: lairds, gentlemen, ordinary Scots, some English military experts who had slipped into the castle to help and, of course, John Knox. Conditions on board were cramped, to say the least, for each galley, 100 to 150 feet long and 30 feet wide, already had its own crew and the complement of 150 rowers needed to propel the vessel forward whenever the wind fell. After a delay of several days during which the French crammed into their vessels more than £100,000 worth of booty, most of it from Cardinal Beaton's private apartments, they were ready at last. On 7 August they set sail.[8]

Although they were bound for enemy territory, Knox and his friends were not as dismayed as they might have been, for they were looking forward to their release and, even if they were captured by the English on the way, they would presumably be set free at once. In the event, there was no sign of any ship putting out from the east coast of England, and they turned, unchallenged, into the Straits of Dover. They almost ran aground, probably on the Goodwin Sands, but they managed to get off again in the nick of time and before long they were sailing into the estuary of the River Seine. They were not, however, going as far as Paris. Their destination was Rouen, where the galleys were based.[9]

The city of Rouen lies in pleasant, hilly countryside. Then as now, it was a busy port, and indeed in Knox's day it was the second largest town in France. Protected by the medieval city walls, handsome new stone buildings with ornate Renaissance façades loomed over old timber houses in the narrow streets running towards the Gothic Cathedral of Notre Dame. The cathedral stands near the river, its great lantern tower and the two ornate towers at the west end clearly visible from the quays. If Knox looked further along to the right, he would have seen the spire of the recently completed Church of St Maclou and, beyond that, the high, graceful nave of the big abbey church which the workmen were just finishing. The Archbishop of Rouen had his palace conveniently near the cathedral, and there was a royal palace in the city too, as well as the formidable tower where Joan of Arc had once been held captive and a large armaments depot.[10]

When the galleys moored at Rouen, Knox and his friends waited confidently to be set free. Instead, to their horror, they found that they were still prisoners. While the lairds and well-born gentlemen were taken ashore to be held captive in various fortresses throughout northern France, Knox and the others were not even allowed to land. They were informed that they were now galley slaves aboard the French fleet. When they protested, they were told that no assurances about their future had ever been given. The Scots in St Andrews Castle had surrendered unconditionally, the French said, and it does seem that Strozzi had granted them their lives but had not actually made them any promises. He had not been in any position to do so, for he was employed by the King of France, and Henri II had been urged by the Pope himself to deal severely with the murderers of Cardinal Beaton. Knox was given a galley slave's brown woollen robe to wear, and chained by the legs to a rower's bench.

For several months the fleet lay at Rouen, and then orders came that the galleys were to move to Nantes, on the west coast of France. They set sail. It took six men to ply one of the great oars, and Knox and the other galley slaves worked in shifts, an overseer standing over them, ready to use his whip if they showed signs of flagging. They were given water to drink and ship's biscuit to eat, with vegetable soup three times a week. It was hard, unremitting, physically exhausting work. They reached Nantes at last, and the galleys dropped anchor. Unable to go to sea in bad weather, they would spend the winter there.[11]

With no rowing to do, the men were put to work repairing the sails and undertaking other maintenance tasks. They were also expected to hear Mass. Their fellow prisoners in Cherbourg, Mont-Saint-Michel, Brest and Rouen refused, but that was not an option available to the galley slaves. From time to time they were taken to attend services on shore, but, for the most part, Mass was heard aboard their galleys. They had their own way of dealing with the problem, however, and when the French on board Knox's galley sang *Salve Regina* on Saturday nights, the Scots pulled their caps and hoods down over their ears and refused to listen.

Not long after they reached Nantes, a painting of the Virgin Mary was passed round the rowers, and they were instructed to kiss it. 'Trouble me not', Knox said quietly when it was held out towards him, 'Such an idol is accursed and therefore I will not touch it.' The officers in charge ordered him to take it, and 'violently thrust it to his face and put it betwixt his hands.' Determined not to give way, he took the picture, looked meaningfully at his friends and then threw it into the river, saying, 'Let Our Lady now save herself: she is light enough; let her learn to swim.' After that, he noted with satisfaction, none of the Scots was bothered again with any such idolatry.

No doubt Knox's companions laughed appreciatively at his grim humour. He was always ready to keep up their spirits, and, whenever his friend James Balfour of Pittendreich despaired, he would turn to Knox for encouragement. From the very start of their time in the galleys, Balfour would ask Knox if he thought they would ever be free again, and Knox always replied robustly that 'God would deliver them from that bondage, to his glory, even in this life'. Be that as it might, their liberation seemed a long time in coming.[12]

Winter passed, and in the spring the commander of the galleys was told to make ready for another voyage. They were to sail for Scotland. During their absence, the Duke of Somerset had finally marched north and routed the Lord Governor and his forces at the Battle of Pinkie, not far from Edinburgh, on 10 September 1547. Many Scottish noblemen had been killed or captured. Less than a fortnight later, the English had withdrawn, but everyone knew that when spring came they would be back again.

Furious with Arran for the debacle at Pinkie, Mary of Guise had pleaded with the French to send more help, and Henri II had been quick to respond. It was not in the interests of France to allow Scotland to be overrun by the English. Scotland had always been useful to the French, for, whenever France was attacked by the English, the Scots could be called upon to create a useful diversion by invading England from the north. Henri had thought of a new scheme to settle the situation once and for all. He suggested that five-year-old Mary, Queen of Scots should marry his four-year-old son and heir, the Dauphin François. Scotland would then be bound to France forever, with England trapped irrevocably in between the two countries.

The prospect of their realm becoming a mere satellite state of France did not appeal to the Scots, and they demurred. Henri then proffered bribes. He would send immediate military assistance and the Lord Governor would be rewarded with a French dukedom. The Scots remained reluctant. On 21 February 1548, however, the English invaded Scotland yet again by the eastern route, and Mary of Guise moved her daughter to Dumbarton Castle in the west. From there, the little Queen could more easily be whisked away to France.[13]

Desperate for help, the Scots finally agreed to Henri II's proposals. Putting aside thoughts of gaining the throne of Scotland for himself or his descendants, Arran accepted the dukedom of Châtelherault and the promise of a wealthy French bride for his son. While the English army burned and plundered in the

Borders as usual and took Haddington, Henri II prepared a large fleet. More than 140 vessels carrying 7,000 soldiers set sail from Boulogne for Scotland at the beginning of June 1548, under the command of Durand de Villegaignon, one of the leading French admirals. Among them were 26 galleys, and on board one of the galleys was John Knox.

His feelings as he rowed northwards towards his native land must have been mixed indeed. Above all else, he wanted to be home, but he was returning under the worst possible circumstances. Against his will, he was in the service of the enemies of the true religion, bringing death and destruction to his fellow Protestants. No doubt the Scottish galley slaves spoke desperately to each other of escape, yet how could they ever get away, chained as they were to their benches? Finally, they sailed into the River Forth. The French soldiers landed and marched to East Lothian to besiege Haddington, declaring that they would not take the town until the new treaty between France and Scotland was signed. This was done on 7 July 1548, at the Cistercian nunnery near the town. Mary, Queen of Scots would go to France and in due course marry the Dauphin. In return, Henri II, while respecting Scotland's laws and liberties, would defend it just as he did his own realm.

Villegaignon then took part of his fleet and sailed round the north coast of Scotland and down to Dumbarton, to collect the little Queen. Knox, suffering from a violent fever, was in one of the other galleys sent to besiege Broughty Castle, held by the English since the previous year. French naval surgeons attended any rower who was sick, but by the time he sailed into the estuary of the Tay, Knox was so ill that his friends despaired of his life. He seemed to be only partly conscious, and, in an effort to rouse him, James Balfour urged him to look out towards the shore, asking him if he recognised anything. Perhaps the sight of his own country would put new strength into him.

With a great effort, Knox raised his head and gazed south towards Fife, where the towers and spires of St Andrews were clearly visible. 'Yes,' he said at last. 'I know it well, for I see the steeple of that place where God first in public opened my mouth to his glory'. He then added faintly, but with all his old determination, 'and I am fully persuaded, how weak that ever I now appear, that I shall not depart this life till that my tongue shall glorify his godly name in the same place.'[14]

He was still very unwell when the fleet sailed back to France in September and moored at Rouen once more, but at least no more rowing was required that year, and some of his concerned friends on the shore managed to send messages to him, trying to encourage him by asking his advice. William Kirkcaldy of Grange was being held at Mont-Saint-Michel with Peter Carmichael and Robert and William Leslie. They were plotting to escape, but there was a difficulty. They had sent word of their plans to Kirkcaldy's father, the Laird of Grange, who was imprisoned at Cherbourg. Instead of approving, he had instantly urged them to do nothing. If they escaped, the French would surely take reprisals against the other Scottish captives. What should they do?

Knox replied carefully that they were certainly free to try to escape, provided they caused no bloodshed. Kirkcaldy's father should not fret, for the matter was out of their hands. God would release them all in due course. If He wished them to get away now, He would give them the opportunity to do so, and they must be ready to take it. Satisfied, Kirkcaldy and the others bided their time and at the Feast of Epiphany, they saw their chance. Their French guards celebrated by drinking too much and were easily overpowered. No blood was shed and, disguised as beggars, Kirkcaldy and Carmichael escaped and crossed to England.

That same winter, Henry Balnaves of Halhill also established contact with Knox. He was near at hand, for he had been imprisoned in Rouen Castle and he had passed the time by writing a theological treatise on the doctrine of justification by faith.[15] Once he had completed it, he sent it to Knox, who received it 'lying in irons and sore troubled by corporal infirmity, in a galley named *Notre Dame*'. Delighted to have something useful to do, Knox read the text with enthusiasm. There was nothing particularly new about it. It was a conventional Lutheran essay explaining that faith in God was all-important. Men and women were sinners from birth because Adam and Eve had sinned, but God forgave true believers, because Christ had sacrificed himself for them by dying on the cross. Pardons and pilgrimages meant nothing. People should not put on outward shows of piety in the vain hope that these would somehow purchase them life everlasting. Good works were to be done out of love, not from self-interest.

Knox decided that the treatise could be a useful means of instructing the less well-informed Scottish prisoners, and set about editing it. He divided the text into chapters, added some marginal notes, and took out various references to the New Testament and the Virgin Mary. In one passage, Balnaves mentioned the duty of subjects to obey their rulers. Knox qualified this by stating, as Martin Luther had done, that this rule did not apply if the prince ordered one of his subjects to do something sinful. In that instance, the ruler must be disobeyed.

Interestingly, in view of his later reputation as a male chauvinist, Knox also modified the remarks made by Balnaves about the duty of wives to their husbands, a subject often discussed when what were seen as the corresponding duties of subjects to their rulers were being considered. Again taking the conventional line, Balnaves remarked that wives must listen to their husbands' instructions and must avoid disobeying their commands. Knox amplified this, pointing out that marriage brought about mutual obligations. 'The office of a husband', he wrote, 'is to love and defend his wife, giving to her only his body. The office of the wife is likewise to love and obey her husband, usurping no dominion over him. And the office of them both is to instruct their children in God's law.'

Finally, he added to Balnaves's essay a brisk message for his fellow prisoners. However desperate their circumstances might seem, the godly would triumph in the end, he said. As for the enemy, 'Their vestments of spiders' webs shall not abide the force of the Lord's wind. This fate shall befall them because they hold the wrong opinions, because they call light darkness, and darkness light.' Even as he wrote these words, his time in the galleys was drawing to a close.[16]

When or why he was released remains uncertain. The Duke of Somerset had long been trying to negotiate an exchange of prisoners with the French, so that he could get back his military experts captured when St Andrews Castle was taken. It could be that Knox was included in the eventual agreement. On the other hand, the French may have decided to let him go because his long illness had made him unfit for any further service at the oars. Knox himself merely recorded that when Kirkcaldy and Carmichael reached England after their escape from Cherbourg, they found him already there, waiting for them, for he 'that same winter was delivered, and Alexander Clerk in his company'. Whatever the circumstances, he was free.[17]

3

The English Years

KNOWING THAT IT WAS far too dangerous for him to return to Scotland, Knox had probably crossed from Dieppe to Rye or one of the other ports on the south coast of England. He then travelled to London, where he received a warm welcome from the Protestant community. His name was already well-known, for the English and Scottish Protestants were constantly in touch with each other and his recent months as a captive of the French had enhanced his standing with them still further. His new English friends lost no time in introducing him at Court. Quite possibly he preached before Lord Protector Somerset and on 7 April 1549 the Privy Council gave him £5, 'by way of reward'.[1]

The Protestant Church in England desperately needed good men, for the country was still in a state of transition. Despite his break with Rome, Henry VIII had continued to regard himself as a Catholic. Since Henry's death in 1547, Somerset had been working with Thomas Cranmer, Archbishop of Canterbury, to take the Reformation a stage further. The English parliament had now repealed the laws against heretics, ordered the removal of all images and crosses from churches and said that henceforth services must be conducted in English. Men and women should be able to follow what was being said for themselves, rather than listening each week to the familiar but incomprehensible Latin of the priest. There were to be no more prayers to the Virgin Mary and the saints. People should pray directly to God, with no need of any intermediary, earthly or angelic. Cranmer had recently produced a Book of Common Prayer, and this was to be used in all churches after Whitsun 1549.

Legislation was all very well, but these measures were difficult to implement because there was an acute shortage of preachers. Certainly crosses and statues had been removed from most of the London churches, but elsewhere nothing had been done. Somerset and Cranmer invited scholars from the continent to settle at Oxford and Cambridge so that they could train the new generation of men entering the Church, but that would take time. Soon after Knox's arrival, the Privy Council set about identifying qualified preachers who could be deployed throughout the country and drew up a list of eighty suitable men. Knox was one of them and he was told that he was to go to Berwick-upon-Tweed.[2]

It is hard to believe that he did not have a hand in the decision, for in Berwick-upon-Tweed he could not have been closer to Scotland. Indeed, for most of its history, Berwick had actually been Scottish, standing as it does on the north bank of the River Tweed which, for much of its eastern course, forms the border between Scotland and England. As a prosperous port Berwick was a valuable asset and in 1174 it had been captured by the English. It subsequently changed hands no fewer than ten times between then and 1482, when Scotland finally lost it. Even then, it was not fully assimilated into England but was regarded as a foreign outpost. It did not become legally part of England until 1836.

Because of its strategic and highly vulnerable position, Berwick was heavily fortified. When Knox arrived there in the spring of 1549, he found an overcrowded town guarded by a medieval wall 22 feet high, with 19 towers, five arched gates and a system of ditches, all designed to keep out the Scots. Close by, on the banks of the Tweed, stood the formidable Berwick Castle, headquarters of the English Lord Warden of the Eastern Marches. The castle had a large garrison, but there were no barracks, and so the discontented, poorly paid soldiers were quartered on the unwilling townspeople. The situation was made worse by the constant arrival of sick English soldiers sent back from Scotland, where the plague was rife.

The atmosphere was tense, to say the least, and the previous November, John Brende, Master of the Musters, had written to Somerset complaining about the lack of discipline and the low morale. 'There is better order among the Tartars than in this town,' he complained. 'No man can have anything unstolen . . . the price of victuals is excessive, the sick soldiers from Haddington, etc., are shut out of houses and die of want in the streets. The whole picture of the place is one of social disorder and the worst police. It will require a stern disciplinarian in the pulpit as well as a stirring preacher to work out a moral and social reform.'[3]

St Mary's, the parish church where Knox preached each week, was in the centre of Berwick, but it was only a short stroll to the town walls and it was a simple matter for individual Scots to slip over the Border and come to his services. Their entry into England might be illegal, but so many people were travelling to and fro that no one was able to stop them. Within weeks of Knox's arrival, increasing numbers of Scots were flocking to hear him, sitting in St Mary's with soldiers of the garrison, members of the resentful families who housed them, and respectable upper middle class ladies from the surrounding area. Many of his congregation were not Protestants but Roman Catholics, curious about the new religion and attracted by his fervour, fluency and sardonic humour.[4]

Knox's confidence had grown during his brief time of preaching in St Andrews before he was captured by the French, and now, even though he had emerged from the galleys physically weak and suffering from digestive troubles and intermittent fevers, he had no difficulty in taking a grip of the situation. The tough soldiers liked his blunt approach and decided that they were willing to listen to him. The respectable ladies were charmed with him, he readily made converts and his powers of leadership soon brought order to the chaotic community. Knox knew exactly what he thought about practically everything, and his brisk assurance attracted those who were still in doubt and felt that they needed to know more about the reformed doctrines. He was always ready to explain and, in particular, he made a point of preaching against the Mass, the service at the centre of Roman Catholic beliefs.

Originally, the Mass had been a re-enactment of the Last Supper, when Christ and His disciples sat down to a final meal together before the Crucifixion. During the early days of Christianity, the whole congregation took part in a weekly service of praise and thanksgiving, sharing bread and wine in memory of that occasion. However, over the centuries, doctrine and practice changed, finally to be defined at the Council of Trent, which sat from 1545–63. All Roman Catholics now had to subscribe to the belief that when the bread and wine were consecrated at the Mass, a miracle took place and these elements were changed into the physical body and blood of Christ. This was known as the doctrine of transubstantiation, and it meant that each time the Mass was celebrated, Christ's sacrifice was re-enacted.

No longer a simple service, the Mass was conducted in Latin, with elaborate ritual. When the priest, standing behind the altar and wearing ornate vestments, held aloft the wheaten wafer and pronounced the words 'This is my body', a special bell was rung to emphasise the holiness of the moment. Moreover, only the priest now took the wine. Members of the congregation came and knelt before him to receive the wafer. So solemn was the service that the people usually took communion once a year only. At other times, they could ask the priest to say Masses for their own souls, for the souls of dead relatives or as a means of requesting God's assistance for particular problems. Masses were said for peace in time of war, for fair weather during harvest, recovery from illness and even for the curing of sick farm animals. Very often a fee was charged for such services.[5]

To Knox, the Mass was anathema. There were many shades of opinion amongst the reformers, but they were all agreed that the bread and wine were not transformed literally into Christ's body and blood. Christ had sacrificed himself on the cross so that God would forgive men and women for their sins. How could He possibly die again and again, every time Mass was said? The elaborate ceremonial with its incense, bells, solemn music and colourful vestments was designed to be spiritually uplifting, but radical Protestants detested it. There was nothing in the Bible to authorise any of these things, they said, and they wanted to revert to a simple service of commemoration, with the congregation receiving the wine as well as the bread. They also wanted readings from the Bible, in their native language, to play a central part in the service. Lutherans believed that, although the bread and wine were not changed into Christ's body and blood, they were imbued with holiness by the priest's blessing, and so the congregation should kneel to receive them. Swiss theologians taught that the bread and wine remained bread and wine, and so people should sit round the communion table instead of kneeling before an altar.

The Church of England followed the Lutheran teaching on the subject. In 1549 Cranmer gave orders that licences were to be issued only to those preachers who signed articles denying the Bodily Presence. The term 'Mass' would no longer be used, and instead the service would simply be called Communion or the Lord's Supper. The altar must be replaced by a table and the congregation would receive both bread and wine, kneeling. Knox, however, preferred the Swiss practice, and when he celebrated the Lord's Supper in Berwick-upon-Tweed he used ordinary bread instead of specially made wafers, and insisted that his congregation sit round a table which was covered with a plain linen cloth.[6]

There were bishops in the Church of England who still believed in the Bodily Presence and Cuthbert Tunstall, Bishop of Durham, was one of them. Berwick lay in his diocese, and when he heard about Knox's sermons against the Mass, he had him summoned before the Council of the North. Tunstall himself was a member of that council, along with such eminent men as the Earls of Shrewsbury, Westmorland and Cumberland, Lord Dacre and Sir Robert Bowes. Knox appeared before them in Newcastle on 4 April 1550 and it was decided that he should preach in the Church of St Nicholas, a large, Gothic building with a handsome lantern tower which is still a feature of the Newcastle skyline today.

As well as members of the Council of the North, his congregation included learned ecclesiastics from Durham Cathedral, and he addressed them respectfully, promising them that, if he was unable to prove his views from his knowledge of the scriptures, he would repent and submit to punishment. He then embarked on a long and closely argued discourse, emphasising that the Bible was God's word and any additions and elaborations thought up by men were entirely wrong and should be discarded at once. If Roman Catholics really believed that they were sacrificing Christ at each Mass, he said, they must feel full of sorrow to be committing manslaughter every day. However, they had no need to feel concerned. 'Be not afraid. Ye do it not, for Jesus Christ may suffer no more, shed his blood no more, nor die no more. And so do ye not slay Christ, for no power have ye to do the same.'

What they had done, however, was almost as bad, for they had deceived the people with their false teaching. Nor should they imagine that he was merely taking up this theme now that he was in the safety of a Protestant country. Even when he had been in the galleys, 'lying in most painful bonds among the midst of cruel tyrants', he had written against the Mass, and he called upon God to record the fact that 'neither profit to myself, hatred of any person or persons, nor affection or favour that I bear towards any private man, causeth me this day to speak as ye have heard'. Obedience to God and love of the salvation of all men were his only motives.

His arguments were logical, carefully thought out and delivered with conviction. Many of his congregation had already accepted the Protestant view of the Lord's Supper and were in agreement with him. As for Tunstall and the rest of the Council of the North, they could see that if they tried to have him arrested they would have a public riot on their hands. They dared not risk that. When he came down from the pulpit, Knox was allowed to go, and he heard no more from either Tunstall or the Council of the North. Some time later, he published his sermon under the title of *A Vindication of the Doctrine that the Sacrifice of the Mass is Idolatry.*[7]

Knox was now greatly in demand as a preacher, and he spent a good deal of time travelling about the area, addressing country congregations. Apart from his normal duties of preaching, baptising children, marrying couples and officiating at funerals, he was converting significant numbers of people to Protestantism. He could not do this simply by preaching. He had to teach them privately, study the Bible with them, enter into lengthy discussions and generally reassure them. After all, the men and women whom he received into the Protestant Church were not following a conventional path. They were abandoning the familiar, comforting religion they had known from childhood in favour of new ways which were still strange and sometimes troubling to them. Knox's strength of character and moral certainty calmed their doubts and encouraged them to persevere.

As the months went by, he extended his activities beyond the immediate vicinity of Berwick and he was receiving more and more invitations to preach further south. In the past, Scotland had always been in the forefront of his mind, but now he was deeply involved with his English parishioners. Indeed, his fellow-countrymen would later mock him for his English accent. In the late spring or early summer of 1551 he decided to move to Newcastle. It was sixty miles away, but he frequently rode north to see his original congregation in Berwick. His reputation was growing fast, and the following year he acquired a powerful new patron.[8]

While Knox had been labouring in the north, Lord Protector Somerset had fallen from power. Once praised for his liberal views, the Duke was blamed for the breakdown of law and order which resulted when he repealed many of the Henry VIII's repressive laws, and his great rival, John Dudley, Earl of Warwick, seized his opportunity. Somerset was arrested, tried for treason and eventually executed. When Knox heard the news, he had been as surprised as everyone else, and he had been quick to blame the Roman Catholics who, he said, had deliberately made trouble between the country's two most important Protestant statesmen.

The Earl of Warwick was a tall, handsome man with a fine military reputation and a liking for a magnificent lifestyle. Now Duke of Northumberland, he accumulated many other titles and offices, amongst them the position of Warden General of the Marches towards Scotland. In the summer of 1552 he decided to ride north to Newcastle to inspect the Border fortifications for himself. When he arrived there in June, Knox was invited to preach a number of sermons before him and the Duke was keenly interested. It was not that he was a fervent churchgoer, but he had chosen to ally himself with the more radical Protestants. He felt that Archbishop Cranmer and his colleagues were far too timid in their approach. The radicals had the fire and energy to drive the Reformation forward and by identifying with them the Duke could criticise the unwarranted luxury enjoyed by various leading ecclesiastics, seize their revenues and put these to his own purposes. As a radical and an extremely influential figure in the north east, Knox could be very useful.[9]

When the Duke travelled around the fortifications that summer, he took Knox with him as his chaplain and, once his tour of inspection was over, he announced that Knox would accompany him south. No direct evidence survives to tell us how Knox felt about this, but there is little doubt that he was reluctant to go. He was satisfactorily settled in Newcastle, there was much work still to be done and whatever would his congregations do without him? However, there was no arguing with the all powerful Duke of Northumberland. At the end of August 1552 he set off with the Duke and his retinue for King Edward's Court.

Edward VI had gone on his first royal progress that summer

to the west of England, and Northumberland and his companions found him at Mottisfont in Hampshire. The Court was on its way back to Windsor, and as they moved slowly east Knox had the opportunity of observing the King and his leading statesmen at close quarters. Edward VI, at not quite fifteen, was a slim boy of medium height, with fair skin, grey eyes and the red-gold Tudor hair. Intelligent and determined, he was already drawing up meticulous memoranda on subjects such as fiscal reform and the reorganisation of the Privy Council. He was also deeply interested in religion, and had an idealistic commitment to the more evangelical form of Protestantism. Northumberland was quick to introduce his new Scottish chaplain, and, at the end of September, Knox was invited to preach before the King in the Chapel Royal at Windsor.[10]

In no way overawed by the royal presence or by the number of illustrious men seated before him, Knox launched with characteristic vigour into a lively attack on the practice of kneeling at communion. There was an immediate stir amongst his congregation. Quite deliberately, he had chosen a highly charged subject. Archbishop Cranmer had recently completed a new prayer book, his First Book of Common Prayer having been sharply criticised as far too close to Roman Catholic practice. After lengthy consultations with colleagues both at home and abroad, his Second Book had been approved by Parliament and was at last with the printers. After All Saints' Day, 1 November 1552, it would be illegal to use any other manual of worship in the Church of England.

The new Prayer Book certainly did away with most of the Roman Catholic rituals to which the Protestants took exception, but the trouble was that it instructed people to kneel when they received the bread and the wine. To Knox, kneeling implied a continuing belief in transubstantiation, and he was not alone in his views. John Hooper, the popular Bishop of Gloucester, was already arguing that communicants should sit and John à Lasco, Polish founder of the Protestant Church of Foreigners in London was equally concerned. Their protests had been brushed aside, but now Knox was re-opening the whole controversy.

With characteristic allusions to Biblical texts, he insisted that there was no scriptural authority for kneeling. If people knelt, they were worshipping a piece of bread, and that was sinful. God alone was to be worshipped and communicants should sit round a communion table in fellowship, remembering the Last Supper. No vestige of the idolatrous Roman Catholic Mass must be allowed to survive. Jean Scheyve, the Holy Roman Emperor's ambassador, was in the Chapel Royal that day and he reported to his master with relish, 'The Duke of Northumberland has fetched hither a new Scottish apostle from Newcastle, who has already begun to pick holes in the new and universal reformation.' The Protestants were falling out among themselves.[11]

After Knox's sermon, the Privy Council decided to suspend distribution of the Second Book of Common Prayer until Cranmer justified the instruction to kneel. The Archbishop, usually so mild-mannered, was furious. His months of careful work were in jeopardy. He urged the Council to ignore these complaints by people who 'like nothing but that is after their own fancy and cease not to make trouble and disquietness when things be most quiet and in good order'. Kneeling was merely a token of respect, not a visible adoration of the Host.

Knox made a vigorous response, and, as a direct result of his arguments, the Privy Council on 27 October 1552 gave orders that, on the authority of the King himself, a special explanation known as 'the Black Rubric' was to be inserted into the new Prayer Book. At the same time £40 was paid to 'Mr Knox, preacher in the north, in way of the King's Majesty's reward'. Gratifying though this was, the Second Book of Common Prayer still told people to kneel at communion, and any who disobeyed would be in serious trouble. Knox therefore wrote hastily to his congregation in the north, telling them that they would have to conform. It was true that he had hitherto always told them to sit, but it was the duty of subjects to obey their magistrates, rulers and princes, even if those people were ungodly. They should, however, pray each day for this idolatrous practice to be reformed.

He did not say so, but he intended to carry on the battle. He had just been appointed by the Privy Council to a small committee of evangelical preachers set up to scrutinise the new Articles of Faith currently being drafted by Archbishop Cranmer. There were 45 articles in all, and as soon as Knox read them, he pounced on number 38. It said that the Second Book of Common Prayer was holy, godly and provable by scripture. At his urgings, he and his colleagues at once drew up a memorandum pointing out that the ceremonies in the Prayer Book were certainly not all provable by scripture. There was nothing in the Bible to authorise kneeling at communion. For good measure, they redrafted the entire sentence, omitting the words 'holy' and 'godly', saying merely that the Book was not repugnant to the Gospel and in many things did agree with it and advance it. Already affronted by the need to submit his draft to a set of radical preachers, Cranmer was even more indignant when he saw their comments. He refused outright to make the amendments, and the argument dragged on for months.[12]

Knox had become a formidable force, and on 27 October 1552, the Duke of Northumberland wrote a long letter to his friend, William Cecil, Secretary of State, declaring, 'I would to God it might please the King's Majesty to appoint Mr Knox to the office of Rochester bishopric.' There were, he said, three reasons why this was advisable. Firstly, Knox would keep Cranmer up to the mark or, as Northumberland put it, be 'a whetstone to quicken and sharp the Bishop of Canterbury, whereof he hath great need'. Secondly, Knox would be 'a great confounder of the Anabaptists lately sprung up in Kent.' The authorities had been trying for years to stamp out that particular sect of heretics. Thirdly, Northumberland was determined to remove Knox permanently from the north of England.

As long as he stayed in Newcastle, far away from Court, Knox was all too likely to deviate from the accepted Church settlement. His habit of telling his congregation to sit for communion had shown that clearly enough. He must be given no further opportunity to take people off in a different direction. Also, once he was gone, 'the family of the Scots, now inhabiting in Newcastle chiefly for his fellowship, would not continue there, wherein many resort to them out of Scotland, which is not requisite.' This colony of foreigners could pose a serious security risk in the future, and that could not be allowed.[13]

Knox was therefore offered the bishopric of Rochester, but his reaction took everyone by surprise. Instead of accepting with alacrity, he went to William Cecil and told him that he did not want the bishopric. Cecil, ever cautious and calculating, replied that, if that were really so, then he must go and tell the Duke himself, which he did. Outspoken as ever, he accused Northumberland of hypocrisy, complained that powerful men were endangering the church and apparently asked permission to retire to the north of England. Northumberland knew that there was no point in ordering Knox to accept the bishopric. He wrote a huffy letter to Cecil about him saying, 'I love not to have to do with men which be neither grateful nor pleasable ... I assure you I mind to have no more to do with him, but to wish him well.' He even allowed Knox to return to Newcastle, although he had no intention of letting him stay there. He was merely giving him an interlude for reflection.

So why did Knox refuse the bishopric? It has often been claimed that he objected to bishops on principle, had egalitarian views on church government and was appalled by the thought of becoming Bishop Knox. In fact, although he frequently spoke out against the unreformed bishops in the Church – men like his old adversary Tunstall who still held what he regarded as idolatrous views – there is nothing in his writings at this time to suggest that he was opposed to the notion of bishops. He simply had no desire to submit to the restrictions such a position would have imposed. His vocation was that of a preacher, not an administrator, and he had to be free to say what he thought and preach the Word of God.

His own explanation of why he refused the bishopric was 'foresight of trouble to come.'[14]

His refusal accepted, Knox left immediately for the north. On Christmas Day he was in Newcastle, preaching a stirring sermon praising Edward VI and warning in no uncertain terms that powerful statesmen were scheming to undermine the Protestant Church in England. These secret traitors were longing for the King to die so that they could bring back Roman Catholicism. By the time he spoke these words, Knox knew the sad secret that was being kept from the public. Young, promising King Edward, until now healthy and energetic, had contracted tuberculosis and was gravely ill. According to Henry VIII's will, which had the force of law, Edward would be succeeded by his elder half-sister, Princess Mary. Like her Spanish mother, Henry's first wife, Catherine of Aragon, the Princess was a devout Roman Catholic. Were she to come to the throne, a religious crisis was inevitable, and Northumberland himself was among those already making tentative approaches to the Princess. Religious conviction meant nothing to men like the Duke. Opportunism was all.

Knox did not mention anyone by name, but his listeners that day were shocked by his sermon. Many of them thought that what he had said was treasonable and Sir Robert Brandling, Mayor of Newcastle, complained to Lord Wharton. Wharton wrote at once to the Privy Council to protest and Knox was sent a set of articles to answer. Convinced that he was about to be charged with treason, he sent an urgent appeal to the Duke of Northumberland. The Duke supported him at once, writing to tell William Cecil that he had received a letter from 'poor Knox, by the which you may perceive what perplexity the poor soul remaineth in at this present.' The Privy Council must do something for his 'recomfort' and they were to warn Lord Wharton and his friends that the King 'hath the poor man and his doings in gracious favour' and 'no man shall be so hardy to vex him or trouble him for setting forth the King's Majesty's most godly proceedings.' Sir Robert Brandling was to be rebuked for his 'greedy accusation of the poor man, wherein he hath, in my poor opinion, uttered his malicious stomach towards the King's proceedings.'[15]

The Duke's letter to Cecil was dated 9 January 1553. At the beginning of February Knox received a message telling him that he was being made Vicar of All Hallows Church in Bread Street, London in place of Thomas Sampson, who had just become Dean of Chichester. This was even worse. He was not even being offered the lesser appointment, but was being told that he was being sent there. The Privy Council had apparently decided that he must make the move, but he had not the least intention of accepting the vicarage. Once more he sought the help of Northumberland, and the Duke came to the rescue for a second time. No more was said about All Hallows Church, but instead Knox was invited to take part in a series of sermons for Lent which were to be preached before the King.

However, his troubles were not over. Towards the end of February he was telling one of his correspondents that he had just received a letter from Lord Westmorland, Lord Lieutenant of the Bishopric of Durham, summoning him to appear 'as I will answer at my peril'. No record of the charges against him has survived, but he was called before the Privy Council and he travelled south, apparently fearing that he was to be accused of treason. On 1 March 1553 he was in London. We do not have the details of what happened, but he managed somehow to extricate himself.[16]

By 23 March he was safely back in Newcastle, but it had been a dangerous moment. 'Heinous were the delations laid against me,' he told his friend Elizabeth Bowes, 'and many are the lies that are made to the Council.'[17] Tunstall and his circle had been making trouble, it appeared, and they must have told invented tales to Lord Westmorland about him. His friends and enemies alike had thought that Knox could not survive this latest attack by his adversaries, but he was firmly convinced that God would, in the end, destroy all lying tongues. Nevertheless, he remained apprehensive. 'I look but one day or other to fall in their hands,' he said, 'for more and more rageth the members of the Devil against me.'

4

Elizabeth Bowes

KNOX HAS OFTEN BEEN accused of hating women, yet throughout the troubled months of 1552–3 he frequently confided his anxieties to Elizabeth Bowes. She was important in his life and he in hers. Her letters to him are long since lost, but she kept his carefully, treasured them even, and they give us a unique insight into some of his more intimate thoughts. People, both in their time and in ours, have suggested that their friendship went beyond that of preacher and parishioner. So who was this woman, and what was the relationship between them?

Born about ten years before Knox, Elizabeth was the daughter of a Yorkshire landed gentleman, Roger Aske of Aske. In an age when child marriages were the norm for propertied families, she was engaged when she was about five years old to Richard, the youngest son of Sir Ralph Bowes of Streatlam, not far from Durham. By the time she was sixteen, she was married to him, and over the years she had five sons and ten daughters by him, a large family, but perfectly usual by sixteenth-century standards.

Elizabeth's circumstances were comfortable. Her husband became Captain of Norham Castle, a formidable fortress not far from

Berwick-upon-Tweed and one of her brothers-in-law was Sir Robert Bowes, whom Knox had encountered when he appeared before the Council of the North. On the death of Henry VIII and the accession of Edward VI, Richard Bowes found himself serving a determinedly Protestant government, while his wife began to take an interest in Protestant doctrines and discovered that she had serious doubts about Catholicism. In 1549, friends told her about the exciting new Scottish preacher who had come to Berwick-upon-Tweed, and she went to hear him.[1]

Knox's exposition of the scriptures was so logical and so convinced that she listened to him in fascination. Everything seemed suddenly clear to her. Back home again in Norham Castle, with her sceptical husband and her Roman Catholic household, she found it less easy to keep hold of the new certainties, and so she went back to Berwick time and again, sometimes taking one of her daughters with her for company. She sought Knox's advice between sermons, too, both in person and by letter, and she was never disappointed.

She was genuinely suffering all the torments of a recent convert plagued by doubts. Hitherto a devout Roman Catholic, she missed the comfort of the old religion, and she felt that she was constantly in danger of backsliding. When she read her Bible, unwanted questions sprang to her mind. Could she really trust the Word of God? In particular, like many other Protestants, she found great difficulty with the doctrine of predestination.[2] People today tend to be repelled by the idea that, at the very moment of our birth, God has already decided whether we are among the elect, who will go to heaven, or the reprobate, whose destination is hell. Predestination, as defined in the Confession of Faith approved in 1647, is still a doctrine of the Church of Scotland, but in our secular age few give it much thought or indeed grasp the implications.

Those who do have a passing acquaintance with it, often derived from James Hogg's powerful novel, *The Private Memoirs and Confessions of a Justified Sinner*, are inclined to assume that men and women who believe that they are of the elect must feel smugly free to do whatever they like, commit as many sins as they like, for no punishment will befall them. Hogg's book was written in 1824, and it tells the grim story of a Scottish youth of God-fearing background, corrupted by a mysterious stranger (presumably Satan) who assures him that he can safely commit murder because he is one of the elect. It is a brilliant, if misleading, piece of writing which has undoubtedly affected our attitude to predestination and indeed to Knox, its well-known exponent.

Knox was by no means the inventor of the doctrine of predestination, far from it. In the Bible, both Jesus and St Paul had spoken of 'the elect ones' and 'the chosen few', but it was St Augustine who fully developed the doctrine early in the fifth century. Identifying a great gulf between God's grace and sinful human nature, he taught that salvation was not the result of men's and women's efforts to be good. It was a marvellous gift from God, freely given. He went on to wonder why some people are sinful and others are not, and reached the conclusion that God must have chosen some for eternal life, others for damnation. This explanation was too off-putting for most people, and, during the Middle Ages, theologians found ways of modifying what St Augustine had said.

At the time of the Reformation, however, Martin Luther had no hesitation in accepting the doctrine. He was willing to admit that men and women have free will to do as they choose in many areas of life, but not, he believed, when it comes to salvation. Critics have complained that, as one recent theologian has neatly put it, predestination 'turns God into an arbitrary ogre'. Luther, however, took St Paul's view that it was God's will and therefore it was not wicked. The difficulty for Protestants like Elizabeth Bowes was that they could never be really sure if they were members of the elect or not.

Many of Elizabeth's questions to Knox addressed this problem, and she kept his replies because of the explanations he gave her. His letters are perhaps less interesting to the biographer for their theological content than for the light they throw on his personality, but this is not to say that he poured forth his innermost feelings.

Sixteenth-century letters are simply not like that. In an age when no official postal system existed, most correspondents were constrained by the knowledge that what they wrote might well be intercepted and read by other people. Everything depended upon the reliability of the bearer entrusted with the message. Most letters from that time concern themselves with strictly practical matters and rarely are any personal emotions mentioned, but a close examination can sometimes yield subtle hints as to the state of mind of the writer. So it is with the letters Knox sent to Elizabeth Bowes.

We have to remember, of course, that we do not have the original documents.[3] Elizabeth kept them all her life, after which Knox had them and, thirty years after his death, they came to light in the form of copies made by some unknown relative or acquaintance. It is clear from the internal evidence that there are some errors in the dating, and this raises the possibility that the texts have been edited, by Knox himself or by the copyist. There might even be omissions, but, to those familiar with Knox's other writings, the voice is clearly his and there is no doubt that the letters are genuine.[4]

Wherever he went, he was pursued by Elizabeth's anxious enquiries, and his reassuring replies display a kindliness and patience which might amaze his critics. Her anguished appeals arrived when he was studying his Bible, preparing sermons, talking to parishioners, on the point of travelling from one place to another or even lying ill in bed. Sometimes he had no time to reply, sometimes he mislaid her letters, but sooner or later she got her answer. On certain occasions he engaged in detailed discussion of a biblical text, but more often he told her with satisfying confidence that of course she was one of the elect, he had no doubt of it at all.

Knox's method of dealing with Elizabeth's misgivings was very similar to the technique employed by Luther. The German reformer had told his doubters that they should thank God for their torments, for these were the very proof they sought that they were indeed members of the elect. The devil would not bother about the damned. He attacked only those whom God had chosen. In like manner, Knox sympathised with Elizabeth's anguish but told her encouragingly, 'Your troubles be the infallible signs of your election' and, on another occasion, 'There is no danger of everlasting death. Ye lack not faith, as divers times I have written unto you.' When Barbara Lisskirchen, a German Protestant, had confided similar fears to Luther, he had advised her, 'Learn to say, "Begone, wretched devil! You are trying to make me worry about myself. But God declares everywhere that I should let him care for me . . . .' In an echo of his words, Knox asked Elizabeth why she did not laugh the devil to scorn and told her, 'Say to him when he assaults you, "Avaunt, Satan, the Lord confound thee!"'

Nor did he merely respond automatically with the correct ways of reassuring a troubled parishioner. He went out of his way to choose analogies which he thought would appeal to her. When she worried about the truth of the scriptures, for instance, he reminded her of the passage where God said to Eve, 'In dolour shall you bear thy children,' and asked Mrs Bowes, the mother of 15, 'I pray you, Sister, is it not a manifest and impudent lie to affirm and say that this word is vain? Doth not your own heart witness that the Word of God is true?' Perhaps realising that this was not the passage in the Bible most sympathetic to women, he was careful to add that God then promised that Eve's pains were worthwhile, for it was her descendant, Jesus, who would finally defeat the works of the devil.

Occasionally Elizabeth shocked Knox. She told him once that she was guilty of the sins of Sodom and Gomorrah, and he was horrified until he concluded that she did not know what these sins actually were. 'Dear Mother,' he replied, using the term by which he sometimes addressed her, 'my duty compels me to advertise you that in comparing your sins with the sins of Sodom and Gomorrah ye do not well.' He then explained that these consisted of pride, riotous excess, idleness that provoked filthy lusts, resulting in violence and injury to strangers and all abomination and unnatural filthiness. 'In which of these, Mother, are ye guilty? Of none at all, in my conscience I affirm.'

For the most part, he took a cheerful, rallying tone, asking her almost teasingly, 'What! Think ye that God's goodness, mercy and grace is able to be overcome with your iniquity?' But there were times when he felt exasperated with her. 'I must take a care of you and will instruct you to the uttermost of my power, but it is a cross to me to remember how easily the adversary [the devil] wounds you,' he wrote to her after her Sodom and Gomorrah letter, and, when she thought some minor illness had theological implications, 'Alas, Sister, your imbecility [foolishness] troubles me, that I should know you so weak that ye should be moved for so small a matter.'

These moments of impatience were fleeting, however, and although he sometimes tried to hint to her that she should not write so often, he was soon ready with reassurance again. 'Think not, Sister, that I esteem it any trouble to comfort you. Be so bold upon me, in godliness, as ye would be upon any flesh, and no other labours save only the blowing of my Master's trumpet shall impede me to do the uttermost of my power.' When she panicked that he would forget her, he told her plainly, 'Be sure I will not forget you and your company, so long as mortal men may remember any earthly creature,' and he added thoughtful little touches to his letters, remarking that the very moment her latest message had come he had been talking about her to friends, or commenting diplomatically, 'Your infirmity has been unto me occasion to serve and try the Scripture more near than ever I could do for my own cause.'

The man revealed by these remarks is hardly the censorious tyrant of popular legend and indeed there are other passages which show that beneath the overbearing exterior was humility and doubt. Knox took himself to task for vanity, confessing that he sometimes congratulated himself on having suffered great troubles, endured most cruel bondage in the galleys and yet survived with his faith intact. He was inclined to pride himself on the effectiveness of his preaching. He knew, though, that these vainglorious thoughts were sent to tempt him. Similarly, when explaining the importance of the role of the pastor, he admitted that, although he tried hard, he could not satisfy his own conscience. He should be more diligent in travelling, he felt, more careful to comfort the afflicted and less conscious of what people might think of him: 'The slander and fear of men has impeded me to exercise my pen as often as I would.'

To an extent, the relationship between Knox and Elizabeth was that of distinguished teacher and eager pupil, father confessor and anxious parishioner, but was there also a sexual attraction between them? His contemporaries sniggered at his frequent visits to Norham Castle and his enemies were to accuse him of carrying on a torrid love affair with Elizabeth Bowes, but undoubtedly much of the modern innuendo has been based on a curious passage in one of his letters.

In February 1553, in the midst of Knox's troubles in refusing the vicarage of All Hallows, Elizabeth's brother-in-law, Harry Wickliffe, warned him that she was feeling hurt because, at a recent meeting, Knox had seemed to recoil when she started rehearsing her problems. He might indeed have been excused of retreating from yet another session of anguished soul-searching, but when he heard his friend's reproaches, he took the matter seriously and sent her an explanation. 'I remember myself so to have done,' he admitted, 'and that is my common consuetude [custom] when anything pierceth or toucheth my heart.' Here was the sensitive man who hid his feelings beneath his professional manner.

In itself, this admission of vulnerability is interesting, but it is the following paragraph which has given rise to so much speculation. Knox went on to remind Elizabeth of one of their previous conversations. 'Call to your mind what I did standing at the cupboard in Alnwick,' he wrote. 'In very deed, I thought that no creature had been tempted as I was.' Unfortunately for Knox, the artless sixteenth-century phrase 'what I did standing at the cupboard' sounds in our own day like some sort of comic double entendre, and readers are liable to picture Knox leaping upon Mrs Bowes in a frenzy of passion or, at the very least, eager to embrace her. Some have even carelessly quoted him as saying that he was 'standing *in* the cupboard *at* Alnwick', which sounds even more incriminating. The word 'cupboard' in the mid-sixteenth century was in fact applied to what we would term a dresser or a set of open shelves intended for the display of valuable plate, not a walk-in wardrobe. It would probably have saved Knox and everyone else a good deal of trouble had he been standing by the window or sitting eating his supper when he and Elizabeth had their conversation that day.

It is easy to smirk at this little episode, but the notion that the anguished, spiritual correspondence between Knox and Elizabeth had any sexual connotations is little short of ludicrous. Knox himself would have been horrified at the interpretation placed upon a couple of sentences which are almost always quoted out of context. His letter in fact continues, 'And when that I heard proceed from your mouth the very same words that he [the devil] troubles me with, I did wonder, and from my heart lament your sore trouble, knowing in myself the dolour thereof.' The tone of this paragraph is entirely in keeping with the rest of the Bowes letters, and it almost certainly refers, as usual, to the spiritual doubts which plagued them both. When Knox speaks of temptation in these letters, he almost invariably means the temptation to revert to 'idolatry'. What can really be inferred from the Bowes letters is that Knox himself had struggled with many doubts before he finally committed himself to Protestantism.

The so-called cupboard episode can be dismissed once and for all, but this is not to deny that there may have been an element of sexual attraction between Knox and Elizabeth. In the nineteenth century, of course, the very suggestion that the revered father of the Scottish Church might have entertained such thoughts about a member of the opposite sex would have seemed like sacrilege. Today, we do not expect saintly celibacy from public figures and we are readier to accept that even ecclesiastical leaders may have intimate relationships with chosen partners. Knox himself admitted an interest in women, confessing to Elizabeth on one occasion that, amidst various other shortcomings, he committed adultery in his mind, and his heart was subject to 'foul lusts'.

This sounds worse than it really was, for, where religion and morals were concerned, Knox was even harder on himself than he was on other people. Both he and Elizabeth were so deeply serious about their faith that they often give the impression of wallowing in self-recrimination and his biblical terminology heightens the effect. All he meant on this occasion was that he looked at other women from time to time and found them attractive. Few people in our own time would condemn him for that. His moral standards were dauntingly high and his deep sense of vocation would never have allowed him to commit adultery with a married woman, least of all one in his pastoral care. He enjoyed Elizabeth's admiration, was ingenuously surprised by the mental affinity between them, welcomed the opportunity to confide in an understanding friend and felt a deep affection for her.[5]

Elizabeth's feelings for Knox were not so very different from those of many a middle-aged woman for the authority figure in her life, the doctor or indeed the minister. The fact that she was about ten years older than him meant that there was also an element of maternal solicitude in her attitude towards him. In theological matters, it may have seemed to Elizabeth that he was all knowing, but when it came to the practical concerns of his domestic life, she could give him good advice and she soon decided that he needed a wife. His health was not good and he was dreadfully overworked. What he required, although he might not know it himself, was some sensible, educated girl who would run his household for him and act as his secretary. Elizabeth's fifth daughter Marjorie would be the very person. She was sweet natured as well as intelligent and, as befitted the daughter of the Captain of Norham Castle, she had been educated. Unlike many of the women of her day, she could read and write.

Marjorie was, of course, only 16 or 17 while Knox was about 35, but that had little significance. In an era of high maternal mortality, widowers frequently married women twenty, thirty and even forty years younger than themselves. Knox was not in that position, but his career as a priest had meant that he had remained single, his months in the galleys had obviously afforded him no opportunity of finding a wife, and since his arrival in England he had been too busy to look for one, even if the thought crossed his mind. Moreover, until the recent Protestant legislation he would have been forbidden by law to marry at all.

Always ready to find fault, some of Knox's enemies have criticised Elizabeth for suggesting the marriage, as though there were something improper in the notion of a mother finding a husband for her daughter. This situation may strike us as being odd, but, in the sixteenth century, girls had little or no say in their choice of partner. Marriages were made for strictly practical reasons. If affectionate attachment followed, so much the better, but it was by no means a prerequisite for matrimony. The real problem for Knox was that Marjorie's father was unenthusiastic. As the daughter of a propertied family, she needed his permission. Richard Bowes did not like the Scots, and he liked impoverished former priests even less. However, Marjorie and her mother were determined, they managed to persuade him to consent and Knox and Marjorie were betrothed.

The mid-sixteenth-century betrothal was much more binding than a modern engagement. It was not so much a preliminary but the first part of marriage. In the Roman Catholic Church, the betrothal often took the form of a religious ceremony, with the couple meeting before relatives and agreeing to marry in the presence of a priest, who joined their hands and betrothed them. They took an oath, promising to go through with the wedding, and a notary recorded the proceedings. There would be no priest at Knox's betrothal, but he would have taken the necessary oath. After the betrothal, a couple were regarded as being permanently husband and wife, even though they had yet to go on and complete the marriage formally, with a church wedding or informally, by simply living together.[6]

Knox certainly regarded Marjorie as his wife from that time onwards. In his Biblical terminology, he and she had become 'one flesh'. Totally and irrevocably committed to her, he now referred to her as his wife, his spouse, his own flesh, and he addressed Elizabeth unselfconsciously as 'Mother'. In normal circumstances, Knox and Richard Bowes would then have agreed the marriage contract. Marjorie's father would give her a dowry and Knox would have settled either land or money on her in case he died before her. As it was, Mr Bowes grew increasingly unwilling to co-operate and Knox was in no position to make any financial obligation. Throughout 1553, therefore, when he was busy preaching, travelling and rebutting the accusations of his enemies, he was also struggling to finalise his marriage arrangements.

Before he had time to achieve anything, he had to go south again in April to preach before the King at Whitehall Palace. The Lenten sermons in the Chapel Royal there had already aroused considerable controversy, because all the preachers had taken up the subject of corruption among the leading statesmen of the day. Knox enthusiastically pursued the same theme. Even in Biblical times, he said, rulers had often been ill served by their advisers. King David was one of the many examples he gave, and he reminded his congregation that even Jesus had Judas among his disciples. Why then, he demanded, did godly princes employ wicked men as advisers? Either the evil counsellors had such an abundance of worldly wisdom, foresight and experience that they were indispensable to the government, or else they kept their malice so well hidden that no one recognised it.[7]

There must have been many uneasy glances between the courtiers who listened to him that day, and, as a direct result of what he had said, he was summoned before the Privy Council on 14 April 1553. Archbishop Cranmer was present, but the Duke of Northumberland had thought it best to take himself elsewhere. The councillors began by asking Knox why he had refused the vicarage of All Hallows and he replied firmly that he thought he could be more useful outside London. Moreover, the Duke of

Northumberland had given him a contrary command. That took them aback. They could hardly criticise him for obeying the Duke or accepting the invitation to preach before the King.

They then turned to his refusal of the bishopric of Rochester, pointedly enquiring whether he believed that any Christian would be able to serve in the Church of England according to the rules and laws of the kingdom. Knox answered that many things were still unreformed, but that had not been why he had refused the bishopric. As he had already explained to them, he felt that he could be more useful elsewhere. Exasperated, they changed their ground and demanded to know why he did not kneel at communion. He explained, and a lengthy argument ensued.

In the end, they told him they were sorry to see that he had a mind contrary to the common order, to which he retorted that he was more sorry that the common order should be contrary to Christ's institution. However inflammatory his views, he retained the protection not only of the Duke but of the King himself and so, after insisting that he give an assurance that he would kneel in future, they sent him away, telling him that they bore him no ill will but esteemed him. Soon afterwards, he received word that he was to preach in the southern counties of England but would first be allowed to go back to Newcastle to settle his affairs.[8]

As he hurried north once more, Knox had grave forebodings about the future and, if he was hoping to finalise his marriage, he was disappointed. Knowledge of the King's mortal illness was no longer a secret, and people like Richard Bowes were well aware that Edward VI would soon be dead. When he died, Princess Mary would succeed, and, if the public at large did not realise the strength of her devotion to Roman Catholicism, those with Court connections certainly did. Royal officials like the Bowes brothers were ready to abandon the Protestantism they had publicly professed as servants of a Protestant monarch, and were preparing to revert to Roman Catholicism. In the current climate of opinion, Mr Bowes was even less likely than before to accept a renegade priest as his son-in-law.

Overwhelmed as usual by members of his congregation anxiously wanting to consult him, Knox had no time to enter into delicate marriage negotiations, and, after less than two months, he was on his way to preach in Buckinghamshire as the Privy Council had instructed him to do. He went by way of London, arriving there about 23 June 1553 to find a letter from Elizabeth Bowes waiting for him. Naturally, she had been upset at his departure, and all her old fears of being forgotten had been painfully revived. As soon as he could find a moment, he sat down to compose a consolatory reply and in so doing he described more fully than ever how much he valued her friendship.

Just as she had lamented his departure, he was missing her. Addressing her as 'Mother', he told her, 'Since the first day that it pleased the providence of God to bring you and me in familiarity, I have always delighted in your company, and when labours would permit, you know I have not spared hours to talk and commune with you.' His use of the word 'familiarity' does not imply physical intimacy. To the sixteenth-century reader it simply meant friendship.

Their conversations had comforted both of them, he said, and he had always been struck by the affinity between them, what he termed their 'congruence of spirit'. He had been startled to discover in her doubts 'a very mirror and glass wherein I beheld myself so rightly painted forth that nothing could be more evident to my own eyes.' No wonder she felt wretched, when he did too, even he, he added with engaging honesty, 'to whom God has given greater gifts'. Apparently struck by the thought that this sounded a trifle patronising, he added a hasty parenthesis, '(I write to His praise)', in other words, she should not think that he was congratulating himself for his abilities. He was merely thanking God for the gifts he had been given.

As a result of their discussions he had a clearer view of his own shortcomings. He was, he explained, 'compelled to thunder out the threatenings of God against obstinate rebellers,' while being all too aware of his own failings. In conclusion, he told Elizabeth that she must try to console herself with the knowledge that they were promised everlasting life, a thought which was 'my own singular comfort', but in spite of his words he was convinced that the looming political crisis was coming ever closer.[9]

5

Calvin

KING EDWARD, DYING, WAS desperate to safeguard the Protestant succession, for he well knew his sister Mary's unshakeable Roman Catholic convictions. During the long conversations he and the Duke of Northumberland had that spring, they discussed over and over again how they might solve the problem. Since Mary had spurned Northumberland's diplomatic advances, the Duke was equally alarmed at the thought of her succeeding to the throne, for he knew that his own power would then be at an end. Eventually, the King and he decided that Henry VIII's will, naming Mary as Edward's successor, would have to be ignored. Passing over both Mary and Edward's younger half-sister, Elizabeth, Edward would bequeath his crown to Lady Jane Grey, the daughter of his Protestant cousin, the Duchess of Suffolk. This decided, Northumberland promptly married his son Guildford Dudley to Lady Jane.

Edward knew that there would be serious opposition to his plan to alter the succession, and so he called his statesmen one by one to his bedchamber and begged them to support his last wishes. He was in such a pitiful condition that they did not have the heart to refuse, and when he died on 6 July 1553, Jane was duly proclaimed

Queen. She was, to say the least, reluctant. A quiet, scholarly girl, she disliked her pretty, fair-haired husband and had no desire to rule England. She could not, however, refuse.[1]

Knox was still in London at the time of the King's death, but he left almost at once for Buckinghamshire and began preaching to the large number of Protestants who lived there. Although he was particularly impressed by the civility shown to him by the people of Amersham, the situation was worsening daily. When Sir Edward Hastings, one of the local landowners, gathered together an army of 4,000 men ostensibly for Queen Jane and then declared for Mary, Knox knew that he could stay in the area no longer. He preached a final sermon, lamenting, 'O England, how is God's wrath kindled against thee . . . I perceive that the heart, the tongue and the hand of one Englishman is bent against another, and division to be in the whole realm, which is an assured sign of desolation to come.'

Not only did he warn, as he always did, against any return to idolatry, he also pointed out the practical dangers of having a female monarch. A woman ruler must marry to have heirs, and even a Queen had to do as her husband wished. If she married a foreign, Roman Catholic monarch, the consequences would be dire. He did not mention Mary by name, but he explicitly criticised her cousin and friend Charles V, the powerful, Roman Catholic, Holy Roman Emperor. His sermon delivered, Knox went back to London.[2]

Meanwhile, the Duke of Northumberland had marched with an army into East Anglia, intending to confront Mary, but he had found the people of Suffolk hurrying to join her cause. His commanders began to desert him and his ordinary soldiers melted away. When the Privy Council heard reports of what was happening, they decided that they had made a terrible mistake. Mary was obviously the true monarch, not Jane. On 19 July, just as Knox reached the city, the Lord Mayor proclaimed Mary Queen, to tumultuous cheers. 'Men ran hither and thither, bonnets flew into the air, shouts rose higher than the stars, fires were lit on all sides, and all the bells were set a-pealing,' an Italian resident reported, 'and from a distance the earth must have looked like Mount Etna.' It was Knox's darkest moment since the death of George Wishart.

The godly young monarch whom he had so much admired had gone, and the whole country was about to slide into idolatry. With an overwhelming sense of doom he went on preaching urgently against Roman Catholicism, conscious that he was surrounded by fires of joy and 'riotous banquetings'. Queen Jane was now a prisoner in the Tower of London and the Earl of Arundel and Lord Paget rode to Suffolk to deliver the Great Seal of England to Queen Mary. Recognising that Jane's cause was lost, the Duke of Northumberland filled his bonnet with gold coins, went out into the market square of Cambridge, and listened to a herald proclaim the new monarch. Hoping even at this late date to save himself, the Duke threw his bonnet up in the air and shouted three times, 'God save Queen Mary'. The coins showered down, and the local people scrambled to snatch them up, but shortly afterwards the Duke was arrested and taken to the Tower of London. Tried at Westminster Hall on 18 August 1553 and found guilty of treason, he was executed four days later.[3]

By then the new Queen had already issued a proclamation giving orders that anyone who preached must have a special licence from her. Within a matter of days, members of the Protestant clergy were being arrested and imprisoned, while others fled to the continent. Knox rode to Kent, to preach there, but by 20 September he was back in London again, reading an agitated letter from Elizabeth Bowes urging him to come north. Not only did she have her usual spiritual troubles, but there were other difficulties. Knox replied at once with his customary reassurances, but he explained that his 'great labours' would not allow him time to study in detail 'all the process between your husband and you, touching my matter concerning his daughter'. However, he gave thanks 'both for your boldness and constancy'.

Elizabeth had apparently been making one last, desperate effort to persuade her husband to draw up Marjorie's marriage contract. Prospects seemed bleak, but Knox had no intention of abandoning the woman he already regarded as his wife. Elizabeth must not trouble herself too much, he said, for he had decided that 'it becomes me now to jeopard [endanger] my life for the comfort and deliverance of my own flesh' [meaning Marjorie]. He was resolved to come north to visit them, and 'If I escape sickness and imprisonment, be sure to see me soon.' By nature neither a dashing nor romantic figure, he could not help adding, 'Yet, Mother, depend not upon me too much, for what am I but a wretched sinner?'[4]

Relieved and determined not to give up, Elizabeth now suggested that Knox enlist the support of her brother-in-law, Sir Robert Bowes. Knox went to see Sir Robert on 6 November, confidently expecting him to be sympathetic to his cause, but just as he was 'about to have declared my heart in the whole matter', Sir Robert interrupted curtly, 'Away with your rhetorical reasons, for I will not be persuaded with them.' He was under the impression that the entire idea of the marriage had been initiated by Knox and Elizabeth, with no reference to Mr Bowes or Marjorie.

Knox was deeply upset. Sir Robert's 'disdainful, yea, despiteful words, hath so pierced my heart that my life is bitter unto me,' he told Elizabeth, adding indignantly, 'God knows I did use no rhetoric nor coloured speech, but would have spoken the truth and that in most simple manner.' Torn between rage and mortification, he went on, 'I am not a good orator in my own cause, but what he would not be content to hear of me, God shall declare to him one day to his displeasure, unless he repent.' In his agitation, he believed that his prospects of completing his marriage to Marjorie were disappearing rapidly, but he assured Elizabeth that he would go on calling her 'Mother' because of all her past kindness to him.

He did not know what he would do now, or where he would go, he said. Indeed, he no longer cared 'what country consume my wicked carcase', but he realised that he could not stay in England for much longer. Thinking still of Sir Robert Bowes, he said bitterly,

'I cannot abide the disdainful hatred of those of whom not only I thought I might have craved kindness, but also to whom God hath been by me more liberal than they be thankful.'[5] Apart from his own wounded feelings, the House of Commons had passed by 350 votes to 80 an act restoring the Mass and the celibacy of the clergy. Priests who had married would either have to put away their wives or resign. Parliament had also given instructions that until 20 December 1553, worshippers were free to use either the prayer books issued in King Edward's reign or the former ones, but from 21 December onwards no form of service other than the Mass would be permitted. This meant that people would then have to choose between going to Mass, being arrested for heresy or fleeing the country.[6]

It was a measure of Knox's loyalty to Marjorie and her mother that even in those circumstances he made one last effort to see them both. He was urged on by the fact that his latest letters to them had been intercepted. There had been nothing of any great importance in what he had written, but he was worried that, not hearing from him, Elizabeth would think that he had deserted them. He also wanted to see his followers in the north and so, without saying anything to Marjorie or Elizabeth, he set out and rode secretly to Newcastle, where he went into hiding. He was too well known in the area to be able to move about freely without being arrested.

Richard Bowes had apparently forbidden Elizabeth and Marjorie to have any contact with Knox, but someone brought them word of his arrival in Newcastle and they were greatly hurt. Knox had told other people that he was coming, but he had not mentioned it to them. This seemed to Elizabeth to prove what she had always suspected, that she and Marjorie were of no importance to him. She sent him a letter full of reproaches and he wrote a hasty reply. Addressing his letter to his 'Dear Mother and Spouse', he explained about the intercepted letters. He had not dared send her word of his coming, for if any such message had fallen into his enemies' hands they would have learned his movements. 'None is this day within the realm of England with whom I would more gladly speak,' he went on, '(only she whom God hath offered unto me and commanded me to love as my own flesh excepted) than with you.'[7]

It was all very difficult, however, and as the deadline of 21 December 1553 came and went he had still not managed to see them. He wrote again to Elizabeth the following day, explaining that he was not sure if he would manage to come to Berwick at all. He had been very unwell with the gravel, and he would not be able to travel further north for almost a fortnight. In fact, 'almost I am determined not to come at all; ye know the cause.' The interview with Sir Robert was still preying on his mind and in spite of his previously declared intention, he addressed this letter not to his 'Dearly Beloved Mother' but to his 'Dearly Beloved Sister in our Saviour', signing himself 'With troubled heart and weak body . . . Your brother John Knox.'[8]

Where he went next is not altogether certain. Various historians have thought that he went into hiding in some coastal town in the north of England, but it is now generally believed that he went back to London in spite of the danger. Wherever he was, he continued to work on an essay on the sixth psalm which he had promised to write for Elizabeth, and on 6 January 1554 he sent her the first part of it, with the promise that the rest would follow. He would dearly have liked to see her and Marjorie, he said, but it was out of the question. That did not mean, of course, that he had lost interest in all his friends in Berwick. 'My daily prayer is for the sore afflicted in those quarters,' he said, remarking that although at one time he would have thought it impossible for any country to be as dear to him as his native land, England's current troubles were 'double more dolorous unto my heart than ever were the troubles of Scotland.' In spite of that, he was going to have to leave the country and so he bade them farewell, 'in great haste and troubled heart'. By 20 January 1554 he was in France.[9]

He had made the crossing to Dieppe, and, as he sailed into the busy harbour, sheltered by its white cliffs and guarded by its sturdy castle perched high above the town, Knox may have had painful memories of his previous stay in France. However, he knew that

there was a colony of Scottish merchants in this thriving Channel
port and his brother William almost certainly had trading links with
the little community. Knox would be safe there until he decided
where to go next. He found lodgings in one of the narrow streets
and tried to settle down to work on his exposition of Psalm 6, but
he was consumed with feelings of guilt at having left England.

His friends had urged him to go, and it had seemed the sensible
course to take. God had called him to be a preacher, nor a martyr,
and yet what would happen to all his parishioners without him?
He had continually urged Elizabeth Bowes and the others never
to recant, yet if they did not go to Mass they could be arrested
and sent to the stake as heretics. Most of all, he was tortured by
the thought that perhaps he had really fled the country out of
cowardice. In his present frame of mind, the sixth psalm seemed
particularly appropriate, with its prayer, 'O Lord, rebuke me not in
thine anger, neither chasten me in thy hot displeasure/Have mercy
upon me, O Lord, for I am weak: O Lord heal me, for my bones
are vexed . . . I am weary with my groaning . . . I water my couch
with tears . . . Let all mine enemies be ashamed and sore vexed . . .'
He worked on his explanatory essay for six weeks, and by the end
of February it was finished.

He sent it off to Elizabeth on the last day of the month, with a
covering letter, deploring the number of English people reportedly
attending Mass. News of their reversion to Catholicism was more
painful to him than his own death would be, he thought, and
of course that brought him back yet again to the question of his
motives for leaving. 'Some will ask, then, why did I fly?' he wrote.
'Assuredly, I cannot tell; but of one thing I am sure, the fear of
death was not the chief cause of my flying . . . but my flying is
no matter. By God's grace I may come to battle before that all
the conflict be ended. And haste the time, O Lord, at thy good
pleasure, that once again my tongue may yet praise thy holy name
before the congregation, if it were but in the very hour of death.'

She must not think that he had given up the struggle, for
'albeit I have in the beginning of this battle appeared to play the

faint-hearted and feeble soldier (the cause I remit to God), yet my prayer is that I may be restored to the battle again . . .'

Attempting a more philosophical tone, he reminded Elizabeth that he had told her many times that trouble was coming and indeed he was surprised that he had escaped it for so long. The death of Edward VI and the subsequent troubles were God's punishment on the self-seeking statesmen who had ruled the country during the King's minority but these troubles would eventually pass. They were like a medicine which was bitter to drink but would restore health. In the meantime, it was uncertain if he and Elizabeth would ever meet again. Realising as soon as he had written these words how wounded Elizabeth would be, he hastened to promise that 'If God continue you in life and me in corporal health, I shall attempt and essay to speak with you, face to face, within less time than is passed since the one of us last saw the other,' and he vowed that 'neither shall it be the fear of death nor the rage of the devil that shall impede or hinder me, and therefore, I beseech you, take not my words in that part, as though I were not minded to visit you again.' It was simply that 'because our life doth vanish like as the smoke before the blast of wind, my conscience moveth me to write unto you as though I should take from you my last good night in earth.'

Whatever happened, she must continue in the Protestant faith until the end. He had always preached the 'infallible and plain Word of God' and he would never recant one sentence of what he had taught, not 'for all the glory, riches and rest that is on earth.' Both England and Scotland would soon see that he was ready to suffer 'more than either poverty or exile . . . and therefore, Mother, let no fear enter into your heart as that I, escaping the furious rage of those ravening wolves that for our unthankfulness are lately loosed from their bonds, do repent anything of my former fervency.' He finished this long, rambling letter with the words, 'Upon the very point of my journey, the last of February 1554, Yours with sorrowful heart, John Knox.'[10]

That same day, he dispatched a 'Godly Letter to the Faithful in London, Newcastle, Berwick and all others within the realm of

England that love the coming of our Lord Jesus Christ.' Addressing in high rhetorical style all those who 'mourned for the great shipwreck of God's true religion', he urged them to avoid anything to do with idolatry, assuring them that they would win the battle and have everlasting joy. He sent this manuscript to England as well, ending his letter to the recipients, 'From a sore troubled heart upon my departure from Dieppe, whither God knoweth.'[11]

In fact, he did know where he was going. He intended to journey 800 miles south, to Geneva, to consult the great French Protestant authority, John Calvin, who had made his home in the Swiss city, just across the border from France. Moreover, he was not going to ask him about any abstruse theological points. His purpose was strictly practical. England was in a dreadful situation with its female Roman Catholic ruler, and Knox felt that his worst fears were about to be realised. On 2 January 1554, just before he left England, the Holy Roman Emperor's special ambassadors had arrived in London to negotiate the marriage of Charles V's son and heir, Prince Philip, to the English Queen, and the arrangements were progressing rapidly. Philip would soon be King of England, and, as he was a Spanish Roman Catholic, the implications of the match were grave.[12]

Scotland was likewise in a perilous situation. Mary, Queen of Scots was betrothed to a French Roman Catholic. The Duke of Châtelherault who was ruling Scotland for her was not persecuting the Protestants, it was true, but the Queen Mother, Mary of Guise was redoubling her efforts to replace him as regent, and it looked as though she were about to succeed. Hitherto Knox had always advocated passive resistance to ungodly monarchs, and he had even prayed publicly for Mary I at the time of her accession. Now, however, he felt that he could accept the situation no longer.

Perhaps he remembered how, in his university days, John Mair had taught that, if rulers became incorrigible tyrants, they could be deposed by the community and executed. Although Mair had not been thinking of the European situation, the principle was there, and Knox also knew that just four years earlier, in 1550, the Protestant pastors of Magdeburg had rebelled against Charles V and had written an *Apology of Magdeburg* justifying their actions. If people could really depose an ungodly prince, then there lay the solution to all the problems experienced in England and Scotland. However, this theory of rebellion was so challenging and so contrary to the accepted hierarchical view of the world that Knox felt an urgent need to consult his fellow Protestants about it.[13]

He might have gone to Lutheran Germany to seek advice there, but his own beliefs had been much influenced by the teachings of the Swiss reformers, like Ulrich Zwingli. Zwingli was long since dead, killed in battle against the Roman Catholics in 1531, but Calvin was an even greater authority. His classic work, the *Institutes of the Christian Religion*, had first been published in Basle in 1536.[14] In it, Calvin outlined Protestant theology with clarity and precision, and he published with it an address to François I of France, pleading with him to stop persecuting the French Protestants. The book immediately became a best-seller and went into many revised and expanded editions in both Latin and French. It was well-known at the English Court, and indeed Calvin had numbered among his many correspondents Lord Protector Somerset, Lady Jane Grey and Edward VI himself.

Just over three weeks after he left Dieppe, Knox was hurrying past the two storied, red-tiled houses of the walled city of Geneva, and up the narrow, cobbled Rue des Chanoines where John Calvin lived. Ushered into number eleven, he found himself in a noisy, bustling household. Calvin was a widower and his only son had died in infancy, but his two step-children lived with him and so did his brother and sister-in-law and their eight children, as well as a number of other relatives and friends. In the midst of the domestic turmoil, Knox was taken into a quiet, book-filled study, where a thin, ascetic man was sitting hunched in a black, furred gown.

Calvin had a long nose, a wispy beard and a pallid complexion. He had always been delicate, and like Knox he suffered from severe headaches and digestive troubles. He was forty-four years old now, by instinct a quiet, retiring academic who described himself as a timid scholar. He too had lost his mother at an early age and had been intended for the priesthood, but he did so well that his father decided that his clever son could make a more lucrative career as a lawyer and so Calvin changed course. When his father died, however, he abandoned all thoughts of the law and instead studied classical literature.

According to his own account, his conversion to Protestantism was quite sudden. In 1533 his close friend, Nicholas Cop, Rector of the University of Paris, delivered an evangelical address on All Saints' Day which resulted in such an uproar that both he and Calvin had to flee for their lives. From that time onwards, Calvin was committed to Protestantism. He found refuge initially in Basle and then moved to Strasbourg, where he planned to make his permanent home. On a fleeting visit to Geneva, however, he was bullied into settling there by the strong-minded reformer Guillaume Farel, who had recently been instrumental in converting the city to Protestantism and wanted his assistance. The Mass had been suspended in 1535 and the following spring the General Council of Geneva had declared that the city would henceforth 'live by the holy evangelical law and the word of God'. However, much work remained to be done and Farel needed his assistance.

Calvin's subsequent life in Geneva had not been easy. He had even been expelled from the city for three years, and on his return in 1541 people set their dogs on him and shouted him down when he attended meetings of one of the governing councils. Nonetheless he persevered, preaching, writing and travelling all over Switzerland and Germany to confer with both Protestants and Roman Catholics. He was now recognised as a highly distinguished authority, a subtle theologian and an excellent preacher. No account of their first meeting survives, but Knox swiftly became Calvin's admiring disciple.

Each Sunday and often on weekdays too, Calvin walked up the Rue des Chanoines (subsequently renamed the Rue Jean-Cauvin in his honour) and made his way across the wide courtyard to the

Cathedral Church of St Pierre to preach. Knox went regularly to listen to him. Founded in the fourth century, the cathedral building dates from about 1160, and in our own time its two sturdy towers and its elegant spire still look out over the old city, towards the River Rhône where it flows from the Lake of Geneva. A pillared, neo-classical façade was erected to replace the original cathedral entrance in the mid-eighteenth century, but, inside, the vast, arched interior, startlingly plain, is still as it was when Knox knew it.

With the Reformation of 1535, the altars, statues and ornamental pictures had been destroyed, the organs had been demolished and the elaborate wall paintings had been whitewashed over. Instead, the pulpit had become the focal point of the services. Many other churches throughout Europe underwent a similar transformation at the time of the Reformation, but few have preserved that original austerity intact. It is no exaggeration to say that to stand in the Cathedral of St Pierre today, in all its bare, awe-inspiring magnificence, is to gain a whole new understanding of Protestantism and John Knox's concept of God.[15]

Not only did Knox attend the Cathedral to hear Calvin's sermons, he sought his advice on the issues which were now preoccupying him. Was it necessary, he asked, to obey the son of a king if the child succeeds to the throne while he is still too young to rule for himself? Was a woman entitled by divine law to rule and govern, and, if so, was her royal power transferred to her husband when she married? Was it necessary to obey a magistrate who enforces idolatry (meaning Roman Catholicism) and condemns the true religion (meaning Protestantism)? Supposing men – landowners, men of substance, not peasants – wanted to defend themselves by armed force against an ungodly ruler, could they do so? In that situation, should godly men support the right-thinking landowners or the idolatrous ruler?

Knox couched all these questions in theoretical terms, at no time specifying whom he had in mind, but of course it was perfectly obvious why he was asking. Calvin told him firmly that subjects were never justified in resisting an idolatrous ruler by armed force. Law and order had to take priority, otherwise the whole of society might disintegrate. As to women rulers, Calvin took the conventional view that it was against nature for women to govern. There might very occasionally be an exception, like Deborah in the Bible. Her rule had been a blessing, but, for the most part, a woman monarch was sent by God as a punishment for the sins of mankind. In spite of that, it was no more justifiable to disobey a tyrannical female ruler than it was to resist a male tyrant.

Knox was disappointed. This was not what he had wanted to hear. Seeing that he was dissatisfied, Calvin suggested that he discuss the matter further with Heinrich Bullinger, Zwingli's successor in Zurich, and Pierre Viret, the chief pastor in Lausanne. Knox was apparently reluctant, so Calvin supplied him with a letter of introduction saying, 'This brother, a Scot by nationality, seeks the advice of Zurich and is travelling to you, not unwillingly, I hope. They say that, under King Edward, he laboured energetically for the faith. He is now eager to increase his learning.'

Willingly or not, Knox set off once more, and when he arrived in Zurich he submitted his queries in writing to Bullinger. Bullinger's answers were, like Calvin's, cautious. An under-age king such as Edward VI was indeed a lawful ruler, but by the laws of both God and nature, no woman should rule. Of course, if she did succeed to a throne, it would be dangerous for godly men to resist her. As for tyrants, God would give devout people the opportunity to overthrow them in the end.

In one respect, Bullinger did go further than Calvin. It was not necessary to obey a ruler who condemned the true religion and enforced idolatry, he thought. Indeed, the godly should resist such a prince, even if it meant risking their own lives. However, he was unwilling to authorise revolt, and he warned that wicked men often try to persuade the righteous to join them by pretending to have godly motives themselves. Again, any choice between supporting the evil ruler or the right-thinking rebels would very much depend on circumstances. He could not give advice on specific cases. Somewhat encouraged, Knox went on his way and, when he had completed his circuit of the Swiss theologians, he hurried back to Dieppe.[16]

6

Frankfurt

AFTER HIS ARRIVAL IN Dieppe, Knox wrote to tell Elizabeth Bowes that he had come there 'to learn the estate of England and Scotland'.[1] He was hoping to be able to slip across the Channel, but reports from the other side were not good. Three months earlier, Sir Thomas Wyatt, son of one of Henry VIII's favourite courtiers and himself an experienced soldier, had rebelled against Mary I, intending to depose her in favour of Princess Elizabeth. His rising had been crushed, and he had been executed. Until now, Lady Jane Grey's life had been spared, but, amidst fears that she and her husband would become the focus for further plotting, they too had been sent to the block.

The English Privy Council was deeply divided and Parliament was in a state of disarray. The Queen was determined to introduce acts against heresy, in spite of the fact that powerful noblemen were opposing the new legislation because it would force them to give back the church lands they had acquired as a result of the Reformation.[2] As for Scotland, by dint of bribery and promises of future advantage, Mary of Guise had finally succeeded in wresting the regency from the Duke of Châtelherault. The official transfer of power had taken place on

12 April 1554 and prospects for the Protestants looked bleak.[3]

Greatly troubled by these developments, Knox wrote a long letter to the English Protestants on 10 May 1554. He later published this letter under the title *An Epistle to his Afflicted Brethern in England* and followed it up on 31 May with *A Comfortable Epistle sent to the Afflicted Church of Christ.* Desperately worried about the welfare of his friends in England, he could only advocate passive resistance. They must leave vengeance to God, and pray for tyrants. It was a Christian's duty to forgive affronts. It was, however, permissible to resent injuries to Protestantism in a spirit of righteous indignation. God would have no objection to that, and He would in due course 'execute his vengeance upon these bloodthirsty tyrants and obstinate idolaters.'[4]

That spring, Knox also revised his *Letter to the Faithful in London, Newcastle and Berwick* and completed *A Faithful Admonition made by John Knox unto the Professors of God's Truth in England,* which he must have begun before he left for France. All these tracts were published secretly under the names of fictitious printers. Sometimes he humorously gave 'Rome' or 'The Pope's Castle of St Angelo' as the place of publication. Wherever they were actually printed, they were intended for circulation among the Protestants of England and his merchant friends smuggled them across the Channel. In the lengthy *Admonition* he returned to a previous theme, vigorously denouncing the English Protestant nobles for their self-seeking greed during Edward VI's reign and their ready acceptance of Roman Catholicism under Mary I. He even blamed himself for not publicly accusing the Duke of Northumberland of corruption in those sermons which he had preached towards the end of the Duke's period of power.

He then boldly addressed the question of Mary's marriage. Who would have believed that people like Bishop Tunstall of Durham would have handed over the crown of England to a Spaniard, he asked, and he said bluntly that if Mary and certain members of her council had been put to death during Edward VI's reign, she would never have been in a position to persecute Protestants. Until she had come to power, people had believed that she was earnest, merciful and loved the commonwealth of England. No one could have credited the fact that 'such cruelty could have entered into the heart of a woman, and into the heart of her that is called a virgin, and that she would thirst the blood of innocents.'

When she had been in East Anglia in July 1553, at the very start of her reign, Mary had given an undertaking that she would uphold the Protestant religion and refrain from marrying a foreigner, but she had later ignored her promises. Knox could only conclude that 'under an English name she beareth a Spanish heart', and he ended his letter by hoping that God would send a Jehu to execute judgement against idolaters, Jehu being the biblical prophet who slew the wicked Jezebel. Those who read the *Faithful Admonition* were shocked by certain passages in it for they thought, not surprisingly, that Knox was actually calling for the Queen to be assassinated. As so often happened, he had been carried away by the power of his own rhetoric.[5]

Mary and Prince Philip had been formally betrothed on 8 March 1554 and on 12 July Philip set sail from Spain. Their marriage was imminent and so any prospect of Knox being able to return in the near future had vanished. On 20 July he wrote a long letter to Elizabeth Bowes, telling her that he was uncertain when God would grant him any opportunity to visit her again, much as he would have liked to do so. He would, however, keep on writing to her. He was sure that by now she had little need of his admonitions, but it was his duty to comfort her and, he would do so 'for that most unfeigned familiarity and tender love, according to godliness, that we have kept since our first acquaintance.' He ended his letter on a personal note. 'My own estate I cannot well declare,' he said, but 'if any collection might be made among the faithful, it were no shame for me to receive that which Paul refused not in his time of trouble,' and he signed himself, 'your son, with troubled heart, John Knox.' Soon afterwards, he rode south once more to Geneva, in a mood of deep depression.[6]

Back in Calvin's city, he decided to use this unwanted interlude to improve his already extensive knowledge of the Bible, with a view to the day when he could return to his real work of preaching and looking after his congregation. He had never had either the time or the opportunity to learn Hebrew and Greek, but he would do it now, and he would study in detail Calvin's theological writings as well as listen to him preach. Hardly had he settled down to his studies when he received a disturbing letter. A group of English exiles in Germany wanted him to come and be their pastor.

During the previous spring, about 800 Protestants had fled from England and they were now scattered through various towns on the continent, mainly in Germany and Switzerland. Strasbourg, for instance, was a free, Protestant city within the Roman Catholic Holy Roman Empire, granted special privileges in the Middle Ages by the Emperor himself. This allowed it to be virtually self-governing, and much as Charles V would have liked to eradicate Lutheranism from his territories, his empire was so large and unwieldy that he could not possibly attend to everything. As a result, Protestants were able to worship as they wished in these free cities and Strasbourg had become the centre for more than half of the exiles. Other congregations had recently been established at Emden, Wesel and Frankfurt am Main.

Frankfurt was another largely independent city within the Holy Roman Empire, and it had already provided shelter for a congregation of French Protestant weavers who had fled there from Glastonbury in England, where they had been living. Their leader, Valérand de Paullain, had been given the use of the Church of the White Ladies in Frankfurt, and he offered to share the premises with the English refugees. The city authorities agreed, on condition that the English used a form of service similar to that of Paullain and his French Calvinists.

Not all the English exiles were pleased by this, for they would rather have used their own Book of Common Prayer. William Whittingham of Christ Church, Oxford, who was not yet ordained, was acting as their temporary pastor. He preferred the French,

Calvinist form of worship and accordingly devised a new service which, although based on the Second Book of Common Prayer, differed from it in various important ways. Vestments and responses were discarded, Whittingham wore a plain black gown, and the congregation sang psalms and remained seated for communion. Having organised themselves, they wrote to their fellow exiles in Strasbourg and elsewhere, inviting them to move to Frankfurt. It would be best if the English were united in one place until the day came when they could return home. Of course, they would need pastors and elders, and it was at this point that they wrote to Knox. They also invited two of the other preachers who had taken part in Edward VI's Lenten services to come and serve as pastors along with Knox.

James Haddon in Strasbourg wrote back at once, saying that he preferred to stay where he was. Thomas Lever, formerly Master of St John's College in Cambridge and now living in Zurich did not reply and, left to himself, Knox would have declined. A move to Frankfurt would be a distraction from his studies. Calvin, however, had other ideas. Although he had himself originally been attracted to a quiet existence, shut away with his books, he was now of the opinion that, regardless of how much people might admire celibacy or a philosophical life cut off from everyday matters, the men best fitted to govern both church and society were those who had extensive experience of practical matters. He spoke to Knox and, on his instructions, Knox unwillingly agreed to go.[7]

He set out in November 1554. It was a lengthy journey, along Lake Geneva, skirting the edge of the rocky Jura Mountains and then riding northwards through the wide, flat valley of the Rhine, with the Vosges mountains of France away in the distance to the left and the closer hills of the Black Forest to the right. He would have stopped at little villages to change his horses and speak to the local Protestant pastors. He did not speak German, but they would have been able to converse in Latin. Finally, turning east at Mainz, he followed the course of the River Main through pleasantly rolling, wooded countryside until he finally came to Frankfurt.

A great many routes converged at Frankfurt, making it an important trading and communications centre, and since the invention of printing it had become famous for publishing and the book trade. The English exiles he was seeking were housed in a disused plague hospital in the north-eastern corner of the city. Set back from the other houses, its gable end right against the city wall, it was an imposing building. Four storeys high, it had a steeply pitched roof and rows of windows on the gable facing the city as well as along the sides. The extensive walled garden looked over an open area called the Klapperfeld, towards crowded streets.

The Church of the White Ladies was right across the city, just inside the south-west stretch of the encircling wall and only a couple of streets away from the river. Its main external features were a tall, narrow spire and an adjoining cloister, dating from its previous existence as part of a Roman Catholic convent. Inside, there was a sturdy, arched ceiling above a plain interior stripped of its former statues and paintings. Neither the plague hospital nor the Church of the White Ladies survives. However, the hospital can clearly be seen on a detailed plan of the city, which was engraved by Conrad Faber and Hans Grav, just two years before Knox's arrival. This bird's-eye view also shows the Church of the White Ladies, which stood unaltered until its destruction in the air raids of World War II.[8]

When Knox arrived to take up his duties in the late autumn, he was perturbed to find his new congregation still arguing about the form their services should take, for Whittingham's invitation to the other English congregations to move to Frankfurt had exacerbated the problem.[9] The Zurich group had promptly replied that they could only unite with their Frankfurt brothers if the Second Book of Common Prayer was in use, and the Strasbourg community had taken the same viewpoint and had complicated the situation further by offering to send three of their number who had been Church of England bishops to take charge in Frankfurt. This offer had been briskly rejected, but it was not going to be easy to reconcile the various interests.

As soon as Knox arrived, his new congregation elected him to be their pastor and he set to work. He had no intention of bludgeoning them into submission. The whole purpose of his being there was to reconcile their differences, not make matters worse. After his successes in the north of England, he was confident enough that he could establish peace and good order. After all, his fellow exiles were intelligent, educated people. Many of them were eminent Protestant scholars and theologians who would surely listen to reason, or so he thought. In practice, the very fact that they were knowledgeable added to the difficulty of his task. Far from home, upset and out of their usual, worried about the families and the colleagues they had left behind, and well used to engaging in academic disputes, they now expended a good deal of energy on bitter arguments about theological issues, great and small.

A fortnight after his arrival, a letter came from Strasbourg and Knox discovered that the Protestants there who wanted to keep the Book of Common Prayer felt as they did not only because they were used to it, but because they were very conscious that, since their departure, Archbishop Cranmer had been arrested, tried and found guilty of heresy. He was now awaiting execution. If they rejected his Book, it would seem that they were abandoning him too. After careful discussion, Knox and Whittingham composed a diplomatic reply. They explained that they were allowed to use the Church of the White Ladies on condition that they followed the French pattern of worship. The Frankfurt authorities would never agree to some of the ceremonies included in the Book of Common Prayer. Whittingham had made as few alterations to it as possible, and the amendments which he had made implied no criticism of the Book itself.

So far so good, but no sooner had the letter been sent to Strasbourg than a new problem arose. Some of the Frankfurt congregation suggested that instead of continuing with the order of service devised by Whittingham, they should change to the one used in Geneva, which had been drafted by Calvin himself. They knew that Knox would approve of that. Tempting though the idea must have been, Knox had to point out that if they made the change, they would cause a deep rift among the Protestant exiles. Even if everyone in Frankfurt agreed to it, there were the English people elsewhere to be considered. He could not possibly use the Genevan service unless he first obtained the agreement of the brethern in Strasbourg, Zurich and Emden.

Hearing what was afoot, the members of his own congregation who favoured the Second Book of Common Prayer redoubled their efforts to have it reinstated. Beginning to lose patience, Knox pointed out that he personally could not use the Book at Communion, because of its instruction to communicants to kneel. He had been forced to accept it in England, but he was no longer willing to conform to something which he believed to be completely wrong. If people objected to him administering the Lord's Supper to seated communicants, then he would no longer officiate at Communion services, and if that was not enough to satisfy his critics, he would ask them to release him altogether from his charge. That, of course, threw them into a flurry of dismay. They refused to let him go and agreed that he should continue to use Whittingham's order of service.

Peace was restored, but all too briefly. Soon afterwards, a new group of refugees from England arrived, including among their number Edmund Grindal, a future Archbishop of Canterbury, Edwin Sandys, who was to become Archbishop of York and Thomas Becon, formerly chaplain to Archbishop Cranmer. These were men used to organising and instructing. They were not going to sit meekly and accept whatever Knox or anyone else told them, and as it happened they were all supporters of the Second Book of Common Prayer. They joined forces with the like-minded Frankfurt minority, while one or two new arrivals from elsewhere supported Knox and Whittingham. John Foxe had been in Basle, where he had published his celebrated *Book of Martyrs*, while Christopher Goodman was an important political theorist and

Lady Margaret Professor of Divinity at Oxford in Edward VI's time. He now became Knox's close friend. Despite Knox's best efforts, the congregation split into two distinct groups and the battle lines were drawn.

In December 1554, the situation deteriorated still further when Thomas Lever appeared from Zurich, to announce belatedly that he was accepting the Frankfurt congregation's invitation to become their pastor. Knox and his followers were taken aback by this development. Lever was a strong supporter of the Second Book of Common Prayer and it seemed to them that his arrival now was no coincidence. They suspected that he had come to lead the opposition. However, he agreed to use Whittingham's service for the time being, provided the situation was reviewed the following Easter. In a further bid to promote unity, the congregation elected him joint pastor with Knox.

Deeply worried about the situation, Knox decided to write to Calvin for advice. Whittingham composed a letter from them both, strongly criticising the Book of Common Prayer. They sent it off on 11 December 1554, with a Latin summary of the Book. Calvin replied early the following month, regretting such unseemly arguments. He said that although the Prayer Book did still include some dregs of popery, there was nothing obviously wrong with it. Rather than falling out among themselves, the exiles should take this opportunity to put right these minor imperfections, which the English church authorities themselves would undoubtedly have corrected had Mary I not come to the throne.

This did not satisfy those members of the Frankfurt congregation who were still agitating for the Genevan service to be adopted. After further lengthy wrangling, the congregation decided that what was needed was a new form of service altogether, and they asked Knox, Whittingham, John Foxe and Anthony Gilby and Thomas Cole from Geneva to undertake the task. This group obediently drew up a new order of service, presented it to the congregation and the arguments broke out all over again, even more fiercely than before. Thomas Lever and his friends accused Knox and his colleagues of deliberately trying to split the community and they retorted that if the congregation were not satisfied, they should choose a new committee to draft another order of service. That was agreed, and Foxe, Gilby and Cole were replaced by Lever and one of his supporters, Thomas Parry.

Until their new text was ready, the congregation would use an order of service which was closer to the Book of Common Prayer than Whittingham's version had been. All members of the Frankfurt congregation were to agree in writing to this arrangement, and any complaints were to be sent to a group of leading Protestant preachers including Calvin, Bullinger and Viret. On 6 February 1555 there was a grand reconciliation between the two opposing factions. Knox had worked hard for this for this compromise, and for nearly five weeks everything went smoothly, but on 13 March a new band of English exiles arrived in Frankfurt, led by the redoubtable Dr Richard Cox.

If Knox had a strong personality, he was easily matched by Dr Cox, one of Edward VI's tutors. An energetic, overbearing man, Cox had originally been a persecutor of Protestants during the reign of Henry VIII but, at the time of the King's divorce from Catherine of Aragon, he had changed sides and become tutor of Edward VI, Dean of Christ Church and a vice-chancellor of Oxford University. Set on rooting out all evidences of popery in the University, he earned himself the nickname of 'the Cancellor' because he ordered the destruction of ancient manuscripts, rare books and fine paintings on the grounds that they contained Roman Catholic imagery or ideology. He sat on the commissions considering both the First and Second Books of Common Prayer, and he became a stout supporter of the Second Book.

On the accession of Mary I, Dr Cox was arrested and imprisoned on a charge of treason. He was later released and placed under house arrest, but in May 1554 managed to escape to Antwerp. He had been visiting various groups of English exiles when he heard rumours of what was happening in Frankfurt, and he set off at once, arriving in the city on 13 March 1555. He had brought a group of supporters with him, and within a couple of days they attended a service in the Church of the White Ladies. Thomas Lever was officiating that day. Instead of joining in quietly, Dr Cox and his friends interrupted, giving in loud voices the responses set out in the Book of Common Prayer.

Disconcerted, Lever did not try to stop them, but the elders ordered them to be quiet, to no avail. Knox was himself in the congregation, and he tried to remonstrate with the newcomers, but Dr Cox insisted that 'they would do as they had done in England', and that 'they would have the face of an English Church.' Knox replied tersely, 'The Lord grant it to have the face of Christ's Church'. Afterwards, Knox asked Lever to support him. To his dismay, Lever replied that he was in complete agreement with Dr Cox. In future, he said, they must use the Church of England litany in their services. Knox retorted angrily that he could never allow that. The compromise worked out a month before had been accepted unanimously. How could Lever go back on it now?

The following Sunday, 17 March 1555, one of Dr Cox's colleagues entered the pulpit uninvited and read out the litany. Cox and his friends joined in with the responses. When Knox preached that afternoon, he reminded his listeners of the recent compromise. It had been achieved after so much effort, and now it had now been wrongfully violated. The Second Book of Common Prayer contained impure superstitions, he said, and he would oppose any attempt to introduce it. Indeed, he added, England's current troubles were in part the result of God's displeasure with the English for being slack about reforming their religion.

Needless to say, that did not go down well. Infuriated, Dr Cox and his supporters accused Knox of slandering their mother church. They complained loudly about his sermon, and a fierce argument ensued. Knox called a meeting of the congregation for that evening, and demanded a return to the agreed compromise. Dr Cox and his supporters were not present, of course, because they were not actually members of the congregation, but their views were put by

Lever and his followers. No agreement could be reached and the meeting was adjourned.

When they reconvened the following Tuesday, Lever said that Dr Cox and his colleagues ought to be admitted as members of the congregation right away. Most of those present were against the idea, and Knox pointed out, reasonably enough, that the newcomers would have to agree to accept the discipline of the congregation before they could join. Moreover, those who had attended Mass in England could not possibly be accepted as members until they gave evidence that they had repented. This provoked more furious argument, and Lever's supporters walked out twice.

Desperate to prevent a complete breakdown in relations, Knox told his own supporters that Dr Cox and his group would have to be admitted. He was well aware, of course, that this would greatly strengthen his own opponents. The proposal was passed without enthusiasm, and Dr Cox and his companions were invited to join. Dr Cox promptly proposed that Knox should be dismissed and forbidden to preach in the church, leaving Lever as sole pastor. The followers of Cox and Lever voted in favour of the motion, and it was passed. On 19 March 1555, Knox was dismissed from his post and told that he must neither preach nor meddle in congregational affairs.

Horrified, Knox's supporters sent Whittingham to complain to the magistrates of Frankfurt. This he did the following day, saying that the new arrivals were trying to prevent the rightful minister from carrying out his duties. If that were to happen, serious disturbances might well ensue. The magistrates forbade the congregation to hold their usual service that day and told them to elect yet another committee to draw up yet another order of service acceptable to both factions. The new committee, chaired this time by Valérand de Paullain, met in his house that same afternoon. Despite all the trouble, Knox was a member, along with Whittingham, Lever and Cox.

Predictably, the discussions were long and involved, but by the end of the second day they had managed to agree on various points.

At their third discussion, however, they encountered insuperable difficulties over the wording of the service of matins. Cox and Lever wanted to use passages from the Prayer Book: 'O Lord open thou our lips' and 'We praise thee O Lord'. Knox said these were not to be found in the Bible. They had come from Roman Catholic services and were not acceptable. Cox and Lever were so annoyed that they walked out.

Knox and Whittingham then met their own friends and sent a supplication to the Frankfurt magistrates attacking both Dr Cox and the Book of Common Prayer and asking the magistrates to refer the whole dispute to Calvin, Bullinger, Viret and others. These eminent theologians should be invited to draft the new order of service. Thoroughly exasperated, one of the magistrates went in person to the Church of the White Ladies and told the congregation in no uncertain terms that the city authorities were most annoyed with them. They must immediately adopt the form of service used by Paullain and his French Protestants. If there were any further argument, they would no longer be allowed to meet in the church.

As soon as the magistrate had finished speaking, Dr Cox was on his feet, telling him that of course they would obey, and saying how sorry he was about the congregation's behaviour. The following day, Paullain's order of service was indeed used, and Dr Cox and his friends were suspiciously quiet. They did not utter a single response, and offered no objection when arrangements were made for Knox to preach that Sunday but, when Saturday came, two of Dr Cox's supporters went to one of the city councillors. They told him that while Knox was in Amersham at the time of Mary I's accession, he had preached a sermon comparing the Emperor Charles V to Nero and had later published it in a treasonable pamphlet. Producing Knox's *Admonition to England*, they pointed out nine passages which they said were seditious.

Dr Cox had planned his revenge well. In 1547 the city of Frankfurt had defied Charles V and had narrowly escaped his wrath. Ever since, the councillors had made strenuous efforts to avoid antagonising the Emperor. Thoroughly alarmed, the councillor told his colleagues and Whittingham was summoned and questioned. He did his best, assuring them that Knox was 'a learned, grave and godly man', but it was no use. Handing him the pamphlet, they ordered Whittingham to bring them a Latin translation of the offending passages by one o'clock that same day, so that they could read them for themselves. Whittingham complied, the council met again, and Knox was forbidden to preach the following day.

Although forbidden to enter the pulpit, Knox decided to attend as a member of the congregation, which he often did. No sooner had be set foot in the church, than Dr Cox and all his supporters rose and walked out, saying loudly that they could not stay if he was there. The next day, Frankfurt Council decided to expel Knox from the city. Summoning Whittingham once more, they advised him to persuade Knox to leave quietly, for, if he were denounced to the Emperor, they would be forced to hand him over. On the evening of 25 March 1555 Knox preached a farewell sermon to about 50 of his sympathisers who had gathered in his lodgings. They were all angry and indignant, but he stressed the eternal joy awaiting those of God's elect who were persecuted in this life. The next day, he set out for Geneva, accompanied for the first few miles of the journey by a group of friends.

Immediately after Knox had gone, Dr Cox went to the Frankfurt magistrates and got them to withdraw the order that the English congregation must use Paullain's form of service. Instead, they reverted to the Second Book of Common Prayer and Dr Cox announced that in future he would deal with all disciplinary matters. Whittingham and the others stayed on for a time in Frankfurt in an attempt to mend matters, but by the late summer they had had enough, and when Calvin invited them that August to move to Geneva, they accepted with alacrity. Furious, Dr Cox accused them of causing deep divisions within the Church but they retorted that they were not the cause of the schism. He was to blame for that.

John Foxe departed for Basle, the others rode to Geneva and

Dr Cox and his colleagues sent off a letter to Calvin trying to justify their actions. They claimed that Mary I had reintroduced the medieval heresy laws and burned Protestant martyrs because of what Knox had written in his *Admonition*. If Knox had been allowed to continue as pastor, the Frankfurt authorities would have closed down the exiles' church. Satisfied that he had won his Prayer Book battle, Dr Cox then departed for Zurich, leaving his supporters to quarrel among themselves. The following year the English church in Frankfurt was said to be 'almost ruined' as a result of all the dissension.

Knox wrote a measured account of the unedifying troubles in Frankfurt. It was much more restrained in tone than his usual tracts. He could not condemn his fellow Protestants in the way that he lashed out at the Roman Catholics. He did not even denounce Dr Cox, and indeed he said that he forgave his enemies in Frankfurt from the bottom of his heart. His only real criticism was reserved for Thomas Lever, whom he felt had betrayed him, but they made up their quarrel in the end and Lever came to Geneva to join Knox's congregation there.

Knox's months in Frankfurt had been worrying, irritating and frustrating. Diplomacy never was his strong suit, but he had tried hard to be patient and tolerant and he had really gone to extraordinary lengths to appease his adversaries and achieve some form of compromise. It was hardly his fault that he did not succeed. Calvin was shocked when he heard what had happened, and in May 1555 wrote to Dr Cox and his friends, pointing out all the imperfections of the Book of Common Prayer and declaring, 'Mr Knox was, in my judgment, neither godly nor brotherly dealt with'. It would have been better if the exiles had stayed in England rather than bringing the 'firebrand of cruelty' to destroy all those who opposed them.[10]

7

Back to Scotland

ON HIS RETURN TO the calm of Geneva, Knox intended to settle down to his interrupted studies, and yet just four months later he was on his way back to Scotland. He had as usual kept in close touch with what was going on there, and his friends were telling him that the situation was more hopeful now than it had ever been. Mary of Guise, ruling as Regent, seemed gracious, approachable and indeed almost sympathetic to the Protestant cause. Although she was a devout Roman Catholic, she had no desire to stir up religious troubles.

The truth of it was that, like her friends in France, she regarded Scotland as a primitive, infant nation which she meant to transform into a modern, well-organised state, a reliable ally for her own country. Her chief priority was to make sure that Henri II went ahead with the promised marriage between his son and her daughter, and so she set about trying to persuade the Scottish Parliament to grant the Dauphin the crown matrimonial, as Henri II desired. This was no easy task, for it would mean that François was not merely the consort of Mary, Queen of Scots, but King of Scots, joint ruler with her, and, should she die, he would go on governing the country. To accomplish her plan, the Queen Regent needed as much support as possible, and she began to cultivate her Protestant Lords.

She met with considerable success. She now numbered among her advisers Alexander, 4th Earl of Glencairn, Archibald, 4th Earl of Argyll, Andrew, 1st Lord Ochiltree and her own step-son Lord James Stewart. Lord James was one of James V's illegitimate sons, and Mary of Guise had known him since he was a child. He was a handsome, intelligent young man with his father's aquiline features, and a distinct presence. There were those who regretted that an accident of birth had deprived him of the throne. If only he had been legitimate, he would have become king when his father died. As it was, he seemed entirely loyal to the Queen Regent and her daughter, but like the other three men he displayed an increasing commitment to the Protestant cause. In this new climate of toleration, several English Protestant preachers had sought refuge in Scotland in recent months and people began to say that the Queen Regent herself would convert to Protestantism.

This view may strike us as being singularly naïve, but we have to remember that almost all the Protestants in the country were very recent converts. If men like Lord James and Argyll could adopt the new religion, why should Mary of Guise not do so too? An experienced and worldly-wise woman, she must have been well aware of the abuses of the Roman Catholic Church. Various Scottish Protestants felt that, if the reformed religion were explained to her properly, she would surely see that it was the only way. We know that this was wishful thinking, but in the summer of 1555 it seemed a real possibility.[1]

The Scottish Protestants realised that they needed a leader, a preacher who was above political manoeuvrings and could concentrate on the spiritual transformation of the country. Knox was the obvious choice. He therefore began to receive messages indicating that the time had come for him to return home, but he had considerable misgivings. He was not convinced that there was a real opportunity to advance the Protestant cause, and he had been looking forward to a peaceful interlude after the recent turmoil of Frankfurt. In the end, it seems to have been a letter from Elizabeth Bowes which made up his mind. 'Albeit my journey towards Scotland, beloved Mother, was most contrarious to my own judgement before I did enterprise the same,' he told her later, 'yet this day I praise God for them who was the cause external of my resort to these quarters: that is, I praise God in you and for you, whom He made the instrument to draw me from the den of my own ease (you alone did draw me from the rest of quiet study).'[2]

He arrived in Edinburgh in late September 1555 and found lodgings in the house of a well-known Protestant merchant, James Syme. Almost at once, a procession of notable people came to see him. Knox had been a prisoner when he had left Scotland eight years earlier, a renegade priest, his career as a preacher scarcely begun. Since then he had experienced great physical hardship, travelled thousands of miles and become an important, authoritative figure engaged in ecclesiastical debate at the highest levels, not only in England but on the continent. His arrival therefore provoked a good deal of interest.

One of the first to visit him was John Erskine, the Laird of Dun, an active supporter of Protestantism. Erskine swiftly arranged a supper party in his own house in the Canongate so that Knox could meet other influential Protestants: David Forrest, Master of the Mint, John Willock, a former Dominican friar who had been in both England and Germany since becoming a Protestant preacher and, even more importantly, William Maitland of Lethington, the subtle diplomat whose desire for friendship between Scotland and England was leading him to support the reformed cause.

Apart from these public figures, other acquaintances of James Syme came to his house to hear Knox preach and their wives came with them, the usual devout, middle-class ladies anxious for spiritual guidance. Elizabeth Adamson, wife of James Barron, an Edinburgh burgess, was dying of a very painful disease, probably cancer, and her conscience was troubled because she was unhappy with the teachings of the Roman Catholic Church. She found great comfort in her talks with Knox, and he was much impressed with her, not least because she refused the offices of priests during her last hours.

Knox could see that there were many matters in need of his attention. During the supper at Erskine of Dun's house, the question of attendance at Mass had been discussed. Far too many Protestants were still going to Mass. Those noblemen who supported the reformed faith and were tolerated by Mary of Guise were in the habit of attending her services at Court in order to please her. Knox was horrified to hear it. They defended themselves by saying that even St Paul had found it necessary to go to the temple and pretend to participate in services. Knox replied briskly that their attendance at Mass was nothing to do with St Paul and his career. They must stop it at once.

They also discussed what was happening in other parts of the country, and Erskine suggested that Knox should stay with him for a time at his House of Dun, about half way between Montrose and Brechin. Knox took up the invitation. He could not risk arrest by preaching openly, but Erskine invited local gentlemen and Montrose merchants to come to Dun to hear him. They were impressed and Knox was surprised and delighted at their response. There was a far greater commitment to Protestantism in Scotland than he had expected. He wrote on 4 November 1555 to tell Elizabeth Bowes, 'If I had not seen it with my own eyes in my own country, I could not have believed it.' In the same letter, he apologised to Elizabeth for spending so much time at his work, telling her that she must bear it patiently if he delayed some days further, presumably before visiting her. From the general tone of the letter it seems that he had not yet seen her, and since he wrote 'from Scotland', she and Marjorie had not come north to be with him, as has sometimes been supposed.[3]

Knox spent a month at the House of Dun, preaching every day, and then he went to stay with Sir James Sandilands at Mid Calder, about fifteen miles west of Edinburgh. During his time there, he was visited by three even more important public figures. John, 6th Lord Erskine, was slightly older than Knox. He had succeeded to his father's title that same year and his family had always been close to the monarchy. Archibald, Lord Lorne was the powerful 4th Earl of Argyll's heir and the third visitor was Lord James Stewart. He and Knox had met once before, in London, in the autumn of 1552, around the time when Knox had been offered the bishopric of Rochester and Lord James was on his way to visit his half-sister, Mary, Queen of Scots in France. Prior of St Andrews from childhood, Lord James was at that time in his early twenties and apparently still a practising Roman Catholic. No one knows why Lord James went to see Knox, or what they discussed, but they were able to meet now with friendly recognition.[4]

Erskine, Lorne and Lord James were so impressed with Knox that they urged him to preach publicly in Edinburgh. The capital remained strongly Roman Catholic, with too few Protestants to make public services feasible, but Knox did visit Edinburgh regularly that winter, presumably to preach in private houses. After Christmas, he resumed his travels, riding to the south west of Scotland at the invitation of John Lockhart, Laird of Barr and Robert Campbell of Kinzeancleuch. The local lairds offered him hospitality and he stayed with James Chalmers at Gadgirth and also with Andrew Stewart, Lord Ochiltree and his family at his House of Ochiltree, not only preaching but sometimes administering the Lord's Supper.

Just before Easter, Alexander, 4th Earl of Glencairn sent for him. The Earl was a genuinely convinced Protestant, and at this time the most powerful supporter of the reformed cause in Scotland. Knox spent a few days in his household at Finlayston in Renfrewshire, celebrating Communion with the Earl, his Countess, two of their sons and various friends. After that, he returned to Calder where, it is traditionally said, he officiated at the first public Communion in Scotland. It was probably during his stay there that he wrote out a sermon he had preached, arguing that there was no scriptural authority for fasting during Lent. This was passed round his followers.

In April he was at the House of Dun again and by that time his activities had come to the attention of the church authorities. He had, it was reported, said that people should stop paying tithes to the Church, since the decadent priests spent the money on themselves instead of on the poor. Copies of all his available writings were being circulated, not only the sermon on fasting but 'Answers to some questions concerning Baptism', an essay which he composed at about this time, criticising the Roman Catholic christening service. Moreover, the presence of prominent members of the Court at his private services had not gone unnoticed.[5]

Inevitably, the Roman Catholic authorities decided to move against him, and he was summoned to appear on a charge of heresy before a special commission led by John Hamilton, Archbishop of St Andrews. The commission would meet on 15 May 1556, in Black Friars' Church in Edinburgh. Protestants summoned to such hearings usually stayed away, for obvious reasons, but Knox must have reckoned that public opinion was so much in his favour that he could risk a trial. He told his friends that he would be there on the day, and Erskine of Dun and other Protestant gentlemen accompanied him when he rode to Edinburgh on 14 May.

Few people had expected Knox to obey the summons, and as soon as he and his little cavalcade rode into the capital, people hurried to tell Mary of Guise. The Queen Regent was an astute politician, and when she heard what was happening she realised that Knox's trial at the Black Friars' Church could be the signal for public riots. Anxious to avoid any civil disturbance, she warned Archbishop Hamilton that he must not go ahead with the prosecution. The summons against Knox was withdrawn on a technicality and, on 15 May 1556, instead of standing trial in the Black Friars' Church, Knox was preaching in the Bishop of Dunkeld's impressive residence on the north side of the Edinburgh's High Street, not far from Mary's own Palace of Holyroodhouse. The largest congregation he had so far attracted in the capital turned out to hear him, and so he preached there twice a day for the next ten days, morning and evening.[6]

The Earl of Glencairn was a regular attender, and one evening he persuaded William Keith, 4th Earl Marischal to accompany him. Very much taken with Knox's sermon, they told each other afterwards that if only Mary of Guise could hear him preach, she would almost certainly decide to support the Protestant cause. The charges against Knox had been withdrawn on her instructions, after all, so surely she would be willing to consider what he had to say. Convinced that this was the way forward, they went to see Knox and persuaded him to write to the Queen Regent.

No doubt conferring with Glencairn and Marischal, Knox made strenuous efforts to word his letter tactfully. He began by expressing gratitude for his continuing freedom although, of course, he did not thank Mary of Guise personally but attributed recent events to God's intervention. Rather than being able to write to her at this time, he said, he had fully expected to be lying under sentence of death. She would be rewarded, he told her, if she continued her moderation and clemency. 'Superfluous and foolish it shall appear to many that I, a man of base estate and condition, dare enterprise to admonish a princess so honourable, endowed with wisdom and graces singularly,' he went on, but he felt that it was his duty to utter a stern warning, since no one else would.

He knew, he said, how rulers were surrounded by flatterers who dared not speak the truth, and so he felt compelled to point out that unless she acted differently from all the other princes, her high position would bring her nothing but torment and pain everlasting. By this, he meant that she should convert and establish Protestantism. He understood the difficulties of her position, he told her, and he would be satisfied if, at first, she could do no more than grant religious toleration. 'Your Grace cannot hastily abolish all superstition, neither yet remove from offices unprofitable pastors which only feed themselves.' However, if the zeal for God's glory was in her heart she would not 'maintain manifest idolatry neither yet will ye suffer the fury of bishops to murder and devour the poor members of Christ's body.'

Knox was convinced that as a preacher of the Word of God he

was sent to offer spiritual guidance to everyone, regardless of how eminent they might be. Roman Catholic rulers had their confessors to offer them advice, so why should he not give guidance on behalf of the Protestant Church? He probably felt that he had gone to great lengths to be polite and respectful, and he may even have imagined that Mary of Guise would be grateful for his concern. It certainly did not cross his mind that she would resent anything he said. The letter finished, the Earl of Glencairn took it to Court and presented it to Mary in person. She accepted it with her accustomed courtesy, and put it to one side to read later. He and the Earl Marischal and Knox waited eagerly for her reply.

One day passed and then two, but no answer came. In the end, they heard indirectly what had happened. To Mary, Knox's well-meaning advice seemed ludicrous. This agitator, worse still, this former priest was actually having the temerity to lecture his monarch for the good of her soul and was telling her to become a heretic. In front of some of her courtiers she handed the letter to James Beaton, Archbishop of Glasgow, saying to him with a little laugh, 'Please you, my Lord, to read a pasquil [satire].' Knox soon got to hear what was happened and he was mortified. It seemed that he had been mistaken in his assessment of the Queen Dowager. She would never convert. Her apparently merciful attitude was all a pretence. The Protestants could hope for nothing from her but persecution and death.[7]

Soon afterwards, Knox received letters from Geneva, announcing that he had been chosen by the congregation of exiles there to be one of their pastors. Thoroughly disillusioned with the situation in Scotland and well aware that it would only be a matter of time before the church authorities moved against him again, he decided to accept, and set off on a farewell tour of all the little communities to whom he had preached. Before he left the country, however, he had some important business to finalise. As usual, the evidence is tantalisingly inadequate, but it seems that this was when he finally married Marjorie Bowes, probably in Edinburgh. She and her mother would go with him to Geneva.[8]

It is often said that Elizabeth deserted her husband, but Richard Bowes must have given his permission for Marjorie's marriage and he may well have agreed that his wife should go to Switzerland. She and Marjorie were uncompromising in their support of Protestantism and it must have been obvious to him that they were in real danger of arrest and death if they persisted in refusing to go to Mass. All else apart, their presence in his household must have been an embarrassment to him. If they took refuge on the continent they would be safe, he would not be in trouble with the Roman Catholic Church and he would have to endure no more endless arguments with his earnest, woebegone wife.

Knox's friend Robert Campbell of Kinzeancleuch now brought him an invitation from Lord Lorne's father, Archibald, 4th Earl of Argyll, who wanted to meet him. As Argyll was an extremely influential landowner in the west of Scotland, Knox felt that he could not refuse, and so he arranged for Marjorie and Elizabeth to set off ahead of him. All three were unhappy about this parting, but it seemed the safest course. He put them on board a ship sailing to Dieppe and told them to wait for him there, while he set off with his friend Robert Campbell of Kinzeancleuch to see Argyll at Castle Campbell near Dollar, in Clackmannanshire. He spent several days there, preaching and instructing but, when one of Argyll's relatives tried to persuade him to stay on for longer, he refused, saying that 'he must needs visit that little flock which the wickedness of men had compelled him to leave'.[9]

He did, however, compose *A Letter of Wholesome Council addressed to his Brethren in Scotland* for their guidance. Dated 7 July 1556 and later published, it told lairds and householders that they had a duty to see that their families, tenants and servants lived a Christian life for, as he put it, 'within your own houses . . . ye are bishops and kings; your wife, children, servants and family are your bishopric and charge'. There should be prayers for the whole household at least once a day, and Bible readings once a week. Congregations should meet together for weekly Bible study, confessing their sins and saying special prayers for the persecuted Protestants in France and England. If any unanswerable problems arose from the Bible readings, they should seek the opinion of someone they respected, and he indicated that he would always be ready to send advice. He would rather spend fifteen hours interpreting some passage of the scripture for members of the congregation than pass his time in any other way, he said.[10]

It is difficult to gauge the effect of Knox's visit to Scotland. He himself had been excited by the response to his preaching, and certainly he had attracted larger audiences than ever before in Edinburgh when he spoke in the Bishop of Dunkeld's house. Some recent historians have pointed out that most of those who came to hear him were already converts to the Protestant cause. He made no attempt to preach in churches, as George Wishart had done, nor did he regularly celebrate Communion in public. Although he had not tried to convert large numbers of ordinary people, he had exercised a considerable influence over the nobility and he had made himself doctrinal leader of the Scottish Protestants, thereby ensuring that the Calvinist rather than the Lutheran form of worship was adopted.

It was mid-July 1556 when Knox crossed to France and joined Marjorie and Mrs Bowes in Dieppe. As soon as he had gone from Scotland, the bishops summoned him again for heresy. When he failed to appear, an effigy of him was burned at the market cross in Edinburgh. After a few weeks in Dieppe, Knox escorted his wife and mother-in-law to Geneva, taking along with him a servant, James, and a student named Patrick, who must have come from Scotland with him. On 13 September 1556, all five were admitted as members of the English congregation in Geneva.[11]

Geneva was always thronging with refugees. Indeed, by this time they made up more than a quarter of the town's population. Most of them came from France, but there were also Italians, Spanish, Dutch, Scots and English. The previous October, the English refugees had been given permission to hold services in the Church of Notre-Dame-la-Neuve, which they were to share with the Italians. Tucked in behind the cathedral, the little church, now known as 'The Auditory', is a sturdy, thick-walled building with small windows. Church of Scotland and other Protestant services are still held there to this day, and at the entrance a plaque in French proudly proclaims the fact that John Knox, Scottish Calvinist reformer, was elected pastor of the English colony and preached there from 1556 to 1559.

His congregation comprised more than a hundred members and many of them were themselves well known figures. Knox's Frankfurt colleague Whittingham was there, as was their former opponent Thomas Lever and Knox's friend Christopher Goodman. During Knox's absence in Scotland, Goodman and Anthony Gilby, another former member of the Frankfurt congregation, had been acting as pastors. Their order of service was the one drawn up in Frankfurt by Knox, Whittingham, Gilby, Foxe and Cole and adopted there until the differences with Lever forced them to abandon it in favour of the compromise version they were using when Dr Cox arrived. The pastors of the English congregation in Geneva were elected every twelve months and, on 16 December 1556, Knox and Goodman were chosen to officiate for the following year.[12]

At last, Knox could settle down. No longer would he have to spend his time riding hundreds of miles in all weather, arguing with intransigent idolaters and even more intransigent colleagues, going into hiding to avoid the threat of arrest and even death. He could do God's work now under very different circumstances. Calvin himself did not think that Geneva was an ideal world, and to his dying day he complained of the perverse and unhappy behaviour of the inhabitants. This was not perhaps surprising, for he had spent years struggling to impose what he regarded as a godly way of life on the wayward citizens.

The initials of Jesus Christ had been placed on the gates of Geneva and under Calvin's supervision every aspect of daily existence was scrutinised and any lapse from morality was punished by public humiliation, fines, banishment, whipping, imprisonment or, in the worst cases, by execution. Theoretically, heretics could be burned, but only one man had ever been sent to the stake, although others had been beheaded. Adultery was also punishable by death, but only after a long series of warnings and more minor punishments. Viewed by modern standards, the system seems hideously intrusive, but, in fact, the punishments were milder than they had been under previous regimes.[13]

Even so, not everyone liked the Calvinist way of life, and Calvin was consistently criticised by a group of opponents known as the Libertines because of their love of freedom. For his part, Knox viewed Calvinist Geneva with deep satisfaction, believing it to be a truly godly society in which people acted with respect for each other and obedience to God. That same month he wrote to tell Mrs Anna Locke, one of his London friends, that Geneva, 'I neither fear nor am ashamed to say, is the most perfect school of Christ that ever was in earth since the days of the Apostles. In other places, I confess Christ to be truly preached, but manners and religion so sincerely reformed, I have not yet seen in any other place.'[14]

At a personal level, Knox's life was more comfortable than it had been for years. His mother-in-law was on hand to help with the running of the household, leaving Marjorie free to act as his secretary, keeping his papers in order and writing his letters to his dictation when he was unwell or too busy to do it himself. Marjorie was a great asset in every way, for she was diplomatic as well as charming and she soon became very popular with all his friends. John Calvin thought her delightful. Moreover, nine months after she and Knox arrived in Geneva, their first son, Nathaniel, was born. He was christened in The Auditory on 23 May 1557 with William Whittingham acting as his godfather.[15]

Refugees were continuing to pour into Geneva, and that same month Anna Locke arrived from London with her small son and daughter and a servant. Knox was greatly relieved. He had often stayed with Anna and her husband Harry Locke, a prosperous mercer, and they had treated him like a son, he thought, although Anna must have been at least fifteen years younger than he was. Well-educated and devout, she had translated some of Calvin's sermons into English and she had come to rely greatly on Knox's

St Mary's Church, Haddington with the River Tyne, and Giffordgate running parallel to it, on the extreme right of the photograph (Crown Copyright: RCAHMS).

George Wishart being burned at the stake, a woodcut from R. Holinshed, *Historie of Scotlande...unto the yeare 1571* (Glasgow University Library, Department of Special Collections).

Cardinal David Beaton, Archbishop of St Andrews by an unknown artist (In a private collection; photograph, Antonia Reeve).

Rudera Arcis Sancti ANDREAE. The Ruins of the Castle of St ANDREWS.

St Andrews Castle in ruins after the siege by the French, engraved by John Slezer, *Theatrum Scotiae*, 1718 edition (Crown Copyright: RCAHMS).

Edward VI and the Pope, with Henry VIII on his deathbed, a satirical painting by an unknown artist (National Portrait Gallery, London).

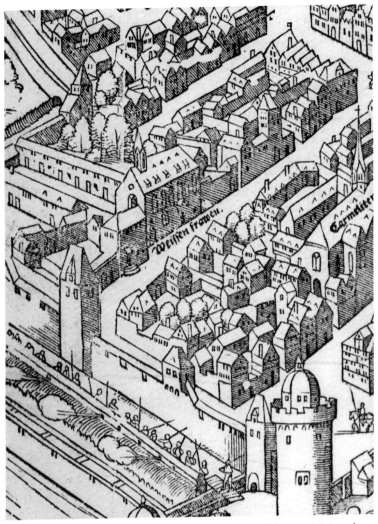

The White Ladies Church ('Weissen frawen') in Frankfurt am Main, where Knox preached: detail from Conrad Faber and Hans Grav's plan of Frankfurt in 1552 (Historisches Museum, Frankfurt am Main).

John Calvin in his study by an unknown engraver (Scottish National Portrait Gallery; photograph, Antonia Reeve).

Mary I of England, Knox's Jezebel, by Hans Eworth (National Portrait Gallery, London).

IOANNES CNOXVS.

John Knox, the famous woodcut from Theodore Beza, *Icones* (Scottish National Portrait Gallery; photograph, Antonia Reeve).

James Hamilton, 2nd Earl of Arran, Lord Governor of Scotland, attributed to A. Bronckorst (The Hamilton Collection, Lennoxlove).

Mary of Guise by Corneille de Lyon (Scottish National Portrait Gallery; photograph, Antonia Reeve).

St John's Kirk, Perth, where Knox preached his famous sermon in 1559 (Crown Copyright: RCAHMS).

James Stewart, Earl of Moray by Hans Eworth, 1561 (In a private collection).

Mary, Queen of Scots in white mourning by François Clouet (The Royal Collection © 2000 Her Majesty Queen Elizabeth II).

Queen Elizabeth I of England by Nicholas Hilliard (National Portrait Gallery, London).

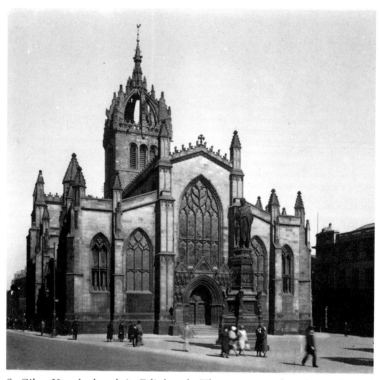

St Giles, Knox's church in Edinburgh The cemetery where he was buried lay to the right. (Crown Copyright: RCAHMS).

Sir William Kirkcaldy of Grange by François Clouet (In a private collection)

James Douglas, 4th Earl of Morton attributed to A. Bronckorst (Scottish National Portrait Gallery; photograph, Antonia Reeve).

spiritual guidance. Because her Protestantism was well known, she was in grave danger in Mary I's England, and Knox had long been urging both her and another friend, Mrs Hickman, to come to the safety of Geneva.

Just a few months earlier he had been telling Anna, 'Ye write that your desire is earnest to see me. Dear sister, if I should express the thirst and languor which I have had for your presence, I should appear to pass measure . . . Sometimes I sobbed, fearing what should become of you . . . I weep and rejoice in remembrance of you, but that would vanish by the comfort of your presence, which I assure you is so dear to me that if the charge of this little flock here gathered together in Christ's name did not impede me, my presence should prevent my letter.' This emotional language may seem a trifle extreme between a pastor and a religious friend, but Knox had read the Bible so much that his vocabulary tended to be that of the Book of Psalms, filled with sighing, groaning and sobbing. At any rate, Mrs Locke's husband saw nothing amiss in their friendship and he willingly agreed that his wife should travel to the safety of Geneva and stay there in the protection of their old friend until the situation in England changed for the better.[16]

Happy as he was taking care of 'this little flock' in Geneva, Knox was considerably disconcerted when two unexpected visitors arrived to see him that same month, May 1557. His old Edinburgh friends James Syme and James Barron had made the long journey to Switzerland deliver to him a letter from the Earl of Glencairn, John Erskine of Dun and Lord James Stewart. They wrote to invite him to come back to Scotland again, saying that they were ready to risk their lives as well as their goods in the Protestant cause. Mary of Guise had not converted to Protestantism, it was true, but neither was she persecuting and so it would be perfectly safe for him to return.[17]

Knox was dismayed. He had always been reluctant to leave Geneva before, and now that he was so happily settled with his well-organised congregation, his wife and his baby son, he had no desire to abandon his pleasant security for yet another difficult, dangerous visit to his native land. He could not, in all conscience, turn down the invitation out of hand, and so he consulted his congregation. Upset though they were, they felt that he could not refuse. He asked Calvin for his opinion and received a similar reply. With a heavy heart, he wrote a letter to Glencairn and the others, telling them that he would come to Scotland with 'reasonable expedition', as soon as he had made the necessary arrangements for his congregation during his absence.

He did not set out for another five months, taking a painful farewell of Marjorie, Elizabeth, little Nathaniel and all his friends. When he finally reached Dieppe on 24 October, he found waiting for him two letters which he read with growing astonishment and indignation. One was addressed to him and came from a Protestant in Scotland. It said that those who had previously invited him to return were on the verge of changing their minds, and it urged him to wait in Dieppe until he had further news. The second letter was not to him but to one of his Dieppe friends, and its message was similar. The Protestant leaders in Scotland no longer thought that the moment was right for action.[18]

8

The First Blast of the Trumpet

NOT SURPRISINGLY, KNOX WAS angry and astonished. He had gone to all the trouble of arranging a substitute pastor in Geneva, he had parted from his wife and their baby son and, when he had left the city on what was undoubtedly a dangerous mission to Scotland, his family and friends had been in tears, not knowing if they would ever see him again. He had then ridden the 800 miles to Dieppe, only to be told that he was not wanted after all. He did not set pen to paper immediately, but three days later he wrote an indignant letter to Glencairn, Erskine of Dun, Lord Lorne and Lord James Stewart, reproaching them for their lack of resolution.

If he gave up and went back to Switzerland, it would reflect badly on all of them, he said. Everyone would think that they had been very imprudent. It would also look as if he himself had been far too forward in undertaking the journey in the first place. Nothing would persuade him ever again to endure such painful farewells as those he had made when he set out, and what was he to tell his friends when he suddenly reappeared in Geneva? More importantly, what was going to happen in Scotland now? The relationship of the Protestant leaders with Mary of Guise was like that of Moses and the Pharaoh, he thought. It was plainly their duty, because of their position in society, to 'vindicate and deliver your subjects and brethren from all violence and oppression, to the uttermost of your power.' They should not imagine that the reformation of religion was the responsibility of the ministers or the monarchy only. It was their business too. Having relieved his feelings, he gave the letter to a messenger and decided to remain in Dieppe to await further developments.[1]

Perhaps he was hoping for a reply from Glencairn and the others saying that it had all been a misunderstanding and that the Protestant Lords were ready and waiting for him to arrive in Scotland, but no such message came, not even an acknowledgement of his reproachful letter. He continued to wait impatiently for another two months. He could, of course, have travelled to Scotland regardless, for the official invitation to go had not been withdrawn, but he had grave doubts about what was happening there. In December, reports reached him that the Scottish Protestant community was being criticised because of the dissolute way of life of some of its members. He wrote at once to say that this should not deter other people from converting. After all, in any organisation there were always some whose behaviour was inappropriate. That was a simple fact of life, and it mattered far less than the realisation that the Protestant doctrines were the right ones.

He was much more worried about the attitude of some of the Scottish nobility. Knox was a mature and experienced man, and he very well knew that many of the lords were not as high-minded as they would have liked him to believe. Self-interest had always been the principal motivation for most of them, and no amount of Protestant preaching would change that. They were always ready to receive bribes, from both sides at once if they could manage it, and that autumn lavish inducements were being offered to them as a prelude to the imminent marriage of Mary, Queen of Scots and the

Dauphin. No longer was this match a distant prospect. It was about to become a reality. Henri II had decided that he needed Scotland's support against England and Spain, and he had asked the Scots to send over commissioners to negotiate the marriage contract. Mary of Guise had therefore redoubled her efforts to gain the support of the nobility, and large bribes were being offered and accepted. Support for the Protestant cause was ebbing away, and that was the reason why Knox's friends had told him to stay where he was.

Knox had also identified a more sinister danger in the present situation. He was particularly concerned about the influence of the Duke of Châtelherault. Since accepting his French dukedom, Châtelherault had ostensibly been a supporter of Mary of Guise, the Roman Catholics and the French, but now he had changed his mind yet again. When Mary, Queen of Scots married, the Dauphin became King, and they had children, Châtelherault's position as heir to the throne would vanish. He therefore decided to do everything he could to prevent the wedding from taking place, and in order to gain friends he began to tell people privately that he had really been a Protestant all along.

Moreover, on 3 December 1557 Glencairn, Argyll, Lord Lorne, Erskine of Dun and the Earl of Morton drew up and signed an agreement which they described as a covenant, promising that they would defend Christ's Evangel and congregation from the rage of Satan and remove all abomination and idolatry. When he heard about it, Knox was far from rejoicing that the lords were doing something positive at last. His worst fears were being realised. Châtelherault and the other Lords were about to pursue their own worldly ambitions under the cover of religion.[2]

Knox wrote to them on 17 December 1557, warning them against 'those that seek authority and pre-eminence of worldly glory, yea, of the oppression and destruction of others,' and he particularly criticised 'him who in the beginning of his authority and government began to profess Christ's truth, but suddenly sliding back, became a cruel persecutor of Christ's members, a manifest and open oppressor of all true subjects.' Although he did not mention his name, everyone knew that he meant the Duke of Châtelherault. He warned them, too against supporting Mary of Guise over the forthcoming marriage. There was a great difference, he said, between 'lawful obedience, and a fearful flattering of princes, or an unjust accomplishment of their desires in things which be required or devised for the destruction of a commonwealth'. The marriage between the Queen and the French Dauphin would have all manner of implications for Scotland, and they must beware. Even so, he said explicitly that he did not wish to begin a civil war or see them plunge into one in the name of religion.

Three leading Protestants, Lord James, Erskine of Dun and the Earl of Cassillis were among the nine commissioners who set off for France that same month to finalise the marriage of Mary, Queen of Scots. Meanwhile, Knox left Dieppe and rode to La Rochelle, France's second port. Like Dieppe it had many trading links with Scotland and a large Protestant community. Knox delivered sermons in private houses, and according to tradition announced that he hoped to preach the same doctrine in St Giles Church in Edinburgh in the not too distant future, perhaps in two or three years' time. Travelling by way of Lyon, he then made his way back to Geneva where, on 16 December 1557, he and Goodman had in his absence been re-elected as pastors of the English congregation for the coming year.[3]

After a glad reunion with family and friends, he began work on what is perhaps his best-known text. Certainly the *History of the Reformation*, produced at a later stage of his career is his major work and the classic source for events in Scotland at that period, but in the late twentieth century *The First Blast of the Trumpet against the Monstrous Regiment of Women*[4] has gained him a whole new notoriety throughout the English-speaking world and beyond from its title alone. As a result, he seems to feature in the public mind as Scotland's first and most vituperative male chauvinist.

Because few people have actually read *The First Blast*, its title is often misunderstood. Knox was not conjuring up a picture of a huge army of women on the march against the opposite sex. In his day, 'regiment' meant rule, and so he was attacking the monstrous (meaning unnatural) rule of women. Worried though he might be about the situation in Scotland, he remained preoccupied with events in England and he desperately wanted to find a means of freeing Mary I's subjects from their obligation to obey her. In so doing, he expressed himself in his usual colourful language and the result is an essay guaranteed to infuriate all but the most docile of his modern female readers. His attitude towards women's place in society was not what surprised his contemporaries, however, for it was no different from their own. What really shocked them was something else altogether. What, then, does *The First Blast* actually say?

It is a rather repetitive tract which runs to some 45 pages. Knox knew that he had come up with a controversial theory, and therefore much of what he wrote was defensive in tone. He was, he said, being forced to set down his thoughts because not a single preacher in what he interestingly termed 'the Isle of Great Brittany' had raised a voice against Jezebel, by whom, of course, he meant Mary I. In Biblical times, prophets constantly admonished those who were going wrong and so someone must now take a stand at a point when England was about to become the prey of a foreign nation and Protestants were being martyred. Knox very well knew, he said, that the sentiments he was about to express could be regarded as treasonable and therefore dangerous, not only for the author but also for his publisher and for his readers. He also recognised the fact that the Jezebel in question was unlikely ever to read what he wrote, but the matter was so important that he must risk these dangers, even though he was aware that what he said would evoke much criticism from 'wise, politic and quiet spirits' as well as from the more rash.

His preface complete, he launched forth with engaging bluntness into 'The First Blast to Awaken Women Degenerate'. 'To promote a woman to bear rule, superiority, dominion or empire above any realm, nation or city', he wrote, 'is repugnant to nature, contumely [insulting] to God, a thing most contrarious to His revealed will and approved ordinance, and finally it is the subversion of good order, of all equity and justice.' He then proceeded to develop his argument with relish. Female weaknesses made women totally unfit to rule. 'Nature, I say, doth paint them forth to be weak, frail, impatient, feeble and foolish, and experience hath declared them to be inconstant, variable, cruel and lacking the spirit of counsel and regiment. And these notable faults have men in all ages espied . . . .'

Moreover, not only was it 'a thing most repugnant to nature that women rule and govern over men', but God himself had specifically forbidden it. Eve should have realised that she was created to be subject to man, but she did not do so, and after she was driven out of the Garden of Eden, God pronounced judgement against her with the words, 'With sorrow shalt thou bear thy children and thy will shall be subject to thy man, and he shall bear dominion over thee.' It followed, then, that when people disobey and promote women to be rulers, a horrible vengeance awaits all concerned.

Knox piously wished to God that there were not so many obvious examples of women's unfitness to govern a country, but he felt compelled nevertheless to rehearse past examples of their instability. There were women who had died for sudden joy, murdered themselves out of sheer impatience, burned with such inordinate lust that they betrayed their country to strangers and out of ambition even murdered their own husbands, children and grandchildren. In support of his argument, he quoted from a variety of authors, ranging from Tertullian, the Carthaginian Christian at the end of the second century AD, who had briskly pointed out to each and every woman, 'Thou are the port and gate of the devil,' to Chrysostom, Bishop of Constantinople in the fourth century, who thought that 'Womankind . . . is rash and fool-hardy; and their covetousness is like the gulf of hell, that is insatiable'.

A paragraph or two earlier Chrysostom had already helpfully told man that woman was put under his power, 'and you were pronounced lord over her, that she should obey you, and that the head should not follow the feet.' The metaphor of the head and the feet rather appealed to Knox, and he began his next section, entitled 'The Empire of Women is Subversity of Good Order, Equity and Justice', with a more elaborate anatomical allusion, likening a country with a woman ruler to a monster with no head, with eyes in its hands, tongue and mouth in its belly and ears in its feet. In case his message was not plain enough, he went on to compare a nation such as that to a painted idol, which had all the necessary limbs and features but lacked the vital animating spirit.

Reminding his readers that 'no man ever saw the lion make obedience and stoop before the lioness', he turned at last to the specific situation in London, where insolent joy, bonfires and banqueting had greeted the proclamation of 'that cursed Jezebel' Mary I as Queen. She was God's punishment for England's evil behaviour during the reign of the 'innocent and tender' Edward VI. Now the English were 'compelled to bow their necks under the yoke of Satan, and of his proud mistress, pestilent papists and proud Spaniards.' In short, the nobility of England and Scotland were inferior to brute beasts because they made reverence to a female.

Having proved woman's inferiority to man to his own satisfaction, Knox turned to a consideration of women and the state. Seizing upon a topic which he knew would be popular with his readers, he declared that the Bible forbade the appointment of a foreigner as monarch of a country. This implied that a Queen's foreign husband could not become King of her realm, and ruled out Philip of Spain very nicely, not to mention the Dauphin of France. Promising to address this point at greater length in a forthcoming *Blast of the Second Trumpet*, he hastened to reassure anyone who thought that these Old Testament rules applied only to Jews. With various biblical examples, he argued that the prohibition against women acting as God's lieutenant was a moral law, applicable to all, Jews and Gentiles alike, and if people flouted it, retribution would surely follow.

Conscious that many of his readers would disagree with him, he anticipated some of the possible objections to his argument. His opponents might draw attention to Deborah, the Old Testament

prophetess who inspired the military commander Barak to lead the
Israelites against the Canaanite general, Sisera, defeating him in
a battle at which she was personally present. While Knox rather
grudgingly admitted that Deborah was a godly woman possessed
of the spirit of mercy, truth, justice and humility, and very
different from 'our mischievous Marys', he hastened to dismiss
her as irrelevant on the grounds that she was not a female monarch
but a prophetess, and what was more she had a husband to whom
she should have been deferring.

Huldah, another godly woman in the Old Testament, had proved
that a previously unknown ancient book of laws was the true Word
of God, but she too was a prophetess, not a woman with any
official authority. Other critics, Knox thought, might cite the
example of Moses, who gave a special ruling that, on the death
of Zelophehad of the tribe of Manasseh, his property should pass
to his five daughters rather than to any male relative. Knox had no
quarrel with property passing from father to daughter, he said, but
the right to rule could never be inherited by a woman, and the
only reason Moses agreed to the arrangement in question was so
that Zelophehad's name should not die out.

The example of Zelophehad brought Knox back to the problem
of the marriage of heiresses, and he noted that, in the Bible, women
were forbidden to marry anyone not of their own tribe. Those who
advocated the rights of women should have considered this tale
before they advised their own people to betray their countries by
permitting their queens to marry foreigners. There was England,
betrayed to 'the proud Spaniard' in order to satisfy 'the inordinate
appetites of that cruel monster Mary (unworthy, by reason of her
bloody tyranny, of the name of a woman)' while Scotland, 'by the
rash madness of foolish governors, and by the practices of a crafty
dame [Mary of Guise]' was likewise giving itself up 'under the title
of marriage, into the power of France.'

Some people claimed that the ability of a woman to inherit a
throne was a long-established custom, but that did not make it
right. God had forbidden it. Others said that, although women

could not really exercise power in person, they could delegate to lieutenants, judges and the like until they chose a husband, who would rule for them. That would not do either, for Knox. 'From a corrupt and venomed fountain can spring no wholesome water,' he said, and no one had the power to give away that which did not belong to them in the first place. Men who received positions of authority or honour from a woman were declaring themselves to be enemies of God and so must refuse to be her officers, because she was a traitoress and rebel against Him. Finally, they must 'study to repress her inordinate pride and tyranny to the uttermost of their power.'

Until this particular condemnation, Knox had said nothing new. The law, as it affected the status of women, had remained largely unchanged since the Middle Ages and a woman's position was technically equivalent to that of a minor. As the eminent Scottish judge, Sir James Balfour, had explained in 1550, 'The husband is principal and head over his wife.' Before she married, a woman had to obey her father. After marriage, she was expected to do what her husband told her. Her property was administered by him, he chose where she was to stay, she could not go and live elsewhere unless he agreed, and she could not raise a court action, act as cautioner for a debt or dispose of her goods without his consent.[5]

Such was the letter of the law. This is not to say that women were really down-trodden creatures with no will of their own. History is full of examples of female energy and enterprise throughout the centuries, but the fact remains that official writings on the subject went largely unchallenged. After all, they were based on the Bible, where St Paul had made perfectly clear the necessary submission of women to men. The first thirty pages of Knox's *First Blast* were therefore in no way startling to his readers. It was only when he came to the discussion of what subjects ought to do about a female ruler that he was breaking new ground.

Those nobles who had promoted a woman to rule must call for the mercy of God and then they 'ought without further delay to remove from authority all such persons as by usurpation, violence or tyranny do possess the same', especially 'that monster in nature . . . a woman clad in the habit of a man, yea a woman against nature reigning above man.' Moreover, if anyone defended the wrongful monarch, they too must be removed and executed. This was startlingly controversial, and Knox knew it.

To hammer home the message, he reminded his readers that Mary I, 'cursed Jezebel of England, with the pestilent and detestable generation of Papists' had boasted of executing Sir Thomas Wyatt and martyring innocent Lady Jane Grey, devout Bishop Latimer, mild-mannered Archbishop Cranmer, learned and discreet Bishop Ridley, and 'many other preachers consumed in the fire.' His readers should not despair, however, for 'the day of vengeance, which shall apprehend that horrible monster Jezebel of England, and such as maintain her monstrous cruelty, is already appointed in the counsel of the eternal.' Her empire and reign were a wall without foundation, and 'that rotten wall, the usurped and unjust empire of women, shall fall by itself in despite of all men, to the destruction of so many as shall labour to uphold it. And therefore let all men be advertised, for the trumpet has once blown.' With that, he ended.

Knox never meant *The First Blast* to be a polemic against women in general, and to see it only in that light is to miss the point. His overriding concern was the reign of Mary I in England, the martyrdom of so many Protestants as a result and the likely prospect of even worse times ahead as a result of Mary's marriage to Philip of Spain. There are one or two allusions to Scotland, but it was not at the forefront of his mind as he wrote. He would address its problems elsewhere. Although formerly convinced that passive resistance was the only way to deal with ungodly rulers, he had come to believe that this led to too much suffering, too many deaths and, in order to justify his controversial new view that Mary I must be deposed, he had hit upon the notion of piling up all the evidence that rule by any woman at all was illegal. This is what *The First Blast* did and this is how it was read by his contemporaries. They passed over the familiar biblical texts about women without a qualm but were brought up short by the explicit instruction that it was their duty to depose their ungodly female monarch.[6]

Knox very well knew that Calvin would never have given him permission to write anything so revolutionary. He deliberately avoided mentioning *The First Blast* to him and arranged to have it published anonymously in Geneva. He meant to follow it up with two more 'Blasts', and he intended to reveal his identity with the publication of the third. Before he embarked upon the sequels, however, he wanted to gauge public reaction to *The First Blast*. He was aware that it would be some months before copies reached England, and so he occupied himself in the meantime by developing his ideas further in three more pamphlets which he wrote in the early months of 1558. All three concerned Scotland, and the first was a new edition of his *Letter to the Regent* of 1556 in which he had thanked God for Mary of Guise's change of heart in ordering the withdrawal of the heresy charges against him and then tried to persuade her to convert to Protestantism.

If the original had been couched in polite and respectful terms, the new version was much fiercer. There were entirely new passages referring in tones of bitter grief to those who had been 'most cruelly . . . murdered in France, Italy, Spain, Flanders and now of late years beside you in England, for no cause but that they profess Christ Jesus to be the only saviour of the world . . .' Mary of Guise had witnessed some of this for herself in Scotland, he said, and she must be very careful, for rulers who permitted such atrocities would burn in the everlasting fire. Not only was idolatry rife in Scotland, but 'the avarice and cruelty as well of yourself as of such as be in authority may be known by the facts'. Word of the heavy taxes she imposed on the poor had reached him in a far country, and God no doubt knew about it too. Unless she truly repented, he warned, she would suffer eternal punishment. Seldom did any woman reign for long with felicity and joy, and God had already begun to punish her. Knox knew that Mary of Guise had suffered a dreadful tragedy when her two sons by James V had died as babies within hours of each other in 1541 and James himself had died the following year.

Now he told her, 'God hath begun very sharply with you, taking from you, as it were together, two children and a husband. He hath begun, I say, to declare Himself angry; beware that ye provoke not the eyes of His majesty.'

If Mary ever read the second version of the letter, her feelings may well be imagined. It is strange that a man like Knox, who enjoyed such close and sympathetic relationships with women, could write with such cruelty, but when he was in the grip of religious fervour any thought of the pain he might be inflicting on his reader was set aside. If challenged, he would no doubt have justified his words by saying that a far worse pain awaited the Queen Regent if she did not mend her ways. There was also an element of personal resentment in everything he wrote about Mary of Guise after her rejection of the original letter. His published version of it included a new paragraph recounting how she had dismissed it with the wounding words, 'My Lord, will ye read a pasquil.' He was not going to forget that insult. 'God move your heart to understand my petition, to know the truth and unfeignedly to follow the same,' he concluded, and he attached a text from Revelation which promised that unbelievers, idolaters and liars would suffer in a lake burning with fire and brimstone.

Two French Protestant refugees working in Geneva, Jacques Poullain and Antoine Reboul, printed the work for him, and, of course, it appeared under his name.[7] The second essay which he composed that spring was addressed to the nobility and Parliament of Scotland. It was about the same length as *The First Blast* and in it Knox argued that the nobles and estates must exercise authority over the bishops. No longer was it the Christian duty of people to obey their ruler because he was God's representative. God had certainly commanded that kings should be obeyed, but it was equally true that He approved and even rewarded those men who stood out against ungodly orders from evil monarchs. The nobility had not only a duty to protect persecuted Protestants from the fury of the bishops. They must also put idolaters to death, for that was what God had commanded. Indeed, it was not only the nobility who had this responsibility. Everyone in the community must ensure that the idolaters were punished.[8]

Knox's third treatise was much shorter but it was even more revolutionary, for this time he addressed 'his beloved brethren, the Commonalty of Scotland'. They, the ordinary men of the country, must act along with the nobility to compel the bishops and clergy to cease their tyranny. He could understand that they would be reluctant to overturn the long established religion, but it was the only course to take if they wished to escape death and damnation. All men were equal in the sight of God, for they were all descended from Adam and so it was not only the rich and powerful who should take action. In pursuit of this argument, Knox even said that 'in Christ Jesus, the Jew hath no greater prerogative than hath the Gentile, the man than hath the woman, the learned than the unlearned, the lord than the servant, but all are one in Him.' If their superiors failed to provide the ordinary people with true teachers, they were permitted to provide their own, and they were at perfect liberty to withhold the revenues demanded by their false bishops and clergy.

To hang back and excuse themselves from acting on the ground that they were mere subjects, too lowly to improve the situation, would not do. God required them to act and, if they failed to do so and consented to iniquity, He would punish them. In a hierarchical society, these were startling words indeed. Others might urge the nobility to act against an ungodly prince, but Knox was telling all the subjects that they must rebel against and depose such a ruler. Quite simply, he was inciting revolution.[9]

The Letter to the Commonalty of Scotland was published in Geneva that summer along with Knox's address to the nobility and Parliament, under the title *The Appellation of John Knox*, a reference to the fact that he was appealing against the sentence pronounced against him by the bishops in his absence. Also in the book was a pamphlet by Anthony Gilby, entitled *An Admonition to England and Scotland to call them to Repentance*.[10] Finally, the volume contained a synopsis of Knox's intended *Second Blast of the Trumpet*. The summary was brief and to the point. In the *Second Blast*, Knox promised, he would explain that birth alone did not make a king. It was all very well to be born royal, but, unless that person was right thinking too, he could not rule. God's instruction about the election of 'inferior judges' was equally applicable to monarchs. No idolater or notorious transgressor of God's laws could hold any position of public authority. No oath or promise made to a tyrant acting against God's will had to be observed, and if people rashly or ignorantly chose a ruler who proved unworthy, then they could, when they saw their error, overturn and punish that ruler. Here again was Knox's theory of revolution. Bold though his words were, however, he had already realised that *The First Blast* was receiving a reception even more hostile than he had anticipated, and he never did write the planned sequels. His *The First Blast* was also his last.[11]

9

The Sermon at Perth

K NOX FULLY EXPECTED MARY I and her Roman Catholic
supporters to be outraged by his *The First Blast* and indeed in
June 1558 the Queen issued a proclamation against the importing of
heretical and seditious books into England.[1] He had not, however,
foreseen the strength of the Protestant reaction against him. One
of the first to object was a friend from his Frankfurt days, John
Foxe the martyrologist. Foxe's reproachful letter to Knox does not
survive, but Knox's reply of 18 May 1558 makes clear the nature
of Foxe's complaints. Knox admitted, 'My rude vehemency and
unconsidered affirmations . . . may appear rather to proceed from
choler [anger] than of zeal and reason' but he defended himself by
saying that he was never one to flatter. 'To me, it is enough to say
that black is not white, and man's tyranny and foolishness is not
God's perfect ordinance.'[2]

There was a general outcry amongst the Protestants in England,
where Matthew Parker, later Archbishop of Canterbury, spoke for
many others when he declared that, if people followed the principles
laid down in the writings of Knox and Goodman, no Lord of
Council would be able to ride quietly through the streets among
such desperate beasts and no master would be safe, even in his

own bedchamber.[3] The groups of continental exiles were equally indignant and one of their leaders, Sir Anthony Cooke, wrote to Theodore Beza, Calvin's close associate and eventual biographer, expressing their outrage.

Until then, the Genevan authorities and indeed Calvin himself had not heard of *The First Blast*, nor did they know anything about Christopher Goodman's new book, *How Superior Powers Ought to be Obeyed*, which advocated rebellion against ungodly rulers in terms even more extreme than those used by Knox. On 24 June 1558, in a peaceful atmosphere, Knox and Goodman were formally admitted to be citizens of Geneva. The entry in the relevant register reads, in French, 'John Knox, son of William Knox, native of Haddington in Scotland, and Christopher Goodman, son of William Goodman, native of Chester in England, minister of the English, have been received [as citizens] free of charge'.[4]

Shortly afterwards, Cooke's letter was delivered to Beza and he took it at once to Calvin. Calvin sent for a copy of *The First Blast* and presumably read it with mounting irritation. He had a sharp temper and he had always urged obedience to misguided rulers, for he believed that the need to preserve the peace was of prime importance. He would never have approved of a tract urging rebellion, let alone the deposition and even execution of an ungodly monarch. That, of course, was precisely why Knox had kept it from him. Calvin wrote back to Cooke disassociating himself from the views expressed in *The First Blast*, and he banned its sale in Geneva. No record of his inevitable confrontation with Knox has survived, but, although the interview cannot have been a pleasant one, it did not damage their relationship.[5]

As well as voicing their complaints, some of Knox's readers set about composing refutations of his theories. John Aylmer, former tutor of Lady Jane Grey and now one of the Strasbourg refugees, was already at work on an answer to *The First Blast*. Entitled *A Harbour for Faithful and True Subjects*, it was published anonymously in Strasbourg in April 1559. It was certainly not intended as a defence of women. In Aylmer's opinion, although 'some women be wiser, better learned, discreeter, constanter than a number of men', most were 'fond, foolish, wanton, flibbertigibbets, tattlers, trifling, wavering witless, without counsel, feeble, careless, rash, proud, dainty, nice [meaning pernickety], tale-bearers, eaves-droppers, rumour-raisers, evil tongued, worse-minded and in every way doltified with the dregs of the devil's dunghill'.

Aylmer's objective was to uphold order and the hierarchical society against Knox's incitement to rebellion, and even though he objected to a Scot telling the English who they should or should not have as a sovereign, he made it clear that he understood why Knox had written as he did. The author of *The First Blast* had produced his misguided text not from malice but from zeal, his judgement blinded by tears caused by Mary I's cruelty. This was an accurate assessment, and it was no doubt Calvin's opinion too.[6]

Apart from the fact that he annoyed so many of his colleagues, Knox has often been criticised for the bad timing of his controversial publication. By the summer of 1558, Mary I was seriously ill. She had been deeply depressed by England's loss of Calais to the French that January, she had shortly afterwards suffered her second phantom pregnancy at the age of forty-two, and she was greatly distressed by the increasing absence of her husband, Philip of Spain, on the continent. She began to suffer from bouts of high fever, possibly the result of tuberculosis, and with each month that passed she became weaker.[7]

For all his excellent contacts in England, Knox does not seem to have realised that his Jezebel was near to death. In the early days of November he was working on *An Epistle unto the Inhabitants of Newcastle and Berwick*, denouncing those of his former congregation who had converted back to Roman Catholicism. The loss of Calais, he said, was a punishment for their backsliding. A week later, on 17 November 1558, Mary I died and the crown passed to her younger half-sister, who now became Queen Elizabeth I. Protestants in England had long looked to Elizabeth as their hope for the future, and there was great rejoicing on her accession. The years of persecution were over at last.[8]

Under other circumstances, Knox could have expected Elizabeth to be his powerful protector, but she, most of all, was infuriated by his theories of revolution. She had been told about *The First Blast* and she knew who had written it. She would have had no quarrel with Knox's views about women in general, which she probably shared. She much preferred men, but after her young years of insecurity she was hypersensitive about her position as sovereign and any suggestion that subjects might tell their monarch what to do was anathema to her.

Knox made matters even worse when, on hearing about Mary I's death, he composed *A Brief Exhortation to England for the Speedy Embracing of Christ's Gospel, heretofore by the Tyranny of Mary Suppressed and Banished*. In it, he declared that the whole population of England was at fault for submitting to Catholicism during Mary's reign and failing to stop the persecution of the Protestants. They must now reintroduce Protestantism and put Roman Catholics to death. In other words, he believed that the religion of a country was determined by its people, not by its monarch. Elizabeth would never agree with that. Knox finished his latest essay on 12 January 1559, and published it later that year in Geneva, along with the recently completed *Epistle*.[9] At the time of Mary's death he had also begun work on a lengthy and convoluted book defending predestination and attacking the Anabaptists. The first draft ran to 170,000 words and in the end he had to let it go to press without revising it, for he was called away to deal with much more pressing matters.[10]

One day in November 1558, John Gray, a Scotsman travelling to Rome in connection with the appointment of a new Bishop of Ross, arrived at Knox's lodgings with letters from Lord James Stewart, the Earl of Glencairn and the other Protestant leaders. They wanted him to come back to Scotland. Not surprisingly, Knox was astonished. His futile journey to Dieppe the previous year was still very much in his mind, and he had vowed never to make a similar mistake again. How was he to know that he would not once more be halted on his journey and sent back? What would he find in Scotland? Had the situation really changed?[11]

Presumably Gray explained what had been happening. Mary, Queen of Scots had married the Dauphin in Paris on 24 April 1558 and ever since then, Scottish opposition to the French alliance had been growing. There had been disturbances, for instance, when Walter Myln, an elderly former priest was arrested in Dysart, tried for heresy and burned at the stake in St Andrews on 28 April. The Scottish Protestants feared that now that her daughter was safely married to the French king's son, Mary of Guise was about to follow the example of Mary Tudor and begin a campaign of persecution. When they complained bitterly to the Queen Regent, she said she had not known about the execution and deeply regretted Myln's death. As a former priest he had come under the jurisdiction of the Church and so she had not been informed of his prosecution. In fact, sentences passed by the Church courts were implemented by the civil authorities.[12]

In a climate of increasing hostility to Roman Catholicism, Paul Methven, the son of a local baker, began to preach to large crowds in Dundee, while John Willock returned from Emden. Although ill, Willock encouraged the Protestants from his sickbed in Edinburgh. In the early autumn, violence erupted in the capital. The principal church was dedicated to St Giles. Statues were being taken from churches in various parts of the country, and now the great image of St Giles was stolen, 'drowned' in the nearby Nor' Loch and then fished out again and burned. This was particularly upsetting because on 1 September each year, the Feast of St Giles, the statue was carried through the streets in procession. Determined that the celebrations should go ahead as usual, the clergy borrowed a much smaller image of the saint from Greyfriars Church, and nailed it to their portable shrine.

When the day came, Mary of Guise herself pointedly led the procession. Trumpets sounded, drums were beaten and ecclesiastical banners floated overhead as they all moved slowly down the High Street from St Giles Church towards the Palace of Holyroodhouse.

On reaching the Canongate market cross, they stopped at the house of Sandy Carpenter, a wealthy burgess who was to have the honour of entertaining Mary of Guise to dinner. As soon as the Queen Regent had entered the house, some Protestants shouldered their way through the crowd and approached the portable shrine, which had been laid on the ground while its bearers took a rest. Pretending to help, the Protestants lifted up the shrine and before anyone realised what was happening, they shook it violently, hoping to dislodge the statue. St Giles did not fall, for the image was held firmly in place by the iron nails, but with shouts of 'Down with the idol! Down with it!' the Protestants struck it against the ground, until the head and hands were knocked off. A fracas immediately broke out, and while Mary of Guise and her attendants watched in outrage from the windows of Carpenter's house, the various priests and friars in the procession fled. After the commotion had died down, the Queen Regent's escort hustled her back to the safety of Edinburgh Castle.

All attempts to identify those responsible failed, and the atmosphere was more tense than ever. Even as Gray was on his way to Geneva, there was more trouble. On 8 November 1558 Mary of Guise summoned Paul Methven to appear before the Privy Council for his heretical preaching, but he refused to come and was outlawed in his absence. On hearing this, the Protestant lairds in Angus, Fife and Cunningham and most of the adult male residents of Dundee met together and defiantly signed an agreement in the form of a band or covenant, promising to protect Methven. Scotland seemed to be on the verge of a religious reformation. It was time for Knox to come home.[13]

The Scottish invitation presented Knox with a real dilemma. Apart from his obligation to his congregation in Geneva, he was needed in his own household. Marjorie had just given birth to a second son, and the baby was christened on 29 November 1558. He was given the name of Eleazer, an Israelite leader in the Old Testament, and Miles Coverdale was his godfather. Coverdale, a former Augustinian friar and Bishop of Exeter who had converted to Protestantism, was translator of the first complete edition of the Bible to be published in English. His wife was Scottish, her brother was another exiled Protestant scholar, John Macalpine, and the two families must have known each other well.[14]

On 16 December 1558, Knox and Goodman were once more elected pastors of the English congregation in Geneva for the following year, but there was no ignoring the dilemma of the Scottish invitation.[15] The Scottish Lords had not only written to Knox himself. They had also sent letters to Calvin, urging him to make sure that Knox complied with their request. The Lords still believed that Mary of Guise could be persuaded to convert to Protestantism. Knox was less sanguine, but Calvin presumably took the view that the work to be done in Scotland was more important than any other consideration. On 28 January 1559, Knox set out yet again on the long ride to Dieppe.

He arrived there on 19 February 1559 and wrote at once to England for a safe conduct. Now that Elizabeth was on the throne, there was no need for him to travel all the way to Scotland by sea. He could make the far shorter Channel crossing, visit colleagues in London and then call in on his friends in Northumberland on his way north.[16] While he waited for the safe conduct, he spent his time preaching regularly to the large Protestant community in Dieppe and catching up with his correspondence. On 17 March he received a reproachful letter from his friend Anna Locke, complaining that she never heard from him now. He replied almost three weeks later, on 6 April, excusing himself on the grounds that he had no reliable messenger to take letters to London, a problem which was likely to continue.

In much the way that he had reassured Elizabeth Bowes on similar occasions, he told Anna that he had not forgotten her, nor would he do so, even if she heard from him only once a year. 'Of nature I am churlish,' he admitted, 'and in condition different from many, yet one thing I ashame not to affirm, that familiarity once thoroughly contracted was never yet broken on my default.' Perhaps the reason why he would never end a friendship was, he said, that 'I have rather need of all than any hath need of me', an intriguing admission from a man often thought to have been supremely self-confident. 'Whether I write or no,' he went on, 'be assuredly persuaded that I have you in such memory as becometh the faithful to have of the faithful' and he went on to discuss the current state of the Church of England. He ended by assuring her that, although 'To me it is written that my *First Blast* hath blown from me all my friends in England', he stood by what he had said in it.[17]

The First Blast was very much in his mind, for a few days earlier he had received an unpleasant surprise. His request for a safe conduct had been refused, not just once but twice. The author of the tract against the monstrous rule of women was the last person Queen Elizabeth would allow to travel through her realm, stirring up sedition, least of all in the present situation. On 2 April 1559 France and Spain had made peace with each other by the Treaty of Cateau-Cambrésis. Their respective allies Scotland and France were included in the treaty, but Elizabeth and the English were nervous. Now that France was no longer at war with Spain, it was possible that the French might attack England. Certainly Knox was no instrument of the French, but he was all too likely to try to stir up the English Protestants against Elizabeth. They had no need of this complicating factor.

Knox had not expected his application for a safe-conduct to be refused, and four days after his letter to Anna Locke, he sat down and wrote an indignant letter to Sir William Cecil, now Elizabeth's secretary of state. With unfortunate candour, he began by condemning Cecil for having made no protest against the persecutions during Mary I's reign. Cecil deserved to go to hell for that, he said briskly, but God instead had promoted him to a position of honour and dignity. Unless he repented, however, he would not long escape the reward of dissemblers.

Having delivered himself of this salutary advice, Knox then turned to the matter in hand. 'By divers messengers I have requested such privileges as Turks commonly do grant to men of every nation, to wit, that freedom should be granted unto me peaceably to travel throughout England, to the end that with greater expedition I might repair towards my own country, which now beginneth to thirst for Christ's truth.' This was the third time he had asked, and he had thought his request so reasonable that he had almost set out without waiting for the necessary document.

As to *The First Blast*, which he was told had given cause for concern, he could honestly say that he had never intended to offend anyone in England. Those who thought that he was an enemy to Elizabeth or her rule were gravely mistaken. If Elizabeth were willing to confess that she was queen because God had given her an extraordinary dispensation to rule, against the laws of both God and nature, 'then shall none in England be more willing to maintain her lawful authority than I shall be'. If, however, she insisted on claiming that she was queen because of custom and the laws of men, that was a foolish presumption which would offend God and 'I greatly fear that her ingratitude shall not long lack punishment'. Knox asked Cecil to tell Elizabeth this on his behalf, with the warning that 'only humility and dejection of herself before God shall be the firmity and stability of her throne'.

Finally, he pointed out that the members of his own poor flock bore no responsibility for what he had written. His only wish in coming to see them was to bring them the comfort of God's Word, and if he were refused permission once again, then the godly would know 'that England, in refusing me, refuseth a friend'. Had Elizabeth ever laid eyes on this letter, her reaction would have been explosive, to say the least, but Cecil knew that it was more than his life was worth to show it to her and Knox received no reply. He sent Cecil another copy of his letter on 22 April, in case the original had been lost on the way, but there was still no response. By the end of April, he realised that there would be no safe conduct, and he set off to travel to Scotland by sea.[18]

During Knox's voyage to Scotland, one of his fellow-passengers took him aside and showed him, in strictest secrecy, a new Great Seal for Scotland, which the man was carrying to Edinburgh. On it, the arms of England were quartered with those of Scotland and France, and with it was a document describing François II and Mary as King and Queen not only of Scotland but of England too. According to canon law, Elizabeth I was illegitimate because her father Henry VIII's first, Roman Catholic wife, Catherine of Aragon, was still alive when she was born. As far as Roman Catholics were concerned, Elizabeth's mother, Anne Boleyn, had merely been Henry's mistress, not his wife. Mary, Queen of Scots was the great-grand-daughter of Henry VII of England and the French obviously intended to make the most of this fact. Mary was rightful Queen of England, not Elizabeth, they claimed, hence the design of the new Great Seal.[19]

Knox arrived at Leith on 2 May 1559 to find Scotland in a state of ferment. That winter, the Protestants had sent a series of petitions to the Queen Regent, demanding the right to take Communion in both kinds and hear services in their own language instead of Latin. They wished to meet both publicly and privately for prayers and they intended that these should be read out in Scots. They insisted that all acts against heresy be suspended and they urged Mary of Guise to compel the churchmen to reform their lives. On 1 January 1559, they drew up 'The Beggars' Summons'. Written as if from the blind, infirm, bedridden, widows and orphans, it charged all the friars in the country with having taken illegal possession of the hospitals and other properties set up for the assistance of the poor. Copies of this summons were pinned to the doors of friaries throughout Scotland, ordering the occupants to hand over their ill-gotten gains by the following Whitsun or be forcibly ejected. The Queen Regent received the various petitions calmly, promising to take note of what they said and to put all to rights.

Well pleased, the Protestant leaders wrote to Calvin praising her Biblical knowledge and her goodwill towards them, nor did they hesitate to rebuke anyone who doubted her sincerity. For her part, Mary did not believe that this Protestant agitation was inspired by anything like genuinely religious feeling. The complaints about the church were simply a cloak for political dissent. She well knew the selfish ambition of many of her Scottish Lords. They favoured Protestantism because they were determined to retain the church lands they had managed to accumulate in years gone by. As for the ordinary people, they were being deliberately stirred up by preachers who were no less than seditious agitators determined to challenge her authority. They were to blame for all the unrest. Believing that the abuses of the Church must be corrected from within, she ordered the Archbishop of St Andrews to convene a provincial council to consider the Protestant demands. She then summoned the troublesome preachers to appear before her at Stirling on 10 May 1559, intending to have them outlawed and banished.[20] This summons was issued on the very day that Knox arrived back in Scotland.

He spent only two nights in Edinburgh, before riding north to Dundee, where the Protestants were gathering. Lord James Stewart was not there, for he was still officially supporting his step-mother, Mary of Guise, and was at her Court, but there were plenty of other people ready to give him the latest news. Messages had been sent to the Queen Regent begging her not to interfere with the preachers in their ministry unless they were teaching false doctrine, but she had replied shortly that they would be banished from Scotland even if they preached 'as truly as ever did St. Paul'. Shocked, they sent the Earl of Glencairn and Sir Hew Campbell, the sheriff of Ayr, to urge her to perform the promises she had made. She answered that it did not become subjects to burden their princes with promises beyond those that rulers chose to keep. When the two emissaries warned her that there was trouble brewing, she seemed indifferent.

The Protestant leaders decided that they would accompany the preachers to Stirling, where they were to appear on 10 May. Before that, they would assemble at Perth, a thriving royal burgh on the banks of the River Tay. Knox rode there with them. Mary of Guise was sure to hear that something was happening, and so they sent Erskine of Dun to explain to her that this was not an army on the march. They were merely peaceable men, anxious to support their own pastors. They chose Erskine purposely because, although he was a zealous Protestant, he was well-known for his mild and gentle nature and his courteous manner.

Erskine had a lengthy audience with Mary of Guise, and as a result he wrote to the Protestant leaders urging them to stay where they were because she had promised to amend the situation. In the meantime, the appearance of the preachers at Stirling would be postponed indefinitely. When they read his letters, some of the Protestants were highly suspicious of the Queen Regent's promises, but others thought that she should believed and in the end they agreed to disperse. Some of them went home but, even as they did so, the Queen Regent and her council suddenly summoned the preachers again to come on 10 May and, without giving them time to get there, outlawed them and their supporters in their absence, for non-appearance.[21]

During his stay in Perth, Knox had preached regularly and on 11 May he entered the pulpit of St John's Kirk, in the centre of the town. This was the parish church, and it occupied such an important place in the community that the burgh was generally known as 'St Johnstoun'. Rebuilt in the fifteenth century, the church is a large one, its choir flanked on either side by an arcaded aisle. Part of its nave had been designed by royal craftsmen under the patronage of Mary of Guise's father-in-law, James IV. Its interior today is dark but dignified. When Knox preached there, it was a blaze of colour, the walls painted with biblical scenes, ornate statues of saints in niches and glittering chalices and candlesticks on the various altars. The rood screen, which divided the nave from the choir, was beneath the tower above, with the usual great crucifix hanging above it. The pulpit from which Knox preached has long since gone, but it stood where its modern replacement is today, to the left of the rood screen. As usual, he attracted a large congregation, and that day he preached, as he so often did, a sermon which he described as being 'vehement against idolatry'.

This passed off without incident but, shortly afterwards, one of the local priests went into the church to celebrate Mass, approached the high altar and opened the door of the tabernacle which stood there. Most of Knox's congregation had gone home for dinner, but there were a few people still in the church, and, as the priest prepared to take out the Host, a young boy who had heard Knox preach shouted out in protest, 'This is intolerable, that when God by his Word hath plainly damned idolatry, we shall stand and see it used in despite'. Perhaps these words are Knox's rather more literary version of what the boy actually said, but the effect was the same. The priest, hearing him, turned round and struck him a sharp blow. The boy picked up a stone and threw it at the priest. He missed, and hit the tabernacle instead, breaking one of its statues.

Before the priest could do anything, the other men standing nearby began to throw stones and tear down all the statues in the church. Hearing the commotion, people living nearby came running to see what was happening. Eager to join in, but realising that there was nothing left to destroy inside St John's, they ran to the Grey and Black Friaries and the Charterhouse, pushed their way past the guards at the gates and burst in. They attacked and broke all the religious statues they could find, and then they carried off the food and the fine bedding used by the friars in spite of their vows of poverty.[22]

When Knox reported these events to Anna Locke some weeks later, he told her that 'the brethren' had reformed the religious establishments in Perth, but, when he came to write his *History of the Reformation*, he distanced himself from the events of that day, declaring that 'the rascal multitude' were responsible.[23] No doubt in the excitement of the spring of 1559 he was glad to see people rising up against the Roman Catholic Church, but he had no desire to cause a breakdown in public order. During all these past years when he had pondered on the subject of rebellion and urged the overthrow of idolaters, he had regarded the reformation as a movement led and directed by the nobility and the preachers, not as a mass uprising by the people. He might urge his congregations to destroy idolatry, but he did not regard himself as a rabble rouser.

The Queen Regent and her friends must be overthrown, but in a deliberate, controlled manner, by men acting in the name of God.

Mary of Guise, deeply disturbed by the events in Perth, sent for the Duke of Châtelherault. She told him that she was going to confront the rebels, and he must go with her, for 'they stand in no awe of me because I am but a woman'. The Duke, ever resentful that Mary had torn the regency from his grasp, was unwilling, but she reminded him that, as second person in the realm and half-brother of the Archbishop of St Andrews, he had a duty to protect the Church. Irresolute as always, and at the mercy of anyone with a stronger character than his own, the Duke gave way and they set off for Perth together at the head of a small army which included eight or nine hundred French soldiers.

They marched to Auchterarder in Perthshire, where they waited for a week while their artillery was dragged by oxen from Edinburgh and Stirling. They then advanced to a position outside Perth. Meanwhile, the Protestants were doing all they could to put the burgh in a state of defence, and, by the time the royal forces approached, they had drawn up their army of three thousand on the Inch, a flat, grassy area on the edge of the town, confident in the knowledge that the Earl of Glencairn was marching to join them with reinforcements from the west of Scotland.

Realising that she was outnumbered, the Queen Regent decided to negotiate. She sent Lord James Stewart, the Earl of Argyll and Robert, 3rd Lord Sempill, a conservative Roman Catholic, to ask the Protestant leaders why they were holding Perth against her. Erskine of Dun and his companions replied that, if Mary of Guise would allow the true religion to proceed in peace, there would be no trouble. They did not intend rebellion, merely the protection of their unjustly persecuted brethren. Knox was not one of the negotiators, for his friends knew all too well that diplomacy was not his strong suit. On 25 May, however, he spoke to Lord James and the others privately in their lodgings and sent his own message to Mary of Guise.

Repeating that he and his friends were not rebelling but simply defending the true religion, he could not resist adding that this did not mean her religion, which was 'a superstition devised by the brain of man'. If she persisted in her course, 'the end shall be her confusion' and he claimed that he was a far better friend to her than her own people, who spent their time flattering her and deliberately setting her against the Protestants. The envoys promised to repeat his words to the Queen Regent 'as far as they could'. No doubt they presented her with a somewhat edited version of his remarks but, even so, Lord Sempill later reported that she was 'somewhat offended'.

The negotiations continued, however, and on 29 May 1559 it was finally agreed that both armies would disband, leaving the Queen Regent free to enter Perth. None of the inhabitants were to be punished for the recent troubles or for supporting the Protestants, and no Frenchman was to come within three miles of the town. When the Queen moved on, she was not to leave a French garrison behind. All other causes of dispute were to be referred to Parliament.[24]

The following day, Knox preached a final sermon in St John's Kirk before a large gathering which included members of the royal army. He gave thanks that God had prevented the enemy from falling upon them, but he warned that Mary of Guise would never keep her promises. The Congregation, as the Protestants now called themselves, then left Perth and the Queen Regent made her entrance. She gave orders for the repair of the friaries, said that tables should be set up in place of damaged altars, dismissed the Protestant provost of Perth, Lord Ruthven, and garrisoned the town with 400 Scottish soldiers. She then withdrew to her palace at Falkland.[25]

IO

Negotiations with England

CLAIMING THAT THE QUEEN REGENT had broken the agreement already because the Scottish garrison she had left in Perth were in the pay of the French, the Congregation called a meeting at St Andrews on 11 June 1559. Lord James and the Earl of Argyll then changed sides, joining their fellow Protestants. Knox decided to go to St Andrews with the Lords and rode first to the fishing port of Crail, on the south coast of Fife. The provost of the town welcomed him, and on 9 June he preached a stirring sermon denouncing the Queen Regent for violating the truce. The local people promptly destroyed all the altars and images in Crail Collegiate Church. Next day he preached in Anstruther, to similar effect. Alerted to the situation, Archbishop Hamilton hurried to St Andrews with an armed force, swearing that if Knox tried to preach there he would greet him with a round of shot. He would, said the Archbishop, bring Knox to the Queen Regent, dead or alive.[1]

Fearing for his safety, the Lords tried to dissuade Knox from going to St Andrews, but he was adamant that he would keep to his plans. He had preached his very first sermon in the parish church of St Andrews before being torn away by the French and, while he lay in the galleys, he had often promised that he would one day preach there again. God had finally brought him to that place once more and he could not step back from his duty. To those who were worried about him, he could only say that his life was in God's hands. He wanted no one to defend him. All he asked was that a congregation should gather to hear his words. Defying Archbishop Hamilton, he entered the city and on Sunday 11 June he preached in the parish church on the theme of the ejection of the moneychangers from the temple in Jerusalem and the duty of Christians to root out corruption. Furious, Archbishop Hamilton rode to Falkland to tell the Queen Regent about the sermon. That same week, the local people looted St Andrews Priory and the monasteries.[2]

For Knox, the experience of preaching once more in St Andrews was rewarding. 'The long thirst of my wretched heart is satisfied in abundance,' he told Anna Locke when he wrote to her from there on 23 June, adding that, for the past forty days and more, 'God used my tongue in my native country, to the manifestation of his glory'. The longing of the poor people and the nobility alike to hear the Word of God was 'wondrous great', but the task confronting him was a heavy one. He desperately needed the assistance of his old friend Christopher Goodman, even more than he needed his wife's company, he said. If Goodman was still in Geneva, he must be urged to come to Scotland right away, and Knox gave the names of various friends in Dundee and Edinburgh whom he could contact on his arrival.[3]

In spite of this cavalier reference to Marjorie, Knox was anxious to know where she was. As soon as he had arrived in Edinburgh, he had sent for her. If she, her mother and the little boys came to see Anna on their way through London, she was to urge them to hurry on to Knox or at least go to the north of England where he could get in touch with them more easily. By the time he wrote, they were in fact already in Paris, waiting for a safe-conduct to allow them to cross to England. The journey from Geneva had been no small undertaking for a young mother with a baby and a toddler but, nothing daunted, Marjorie and her mother had set out not long after Knox himself, Goodman travelling with them. Sir Nicholas Throckmorton, the English ambassador in Paris, was of the opinion that, in spite of Elizabeth I's attitude towards Knox, the Scottish preacher was such an influential figure that it would do no harm to allow his family this favour. The safe-conducts were duly granted and Marjorie and her companions were able to cross the Channel.[4]

In his letter to Anna Locke, Knox confessed that he was 'being oppressed with hourly cares', and indeed there was much cause for concern. After the visit of Archbishop Hamilton, the Queen Regent sent her army to Cupar, just six miles from St Andrews. As she had been ill for some weeks past and was too weak to lead them in person, the Duke of Châtelherault took command, along with Henri Cleutin, Seigneur d'Oysel, the French ambassador in Scotland. Hearing about her military preparations, the Congregation marched out from St Andrews and drew up their army on the moor just outside Cupar, ready to confront the enemy.

Lord Lindsay, one of the Lords of the Congregation was anxious to mediate. He rode to see Châtelherault and d'Oysel and urged them not to fight. Châtelherault was willing enough to comply, but d'Oysel was reluctant. However, when he climbed the Hill of Tarvit to survey the opposition and saw the much greater size of the other army, he agreed to come to terms. The French and their artillery would withdraw, first to Falkland and then across the River Forth to Lothian. The Queen Regent would be able to ride through Fife as she had always done, provided she did not have any French soldiers with her, and she would promise the Protestants freedom to worship as they chose. For their part, the Protestants would disband their army.[5]

While Mary of Guise retired to Edinburgh Castle, Knox and the Congregation went back to Perth. They ejected the provost chosen by the Queen Regent to replace Lord Ruthven and, excited by their arrival, 'the rascal multitude' poured out of Perth to nearby Scone, intent on destroying the ancient abbey held by Patrick Hepburn, Bishop of Moray, whom they held responsible for the burning of

Walter Myln. Scone was also the traditional coronation place of the Scottish kings and the Lords of the Congregation had no desire to see the abbey destroyed. They dispatched James Haliburton, Provost of Dundee, in a vain attempt to restrain the rioters and then they sent Knox to see what he could do. He did manage to prevent the mob from destroying the Bishop's granary that night, but, although Lord James and the Earl of Argyll came to join him, they were powerless to prevent their followers from looting the abbey and then setting fire to both it and the nearby palace.

Lord James and Argyll left Perth secretly by night with their forces, and Knox rode with them. They captured Stirling and turned east again, making for the capital. Fearing that she would be trapped in Edinburgh, the Queen Regent rode for Dunbar, on the east coast. Perched on the edge of the North Sea, its castle would be a safe refuge until help arrived from France and, if need be, she could make her escape by sea. At 3 a.m. on 30 June 1559 the army of the Congregation marched into Edinburgh. Images in the friaries and churches were pulled down, prayer books were burned and chalices and other precious vessels were carried away.

Knox went to the church of St Giles and preached a sermon, but it was not inflammatory in tone. The 'rascal multitude' needed no further encouragement. The following day, Mary of Guise issued letters declaring that the actions of the Congregation plainly showed that that they were not interested in religion but were intent on subverting her authority. She ordered them to leave Edinburgh within six hours. Ignoring her commands, they stayed where they were and on 7 July they flocked into Edinburgh Tolbooth to elect Knox as minister of St Giles. In some ways it was a moment of triumph, but they all knew that it was merely a matter of time before Henri II sent a French fleet to assist Mary of Guise.[6]

The Protestants' best hope lay with the English, and the Lords of the Congregation had already decided to send Knox south as their emissary. He intended to go no further than the north of England, but Cecil announced that he wanted to speak to him in person and invited him to come to his own mansion house of Burghley, in Lincolnshire. He would see Knox there on 25 July. For some reason, Knox did not go to Burghley. He may have misunderstood Cecil's message or perhaps the Lords had other plans. At any rate, he remained in Edinburgh. He and his friend William Kirkcaldy of Grange had, however, corresponded with the 7th Duke of Northumberland's brother, Sir Henry Percy, who passed on their messages to Cecil.[7]

The English were extremely wary of intervening in Scotland. They had no desire to see their northern neighbour become the satellite state of France, but they were very conscious of the fact that by the Treaty of Cateau-Cambrésis they had made peace with the French. They could hardly launch into a war against them without very good cause. Moreover, Elizabeth I was adamant that she would not have dealings with another monarch's rebellious subjects, no matter how much she might privately agree with their views. Any negotiations between the English Court and the Scottish Protestants would have to be conducted with the utmost secrecy, and no open help could be given.

Another cause for caution, of course, was the fact that they did not know how many people in Scotland truly supported the movement for reform, and they too suspected that the Lords of the Congregation were motivated by self-interest rather than regard for religion. For all anyone knew, the Lords might decide at any time to revert to their traditional alliance with France. The English would have to be very sure indeed that their intervention was truly merited before they would do anything at all, and so Cecil's letters on the subject were vague, reticent and avoided any hint of commitment. Knox worked hard to convince Cecil that they were concerned only with the establishment of the true religion and perpetual peace with England. On 19 July the Lords themselves signed a letter to Cecil which Knox had drafted, emphasising that their only purpose was 'to advance the glory of Christ Jesus'. They would never return to their old alliance with France, as he seemed to suspect.

The next day, Knox himself wrote again to Cecil. After referring pointedly to his previous letters from Dieppe and St Andrews, all of which had gone unanswered, he said that he had heard that he was 'so odious to the Queen's Grace [Elizabeth I] and to her council that the mention of my name is unpleasing to their ears'. Why this should be, he could not imagine, for he had always been the friend of England and had long looked for a perpetual concord between the two realms. Undeterred by the rumours of his unpopularity, he was enclosing a letter for Elizabeth I, 'smelling nothing of flattery'. In such dangerous times, Scotland and England must act together, and if the Reformation in Scotland seemed 'somewhat violent', it was because the adversaries of the true religion were stubborn. Cecil must take care. Just because one godly woman with rare gifts and graces was allowed by God to rule, Elizabeth's reign must in no way set a precedent.[8]

Even as he read this covering note, Cecil must have realised with a sinking heart that the enclosure was not going to be suitable to set before Elizabeth. Sure enough, it was one of Knox's characteristic diatribes. Instead of avoiding the subject of *The First Blast* and hoping that the English Queen might forget all about it, Knox told her that the news of her displeasure at his book was a grievous burden to him. His conscience was clear, he protested, and he was not taking back any of the principal points which he had made. He simply could not understand what had annoyed her. He had not even mentioned her and all he had done was to reiterate that no woman may be exalted above any realm or be allowed to give it into the thrall of a cruel and foreign nation.

Provided Elizabeth admitted that she was queen because God had made her so, she would do well. Only if she showed a proud conceit of herself would her reign be unstable, troublesome and short. 'Forget your birth,' Knox told her, 'and all title which thereupon doth hang, and consider deeply how, for fear of your life, you did decline from God and bow in idolatry.' God had raised her from the dust without her deserving. If she recognised this and humbled herself in God's presence, then Knox would personally defend her authority and her rule with both tongue and pen.

Nothing annoyed Elizabeth I more than references to the alleged inability of women to rule. The Bishop of Winchester had recently infuriated her by insolently reminding the House of Lords of St Paul's remarks about no female being eligible to act as an apostle, shepherd, doctor or preacher, and the Bishop had even had the temerity to ask how any woman could be Head of the Church of England. Elizabeth had responded to such objections by taking the title of Supreme Governor of the Church instead of Head, but that did not mean that she had changed her own views one iota. Moreover, Knox's reference to her behaviour during Mary I's reign, when she had been forced to dissimulate and attend Mass to try to avoid being sent to the Tower, would have sent her into a fury.[9]

Cecil suppressed Knox's letter and tried to give him a hint, heading his reply of 28 July 1559 with a Latin quotation: 'There is neither male nor female, for as saith Paul, they are all one in Christ Jesus.' In fact, Elizabeth intended helping the Congregation first with promises, then with money and finally with arms, but secrecy was all-important and unless the matter were handled discreetly, nothing would be forthcoming. Cecil would have preferred not to deal with Knox at all, but Sir Nicholas Throckmorton, who knew about Elizabeth's reaction to *The First Blast*, nevertheless kept emphasising Knox's abilities and the significance of his role in Scotland. Throckmorton's opinion was not to be ignored, for he had accompanied Somerset's army of invasion to Scotland in 1547 and he had a good grasp of the situation and personalities in the north.[10]

The day after Knox sent off his letters to Cecil and Elizabeth, the Congregation seized Scotland's coining irons from the mint at Holyroodhouse, The Protestants would produce coins themselves, without any hateful reference to French sovereignty. Enraged at such blatant flouting of her authority, Mary of Guise decided to march on Edinburgh. Her advisers warned her that she did not have nearly enough soldiers, but she ignored them. Led by Châtelherault and d'Oysel, her army of some 1,700 men seized and occupied Leith. The Congregation had drawn up their army just outside the capital, but neither side was anxious for an actual conflict. Instead, they negotiated, and agreement was reached at Leith Links on 23 July 1559.

The Queen Regent's representatives promised that the people of Edinburgh would be free to choose whichever form of worship they desired, Roman Catholic or Protestant, and no one would interfere with the Protestant preachers. The Protestants could hold their services in St Giles Church, while Roman Catholic Mass was said at Holyrood. In return, the Congregation said that they would deliver up the coining irons, surrender the Palace of Holyroodhouse and leave Edinburgh the next day. In future, they would obey the authority of Mary, Queen of Scots, the Dauphin and the Queen Regent, according to the existing laws of the country and they would molest neither churches nor churchmen.[11]

In compliance with this agreement, the Congregation gave back the coining irons, handed over the Palace of Holyroodhouse and retired. The Queen Regent returned to Edinburgh and took up residence in the castle once more to await her expected reinforcements from France. Knox preached in St Giles on 29 July, but with Mary of Guise and her forces so close at hand, the Lords of the Congregation felt that he was in grave danger of assassination. This would be an appropriate time to send him on his important mission to England. On 30 July they gave him his instructions.

Knox was to discuss a league of perpetual peace between the Scottish Protestants and Elizabeth I and he was to say that both Châtelherault and the Roman Catholic Earl of Huntly had promised to help the Congregation if the Queen Regent broke the agreement at Leith Links in any way at all. In return for the league of perpetual friendship, Knox would ask for men and money and he would urge the English to capture and hold the strategically important fortress at Eyemouth, so that the French would not be able to seize it when they came. Neither Scotland nor England would then make war or peace without the consent of the other, and all liberties, laws and privileges of both realms would be protected against any foreign power. Even if France asked the Scots to invade England, they would refuse.[12]

Armed with his instructions, Knox sailed from Pittenweem in Fife on 1 August 1559 with another preacher, Robert Hamilton, whom he may have known at St Andrews University. Before travelling on to Lincolnshire to see Cecil, they were to call on Sir Henry Percy. They came ashore at Holy Island, supposedly in secret, but Knox was recognised at once. He had been a familiar figure in the area only a few years before and he seems to have made no real attempt to conceal his identity. Indeed, Sir Henry was to complain that Knox conducted his visit 'in such unsecret sort, that it is openly known both unto England and Scotland, wherefore I think he hath not discreetly used his coming'.[13]

Cecil and his colleagues were prepared to consider an alliance with the Scottish Protestants, but only if it were genuine and effective. They remained suspicious that they were being given fair words by untrustworthy Scots seeking their own advantage, and so they were very cautious. More than that, Cecil knew that, if he pressed Elizabeth I too hard, she would baulk at his plans and refuse to allow negotiations to go ahead. She had to be handled very carefully, and, if Knox made the secret machinations public, then the whole enterprise would fail. Regardless of her Protestant convictions, Elizabeth was first and foremost a monarch, and her status in the eyes of the world was all important to her. She was not going to be seen plotting with a fellow monarch's rebels.

Desperate to conceal the fact that they were negotiating with Mary of Guise's subjects, the English officials hastily smuggled Knox and Hamilton into Berwick Castle. Sir Henry himself was away on business on the border, but they had two days of discussions with the Governor of Berwick, Sir James Croft. Throughout their negotiations, Knox and Hamilton emphasised that, if Elizabeth I supplied them with men and money, the Scottish Protestants were ready to abandon their traditional alliance with France in favour of a firm league with England. Croft remained wary, declaring that he did not see how the English Queen could negotiate a league with the Lords of the Congregation, who had no established authority. With unexpected diplomacy, Knox replied that the Scots would choose from among themselves those representatives whom Elizabeth thought most suitable for the role of negotiators.

In spite of this concession, Croft formed the impression that it would be a mistake for Knox to travel on to Lincolnshire to meet Cecil. He could see that Knox would never make a Machiavellian dissembler and lacked the discretion necessary for this delicate diplomatic mission. Knox may, indeed, have realised it himself. What passed between the two men on this subject is not known but, at the end of two days, Knox made the excuse that he was anxious to return to his flock, and said that he was willing to hand over the negotiations to someone better equipped than he was to discuss such weighty matters. He sailed back to Scotland with Hamilton on 3 August and rode at once to Stirling, to give the Lords an account of his discussions.[14]

Four days later, dramatic news arrived from France. Henri II had died after a jousting accident. Word of his injury had already reached Scotland, but he had been expected to recover. Now Mary, Queen of Scots's husband was King François II of France, she was Queen of France and the two men set to dominate the French Court were her uncles, the Duke of Guise and the Cardinal of Lorraine, brothers of Mary of Guise. They were sure to respond to her pleas for help more swiftly than Henri II had done.[15]

The English quickly devised a new plan. Mary of Guise must be ousted from the regency, and the obvious person to replace her was the malleable Duke of Châtelherault. He was still on the side of the Queen Regent, of course, but that could easily be changed. They had only to persuade him that she and the French were edging him out of the succession and he would gladly support the Protestant cause. On 7 August, Elizabeth sent Sir Ralph Sadler north, officially to inspect the fortifications at Berwick but with secret instructions to rouse up Scottish feelings against the French and persuade Châtelherault to change sides.

Further to facilitate this move, they smuggled the Duke's eldest and favourite son back to Scotland. James, Earl of Arran had been the boy held hostage in St Andrews Castle by Cardinal Beaton and then taken to France as a hostage of Henri II. He was carefully educated and became a captain in the Scots Guard. Henri had meant marry him to a French noble lady so that he and his father would be even more firmly tied to France, but at some point Arran became a Protestant. Hearing rumours that he was being considered as a husband for Elizabeth I, Henri summoned him to the French Court, but Sir Nicholas Throckmorton managed to spirit him away, first to Switzerland, where he spoke to many of the leading reformers, and then to England.

Reaching London towards the end of August 1559, he was taken secretly to Cecil's house for discussions, and the prospect of marriage with Elizabeth was no doubt one of the inducements held out to him. He had a carefully arranged 'accidental' meeting with the English queen in the gardens of Hampton Court Palace. Immediately afterwards, he left for Scotland, travelling incognito in the company of Elizabeth's envoy Thomas Randolph. They reached Alnwick on the morning of 6 September and from there they rode to Hamilton Castle, to see Arran's father.

The English had been told that Arran was the person who could most quickly persuade the Duke of Châtelherault to abandon Mary of Guise and join the Protestant cause, and so it proved to be. After a joyous reunion between father and son, Lord James and Argyll took Arran to Stirling to meet the rest of the Congregation. Soon afterwards, the Queen Regent was writing bitterly to her son-in-law François II, 'Sire, this is to tell you that the Duke of Châtelherault has wasted no time after his son's arrival in declaring himself chief and leader of the rebels.'[16] On 12 October Randolph was able to report for once that the Duke was 'earnest and constant'.[17]

After his visit to Stirling to see the Lords, it had been judged best for Knox to withdraw to the safety of St Andrews, well away from the enemy forces in the capital. He was feeling ill and overworked. He had, however, heard from his wife. Christopher Goodman had arrived in Scotland at the end of August, while Marjorie and her mother presumably broke their journey to visit their relatives and show off the little boys. Elizabeth's husband had died in the autumn of 1558, while she was in Switzerland, but her other children lived in the area. On 23 August Knox wrote to Cecil asking for safe conducts for some men he was sending south to fetch his wife, since 'my wicked carcase, now presently labouring in the fevers, needeth her service'. She arrived in St Andrews on 20 September 1559 and her mother joined them in November.[18]

With his domestic arrangements put in order and Marjorie at his side, Knox was able to devote a good deal of time that autumn to the writing the text which became his *History of the Reformation of Religion within the Realm of Scotland*. His intention was to justify the actions of the Scottish Protestants in rising up against the authorities, and he set out to describe the events of previous months, starting with the various petitions presented to Mary of Guise at the beginning of the year. He wanted to show everyone, particularly the English, that recent events in Scotland had not constituted rebellion, as the Queen Regent and her French advisers were saying, but were the outcome of a genuine religious movement intended to reform a corrupt Church. He was probably also the author of a number of proclamations issued by the Lords of the Congregation that autumn, detailing their grievances.[19]

The Lords met in Stirling on 15 October 1559 and decided that the time had come to depose the Queen Regent. They marched into Edinburgh three days later, only to find that she had slipped away to the safety of Leith, which was garrisoned by French soldiers. On 21 October, the Lords assembled in Edinburgh Tolbooth, where Mary had been invested as regent five and a half years before. In her absence, Lord Ruthven stood up and formally asked if she ought to continue to rule. The Lords said that the preachers should be consulted and Knox's colleague, John Willock, spoke first, emphasising the duty of princes to their subjects and saying that, although God appointed them as his lieutenants on earth, they could still be deprived for just cause.

The Queen Regent had failed to do her duty. She had not ministered justice impartially and she had not allowed God's Word to be freely preached. He called her an open and obstinate idolatress, who had ignored advice and the requests of the nobility.

When Willock had finished speaking, Knox was asked for his views. What he said was surprisingly moderate. He approved of Willock's advice, but he uttered some words of caution, obviously with Elizabeth I and English sensitivities in mind. The Queen Regent's iniquity ought not to make them withdraw their obedience to their sovereigns, François II and Mary, he told his listeners. He warned them, too, that if they deposed Mary of Guise they must do so out of concern for the public interest, not from malice or private envy. Finally, he argued that she should be suspended rather than deprived, for it could be that she might yet repent and she could then be reinstated.

The Lords of the Congregation took his advice and suspended her commission as regent, ordering the Act of Suspension to be read out to the sound of a trumpet at the market cross of Edinburgh. Mary of Guise ignored the suspension and continued to style herself Queen Regent rather than Queen Dowager, but the country was now officially being ruled by a Great Council of 30 leading Protestants, with the Duke of Châtelherault as its president. The Duke was also a member of the unofficial Council of the Congregation. Knox was given a place on a committee set up to advise the Lords on religious matters.[20]

He was still plying his English contacts with requests for men and money, in spite of the fact that Sir James Croft told him again that money would indeed be sent, but only if it were kept secret. 'To be plain with you,' said Croft, 'ye are so open in your doings as you make men half afraid to deal with you.'[21] Attempting to play the political game, Knox suggested that English soldiers could be sent to Scotland unofficially and then denounced as rebels by Elizabeth. That earned him a sharp rebuke from Croft. Everyone would see through the ruse right away. Meanwhile, Cecil told his own colleagues frankly, 'Of all others, Knox's name is most odious here, if it be not Goodman's, and therefore I wish no mention of him' and he confided to Croft and Sir Ralph Sadler, 'I like not Knox's audacity, his writings do no good here, and therefore I do rather suppress them.'[22]

II

The Scottish Reformation

U NPOPULAR THOUGH KNOX MIGHT be at Elizabeth I's Court,
the Lords of the Congregation needed him still. That autumn,
they suffered a series of reverses. A thousand pounds sent to
them by the English was intercepted and seized by one of Mary
of Guise's supporters, ten of Châtelherault's men and a number
of civilians were killed during a skirmish with the French just
outside Edinburgh, the Lords of the Congregation were quarrelling
among themselves and their poorly paid soldiers were drifting
away. On the night of 5–6 November 1559, Protestant morale
abruptly collapsed, and the Congregation decided to withdraw from
Edinburgh. They retreated in considerable disarray to Linlithgow
and Mary of Guise entered Edinburgh again. Knox's Church of
St Giles was reconsecrated by the Roman Catholics and Mass was
said once more.[1]

It seemed as if the entire Protestant movement in Scotland was
disintegrating. Alarmed by the reports he was hearing, Knox rode to
Stirling and, on 8 November 1559, preached one of his most powerful
sermons in the Church of the Holy Rood. Châtelherault was there,
along with the other Lords, and Knox took the opportunity of
analysing exactly what he thought had gone wrong. He chose as

his text Psalm 80, with its metaphor of God rooting out the heathen, planting a great vine and then seeing it attacked by wild animals, burned by fire and cut down. Twice the psalm repeats the refrain, 'Turn us again, O Lord God of hosts, cause thy face to shine and we shall be saved,'

Knox explained that, both now and in Biblical times, God allowed his chosen people to be exposed to danger so that they would realise their own weakness. There were two groups of Protestants in Scotland, he said. Those steadfast men who had supported the reformed cause from the very beginning, when 'we had neither Earl nor Lord (a few excepted)' had of necessity relied on God alone. He had been their sole protector. As a result, there had been no boasting, no rivalries, no concern with worldly reputation. Now, however, there was a second group, comprising members of the nobility and everything had changed.

Ever since the Duke of Châtelherault and his friends had joined them, nothing was heard but 'This Lord will bring these many hundred spears, this man hath the credit to persuade this country, if the Earl be ours, no man in such bounds will trouble us.' God had been forgotten. On three previous occasions, at Perth, Cupar and Edinburgh, the Duke had been a great comfort to the Catholics and 'a great discouragement' to the Protestants and, Knox went on, 'I am uncertain if my Lord's Grace hath unfeignedly repented of . . . his assistance to those murderers unjustly pursuing us.' He was also unsure, he said, whether the Duke regretted the death of those innocent martyrs whose blood had been shed because he had refused to intervene.

God was showing the original Protestants that they had placed too much trust in men, while making the more recent arrivals experience the sort of anguish previously endured by Knox and the rest. What was to be done? The solution was simple. It lay in their own hands. They had only to turn to God for their sadness and confusion to be changed into joy, honour and boldness. In giving this account of his sermon in his *History of the Reformation* Knox does not tell us how the Duke of Châtelherault reacted to such a very public condemnation of his own deficiencies. Perhaps he was not quite as outspoken about the Duke as he would have us believe. At any rate, regardless of the Duke's personal feelings, there is no doubt that Knox's words restored the confidence of the Lords of the Congregation. They went off in a positive mood to hold a meeting of their council, and Knox was called in to say the customary prayers.

Until now, the Lords had been intending to send Knox south again, this time to the English Court to explain the Scottish situation to Elizabeth. Now, however, they changed their minds. Instead, he would be replaced by William Maitland of Lethington. A sophisticated and experienced diplomat, Maitland had been the Queen Regent's secretary until a month earlier when he had joined the Protestants in pursuit of his ideal of a united Scotland and England. He was far better equipped than Knox was to undertake the delicate negotiations. The Lords then dispersed, promising to meet again at Stirling in December.[2]

Knox could not, of course, return to Edinburgh and so he decided to go back to St Andrews. Soon afterwards, he received a letter from Calvin, congratulating him on the progress made in Scotland, and telling him, 'I am not ignorant of how energetic a counsellor you are, and how great readiness and power God has given you for acting such a part.'[3] Heartening as that might be, Knox was well aware that he had been marginalised. The Lords no longer needed him to take the lead. Power had passed to the devious courtiers who would exploit the situation for their own benefit. 'I am judged amongst ourselves too extreme,' he told his friend Gregory Railton, 'and by reason thereof I have extracted myself from all public assemblies to my private study.'[4]

He turned his attention to his pastoral duties. He preached, taught, studied the Bible with his congregation, advised the usual troubled, middle-aged ladies who sought his assistance and generally set about trying to transform St Andrews into the kind of well-regulated, godly society he had seen in Geneva. Berwick had been troubled by its large and unruly community of soldiers, Geneva had struggled with the ever increasing number of foreign exiles, and now St Andrews was suffering from the problem of having a significant number of Roman Catholic ecclesiastics living on in the city.

Knox made no attempt to have any action taken against them. They were an embarrassment, to say the least, but what else could be done with them? Many were elderly, they would die off soon, and some of them, at least, might convert if they saw the error of their ways. He also attended meetings of his kirk session each week, and presided over cases of adultery, fornication and similar misdemeanours, acting with a leniency which might have surprised his critics.[5]

Busy as he was, he could not help but worry about the current situation, and he fretted that the Lords of the Congregation lacked organisation and were too slow to act. The French had marched out of Leith to harass the countryside. In Fife, they managed to capture William Kirkcaldy's house of Grange, and Mary of Guise exclaimed triumphantly, 'Where is now John Knox's God? My God is now stronger than his, yea even in Fife!' They were then rumoured to be marching on St Andrews and word came that a French fleet was on its way to Scotland.[6]

By the end of the year, Knox was suffering from recurring fevers again, a price had been put on his head and he had so much work to do that he was getting to bed for only four hours each night. Marjorie was worn out too. Knox sent a letter to Anna Locke from St Andrews on the last day of 1559, apologising because he had failed to answer her recent religious enquiries. Marjorie had lost the paper on which they were written, and he explained that 'the rest of my wife hath been so unrestful since her arriving here, that scarcely could she tell upon the morrow what she wrote at night.'

As for himself, he had thought himself well used to problems, 'But alas! I now perceive that all my practice before was but mere speculation, for one day of troubles since my last arrival in Scotland hath more pieced my heart than all the torments of the galleys did the space of 19 months, for that torment, for the most part, did touch the body, but this pierces the soul and inward affections.'

When he had lain ill aboard his galley off St Andrews, he had been sure that he would not die until he had preached there once more, and yet, 'having now my hearty desire, I am nothing satisfied, neither yet rejoice. My God, remove my unthankfulness!'[7] At last, however, on 22 January 1560, a small fleet of English ships was sighted at the mouth of the River Forth. Queen Elizabeth had finally sent help.

Admiral William Winter had set sail on 27 December 1559 from Gillingham, with fourteen vessels and instructions that he was to 'annoy' the French. If he were captured, he was to say that he was acting entirely on his own initiative. On the way north he had encountered dreadful storms and lost six of his ships, but at least he had come, a very visible token of English support. When the French outside St Andrews sighted his vessels, they retreated, and Mary of Guise sent an official protest to Elizabeth I. Better still from the Protestant point of view, news came that the same gales encountered by Winter had struck the large French fleet which was also on its way to Scotland. Three-quarters of the vessels were driven to the coast of Flanders and only 900 French soldiers eventually arrived at Leith.[8]

At the end of January 1560, Queen Elizabeth sent Thomas, Duke of Norfolk to Berwick to negotiate with the Scottish Protestants. Châtelherault, Lord James, Lord Ruthven and several other members of the Congregation travelled south to meet him, but Knox was not among them. The Treaty of Berwick was signed on 27 February 1560. Very carefully worded, to answer all Elizabeth I's fears and reservations, it said that the English Queen understood that the French intended to conquer Scotland, suppress its liberties and unite it to the crown of France forever. Having been humbly and earnestly requested by the Scottish nobility, in the name of the whole realm of Scotland, to intervene, she would do so.

Elizabeth would take into her protection the realm of Scotland, the Duke of Châtelherault, heir apparent to the Scottish crown, the nobility and the subjects of Scotland, in order to preserve them in their old freedoms and liberties and keep them from conquest. This agreement would last throughout the marriage of Mary, Queen of Scots to François II and for one year thereafter. Elizabeth would speedily send an army north to expel the French from Scotland. Any fortress won from the French would either be demolished at once by the Scots or handed over to the Duke of Châtelherault and his party, and any fortifications undertaken in Scotland by the English would only be put in place with the advice of the Duke and the Scots. In return, the Scots promised to support the English and resist any attempts on the part of the French to conquer England. If England were invaded by the French, the Scots would send an army to England's aid.[9]

On 29 March, an English army of 9000 men marched north and joined the Duke of Châtelherault and his force at Prestonpans, near Edinburgh. Mary of Guise found refuge in Edinburgh Castle and a force of 11,000 English soldiers and 2,000 Scottish mercenaries hired with English money began to besiege Leith, which was being held by 3,500 French and Gascons and 500 Scots. In mid-April, Knox was able to enter Edinburgh once more. While the English bombarded Leith and started to dig trenches, the French set about countermining and the siege dragged on. Cecil finally lost patience and ordered a full-scale assault. In the early hours of 7 May 1560 the English attacked, but their scaling ladders were too short and they were driven back. The siege continued.[10]

Each time Knox entered the pulpit in St Giles, he preached against Mary of Guise and the French. As his own health declined, his bitterness increased and he both spoke and wrote of the Queen Regent with increasing venom. When he described the siege of Leith in his *History of the Reformation*, he alleged that Mary of Guise gazed out from Edinburgh Castle after the foiled attack and gloated at the sight of the English corpses hung on the walls of Leith. 'Within a few days thereafter,' he wrote, 'began her belly and loathsome legs to swell, and so continued till God did execute his judgment upon her.' Mary had for some time been suffering from dropsy as well as attacks of high fever, both symptoms of grave heart disease, but she could never have seen the corpses from Edinburgh Castle even had she been in the best of health. Knox's vitriolic tone did him no credit.[11]

Mary of Guise decided to summon a deputation of Protestants to discuss the situation with her, and on 12 May 1560 Lord James, Lord Ruthven, Maitland of Lethington and the Master of Maxwell went up to Edinburgh Castle. They complained about taxes, Frenchmen appointed to Scottish offices and attempts to change the laws of Scotland. Mary answered as she always did that the French soldiers had been brought in because of public disorder, and that any appointment of Frenchmen to Scottish offices had been done with the approval of Parliament. When they eventually reached the subject of the Protestant league with England it became clear that there could be no compromise. Nothing would persuade the Protestants to abandon their alliance with Elizabeth I.

At the beginning of June, 400 more English soldiers joined the siege of Leith, and on 4 June their cannon brought down the tower of St Anthony's Church. Mary of Guise was far gone by now. Alarmed at her condition, Lord Erskine the keeper of Edinburgh Castle sent his brother to beg the Lords of the Congregation to allow Nicolas Pellevé, Bishop of Amiens to go to her. The Bishop had been in Scotland for several months on a diplomatic mission. Only the Duke of Châtelherault objected, and, because of him, Mary was denied the consolation of her fellow countryman's presence.[12]

She knew that she was dying, and she sent for her Lords. At 8.00 a.m. on 7 June Lord James, the Earl of Arran, and the Duke of Châtelherault went up to the castle and were shown into her chamber with her other leading nobles. They found her propped up in her chair, pitifully weak but as resolute as ever. She urged them earnestly to favour the alliance with France and turn away from England, telling them that if she had done anything displeasing to them, it was 'rather for lack of wisdom and judgment than for want of any good will'. She went on to ask them to forgive her if she had ever offended any of them during her time in Scotland. For her part, she said, she forgave them for all the offences they had committed against her, and she took each of them by the hand, in turn. Many of them wept unashamedly as they left her chamber.

Lord James stayed in the castle at her request and he and Argyll were with her when she died at about half an hour after midnight on 11 June 1560.[13] Her long and valiant struggle was over at last. Even her enemies had accorded her reluctant admiration as she fought desperately to preserve Scotland for the French, Roman Catholic interest for her daughter, but, in the end, the rising tide of Protestantism and the accompanying anti-French feeling had been too much even for her gallant determination, and her death now made possible the very alliance she had tried so hard to prevent.

Elizabeth I had already sent William Cecil to Newcastle negotiate with French envoys and he now moved to Edinburgh. A truce was arranged, and on 6 July 1560 the Treaty of Edinburgh was signed. The principal clause stated that all foreign soldiers were to withdraw from Scotland. François II and Mary, Queen of Scots would henceforth abstain from quartering the English arms with those of Scotland. Everything relating to religion was to be referred to the Scottish Parliament. Since the Scots had 'spontaneously and freely professed and acknowledged their obedience and loyalty towards their said most Christian king and queen', François and Mary would fulfil all the obligations in the treaty.[14]

After the treaty had been signed, Knox held a great service of thanksgiving in St Giles, praying that God, who had 'partly removed our darkness, suppressed idolatry and taken from above our heads the devouring sword of merciless strangers', would be pleased 'to proceed with us in this Thy grace begun'. His sermon was based on a text relating to the biblical prophet Haggai, and he said a great deal about the work that lay ahead of them all. 'We must now forget ourselves and bear the barrow to build the houses of God,' Maitland of Lethington drawled mockingly to some of his aristocratic friends.[15]

On 10 July 1560, Parliament met in Edinburgh and began passing a series of acts which would make Scotland an officially Protestant country. Some Roman Catholics stayed away, but others, like the

Archbishop of St Andrews, were present to witness the passing of statutes abolishing papal authority in Scotland and forbidding Mass to be said. In future, people who celebrated or even attended Mass would have their property confiscated for a first offence and could be imprisoned, at the judge's discretion. If they offended a second time, they would be banished from Scotland, and if they were brought before the court for a third time, the death sentence would be passed.[16]

Since the previous spring, Knox and a group of other ministers had been working on a report laying down the policy and discipline of the Church of Scotland. This came to be known as the First Book of Discipline, and its detailed proposals were now read out to Parliament. The whole country should be divided into ten dioceses, each to be administered by a superintendent, who would be elected every three years from a short list of candidates drawn up by the ministers, elders, deacons and burgh councils of the diocese concerned.

The superintendents would be paid a stated salary higher than that appointed for ordinary ministers but they were not to be allowed 'to live as your idle bishops have done heretofore'. They would be expected to travel constantly throughout their dioceses, preaching and supervising the behaviour of the ministers. This was not fully-fledged Calvinism, where the Church was governed by ecclesiastical courts, and it should be noted that presbyterianism did not come to Scotland until after Knox's time, with Andrew Melville in the 1570s.

The ministers themselves were to be elected by their congregations with the approval of certain learned colleagues. In those parishes where there was no minister, a reader could be appointed to perform pastoral duties, provided he had the necessary knowledge. If he not only read from the Bible but began to exhort the congregation, he could be paid extra, and it was to be hoped that he might finally qualify as a minister. The most knowledgeable and respectable men in each parish should be elected as elders and deacons, for one year at a time.

The elders would assist the ministers with advice and the judging of ecclesiastical causes, and indeed the senior elders were to pay heed to the behaviour of their minister and admonish him if need be. Every church should have a copy of the Bible in English and the master of every household must be commanded to instruct or make arrangements for the instruction of his children, servants and family in the principles of religion. They would all have to be familiar with the psalms, so that they could join in the singing at services, and there should be common prayers morning and night in private houses.

The Lord's Supper was to be administered no more than four times a year, to the whole congregation. It was not to be given privately in people's houses. Baptisms were to take place on Sundays, after the sermon. All saints days and holy days were to be abolished, and all abbeys, monasteries, friaries, and nunneries would be suppressed as redundant. Churches would have to be repaired, for the Roman Catholic Church had neglected them and some of them had fallen into a semi-ruined state. Every church would provide for the poor of the parish, 'but the stout and strong beggar must be compelled to work'.

One of the best-known passages in the Book of Discipline said that every child in Scotland should go to school. Presumably this applied to girls as well as to boys. Until then, only the daughters of the aristocracy had been educated, but the Reformers, including Knox, were anxious that women should be able to read the Bible for themselves. There would be a grammar school in every parish and a college in every large town, for the teaching of the Arts, logic, rhetoric and languages. The syllabuses of the three Scottish universities in St Andrews, Glasgow and Aberdeen were to be modernised and the old scholastic theology was no longer to have pride of place. Trainee ministers would study not only theology but Hebrew, mathematics, physics, economics, ethics and moral philosophy. The syllabus for medical and law students was outlined too.

People often imagine that these wide-ranging plans were

immediately implemented, but that, of course, was not possible. It would have taken enormous financial resources to set up a school in every parish, let alone address the question of more advanced education. Some new schools were founded, it is true, but more than 50 years later Parliament was still trying to legislate for a school in every parish and a century after the First Book of Discipline was written, the number of girls going to school was small. The question of revenues for the Protestant Church was vital, and it remained a major problem.[17]

One of the great complaints about the Roman Catholic Church had been its extortion of teinds and taxes at every possible opportunity. The teinds or tithes were the tenth part of the produce of a parish, and had been payable to the Church. The authors of the First Book of Discipline pointed out that some Protestant gentlemen were 'now as cruel over their tenants as ever were the papists, requiring of them whatsoever before they paid to the Church'. For that reason, all such teinds were to be abolished forever. The problem was that many of the bishops and priests of the Roman Catholic Church retained their revenues, and a significant proportion of the church lands were in the hands of the nobility. The authors of the Book of Discipline dared not suggest a scheme for financing the Reformed Church, for they knew that anything they suggested would be seen as an attack on the vested interests of the Protestant Lords themselves. Knox and his colleagues therefore turned away from the problem of finance and no new system was suggested.[18]

When the Book of Discipline was presented to Parliament, Knox and his friends waited anxiously. The Roman Catholic bishops as well as Roman Catholic noblemen were present that day and, sure that they would object, Knox and his fellow authors were standing by, ready to answer any criticisms. However, although one or two of the Lords said they disagreed, they could produce no argument other than, 'We will believe as our fathers believed'. The Catholic bishops said nothing at all. Parliament accepted the First Book of Discipline and it was eventually approved on 27 January 1561 and signed in the Tolbooth of Edinburgh by the Duke of Châtelherault and almost all the other Lords. By then, the legislation abolishing papal authority and the Mass had already come into force. From 24 August 1560, Scotland was officially a Protestant country. Two years later, the Book of Common Order, Calvin's service book followed by Knox and the English congregation in Geneva in the 1550s, was introduced. It was intended to replace the English Book of Common Prayer, long in use in Scotland, but it did not entirely supersede it.[19]

Knox's colleagues were eager for him to become one of the new superintendents, but he said that his health was too poor now for him to undertake the constant travelling and they reluctantly accepted his decision. He was given a salary of £200 a year, the highest amount payable to a minister, and the town council agreed to provide him with accommodation. They installed him in a house formerly occupied by the Abbot of Dunfermline on the west side of Trunk Close, one of the narrow lanes on the north side of the High Street, not far from St Giles. Described as 'a great mansion' with a garden and a piece of waste ground, it had recently been let to a tailor, who was paid compensation by the town council when he agreed to move out.[20]

Knox's domestic happiness in his new circumstances was to be all too brief. At the end of November or in early December 1560, Marjorie died. There is no record of what happened. Perhaps she died in childbirth, as so many young women did. We know only that in her last hours she gave her little sons her blessing, and prayed that they would always be as true worshippers of God 'as any that ever sprang out of Abraham's loins'. Knox could only murmur, 'Amen'. He was deeply upset and in his *History of the Reformation* he even mentioned that, during a conversation with Châtelherault and Lord James, they were 'comforting him (for he was in no small heaviness by reason of the late death of his dear bedfellow Marjorie Bowes)'.[21]

Critics have sometimes claimed that Knox's *History* should have been entitled *The Memoirs of John Knox*, but they do him an injustice.

Although he obviously describes events from his particular view-point, he is not at all concerned with chronicling his own every move or his thoughts and reactions. He features from time to time in the pages, either in the third person as 'John Knox' or anonymously, but the reader will look in vain for any intimate revelations. It is therefore a telling moment when he mentions his sorrow at Marjorie's death. Incidentally, the very first letter he had written to her is the only part of their correspondence to have survived. Possibly Marjorie gave it to Mrs Bowes to keep because it consisted of religious advice, but the fact that it was preserved at all may be an indication of the strength of affection between Knox and his young wife.

It seems that Knox did not write to Calvin to give him the tragic news of Marjorie's death until the following spring, for Calvin's letter of condolence is dated 23 April 1561. 'You found a wife whose like is not found everywhere,' Calvin told him, 'but as you have rightly learned where to seek consolation in sorrow, I am sure that you are bearing this calamity with patience.' That same day Calvin wrote to Christopher Goodman, telling him, 'Although I am not a little grieved that our brother Knox has been deprived of the most delightful of wives, yet I rejoice that he has not been so afflicted by her death as to cease his active labours in the cause of Christ and the Church.'[22]

Knox was indeed still battling on. The Treaty of Edinburgh might be safely signed, but it had to be ratified by both England and France. The English ratification presented no problem, but François II was flatly refusing to have anything to do with it, nor would he ratify the recent legislation regarding the church. Instead, he sent word to Scotland that he was highly displeased with the recent proceedings in Parliament. There were rumours of the French preparing to send a new army to Scotland and it seemed that they were about to disown the Treaty of Edinburgh altogether. The Earls of Morton and Glencairn and William Maitland of Lethington hurried to the English Court to ask Elizabeth once more for help. It was unthinkable that the country should slide back into the dreadful situation of conflict which had existed before the death of Mary of Guise.

In November 1560, however, everything changed. François II suddenly fell ill. He had been out hunting one day, and came home complaining of a violent pain in his ear. There had been a bitterly cold wind, but as he had often suffered from earache in the past, no one was too alarmed. Soon, however, he had a raging fever, and although both Mary, Queen of Scots and his mother, Catherine de Medici, nursed him tenderly, he died on 5 December, apparently from an abscess on the brain.[23]

12

The Return of Mary,
Queen of Scots

KNOX WAS THE FIRST person in Scotland to hear that François II was dead, and he hurried at once to Hamilton House, the Duke of Châtelherault's residence at Kirk o' Field, on the edge of Edinburgh. He found the Duke conferring with Lord James and, when he blurted out the news, they did not believe him. François was only fifteen. He had always been delicate, but they had not expected this. It must have seemed to the Duke and Lord James almost too good to be true, and Knox had to spend several minutes assuring them that his informant was reliable, the same messenger who had brought word of the death of Henri II before anyone else knew of it. The prospect of Scotland being forever united to France had dissolved. There would be no royal French sons of Mary, Queen of Scots to rule over Scotland for the French. She was no longer Queen of France as well as Queen of Scots. A dowager was very different from the wife of a reigning monarch.

The implications were even more wide-ranging than Knox and his companions may at first have realised. The death of François meant the end of the Guise supremacy at court. The new king,

Charles IX, was the younger brother of François, and their mother, Catherine de Medici, was going to rule the country until he came of age. She believed in subtlety, not confrontation, and she was more likely to tolerate Protestantism, at least in the short term, rather than risk civil disorder and bloodshed. The Treaty of Edinburgh might remain unratified, but there would be no new French army coming to Scotland.

Confirmation came even as Knox sat talking with the Duke and Lord James. A messenger arrived from Lord Grey in Berwick with a similar report. It was true. François II really was dead. The news spread like wildfire, and, amidst all the excitement, there was much speculation about the future of the Queen of Scots. What would Mary do now? When James V had died, Mary of Guise had been free to return to France, yet she had stayed on in Scotland to look after her daughter's interests. Certainly the situation of Mary, Queen of Scots was rather different. She had no children but an overbearing mother-in-law, and she might not wish to stay on in a secondary role. On the other hand, she had been brought up in France, and many of her friends were there as well as her Guise relatives. Perhaps she would live on the French estates provided in her marriage contract, and some prominent Scottish nobleman could rule Scotland as her regent.[1]

In fact, Mary was genuinely distressed by the death of her young husband, weeping uncontrollably and speaking of retiring to a quiet life in the country. Following French Court etiquette, she put on white mourning and shut herself away in a darkened chamber hung with black, but she did not long remain in this seclusion. Her ambitious Guise uncles were not going to hand over power meekly to Catherine de Medici, and it was obvious to them that Mary must find a powerful new husband as quickly as possible. Within two weeks she was having discussions with ambassadors, bishops and diplomats with a view to marrying Don Carlos, the son and heir of King Philip II of Spain. In the end nothing came of these plans, for Don Carlos was in such poor health that he was hardly fit to marry anyone, and Philip had already confirmed his peace with France when he married Henri II's daughter Elisabeth.[2]

Meeting in Edinburgh on 15 January 1561 to approve the First Book of Discipline, the Protestant leaders instructed Lord James to go to France and ask Mary to return. They might not like her religion but she was their Queen and the Lords of the Congregation had persuaded themselves that, once she was away from the influence of her Guise uncles, she would listen to advice and convert to Protestantism. After all, she was only eighteen, she had led a sheltered life, and people who knew her said that she was quiet and biddable. The Earl of Arran was particularly keen on the idea. The Lords of the Congregation had recently offered him as a husband to Elizabeth I, but this had met with a frosty reception. He himself had always harboured hopes of marrying Mary, whom he knew well from his years at the French Court, and he appreciated that there were many who believed that there would be a far better chance that she would convert if she became the wife of a Protestant like himself.[3]

Before he set out, Lord James took the precaution of speaking to Knox. Mary, Queen of Scots had read *The First Blast* and she had already indicated that she would not set foot in Scotland as long as Knox was there. Knox was therefore prevailed upon to produce some sort of written undertaking, presumably promising not to stir up the Scots to rebel against their female ruler. He was not about to take back one word of what he had said, but he did stress the fact that *The First Blast* had been written in response to Mary I's persecution of the English Protestants, not as an act of rebellion against Mary, Queen of Scots's mother, Mary of Guise. Armed with this disclaimer, Lord James set off on 18 March 1561, the warnings of Knox and the Lords of the Congregation ringing in his ears. He must on no account agree to Mass being said in Scotland either publicly or privately. Travelling through England he crossed the Channel and saw Mary at Diziers on 15 April.

Disappointed over the Spanish match, she was in a receptive frame of mind. Lord James, as he had been told to do, began by asking his half-sister to renounce Roman Catholicism in favour of the Protestant religion. Smiling, she refused, and parried his request by telling him that, if he became a Catholic, she would ask the Pope to make him a cardinal. She then added more seriously that she was prepared to go back, provided she were allowed to attend her own private Catholic services. Setting aside all the warnings he had been given on that subject, Lord James agreed, on condition that she recognise the Protestant Church. She said that she would.[4]

At the beginning of June 1561, Lord James arrived back in Edinburgh with letters from Mary urging her subjects to live peaceably until her homecoming. Meanwhile, she went to Paris to prepare for her departure, but according to Sir Nicholas Throckmorton, the English ambassador, she told people again that she was not prepared to set out unless Knox were banished. She was convinced, said Throckmorton, that Knox was the most dangerous man in Scotland, and not long afterwards there were reports that she was sending Elizabeth I a copy of *The First Blast* to turn her against Knox. Throckmorton hastened to remind Elizabeth that Knox was very useful to England. His zeal made up for his original fault in writing the book, 'and therefore he is not to be driven out of that realm [Scotland].'[5]

Elizabeth was much more taken up with the fact that the Queen of Scots had quartered the arms of England with those of Scotland and France and, even more to the point, she was very conscious that Mary had still not ratified the Treaty of Edinburgh. When Mary sent a request for a safe conduct for her coming voyage to Scotland, in case storms drove her ashore on the east coast of England, Elizabeth refused. Undeterred, Mary went aboard her great white galley on 14 August 1560 and five days later she sailed into Leith in a dense fog at about eight o'clock in the morning. She received an unexpectedly warm welcome. She was ceremoniously escorted to Holyroodhouse that afternoon and in the evening the townspeople gathered beneath her windows to serenade her with psalms, while bonfires lit up the darkening sky.

The ordinary people might rejoice to see James V's tall, handsome, auburn-haired daughter and the nobles might welcome her for their own reasons, but Knox was filled with foreboding. 'The very face of heaven the time of her arrival,' he wrote afterwards, 'did manifestly speak what comfort was brought unto this country with her, to wit, sorrow, dolour, darkness and all impiety.' He had seen it all before. He would never forget how the English had innocently welcomed the accession of Mary I, praising her virtue and her kind nature. He could also remember, all too vividly, the horrors of the persecution which followed and he had no doubt whatever that Mary, Queen of Scots intended the overthrow of the Protestant Church.[6]

Less than a week later, his worst fears seemed to be confirmed when he heard that preparations were being made to hold Mass in the Chapel Royal at Holyrood on Sunday 24 August. Knox was not the only person to be dismayed. The Master of Lindsay and some of the other gentlemen of Fife were loud in their protests and, outside the chapel on the day, there were shouts demanding the death of the priest who was to officiate. Fearing a riot, Lord James stood on guard at the chapel door. When the Protestants asked him angrily what he was doing there, he replied smoothly that he was making sure that no Scotsmen attended the Roman Catholic service. It was hardly surprising that the priest's hands shook with nervousness as he lifted the chalice, and, afterwards, two of James V's other illegitimate sons, Lord John and Lord Robert Stewart, had to escort him back to the safety of his chamber in the palace.[7]

When the Privy Council met soon after, there was much discussion as to what was to be done next. Some of the members were all for refusing to allow the Queen to have any more Masses, but others asked, 'Why, alas, will ye chase our Sovereign from us? She will incontinent [immediately] return to her galleys, and what then shall all realms say of us?' Lord James and Maitland of Lethington insisted that, once Mary settled down to the business of ruling her realm, guided by them, she would surely see the wisdom of accepting Protestantism, for political if not for religious reasons.

If she wanted to assert her claim to be heir to the English throne, she would be well advised to cultivate the friendship of Elizabeth I. Their arguments prevailed, and the Council decided that they would not object to Mass being said at Holyrood.[8]

The following day, no doubt advised by Lord James and Maitland, Mary issued a proclamation emphasising her desire for an end to religious dissension and saying that she would take Parliament's advice on the subject as soon as possible. In the meantime, no one was to disturb the current situation. In other words, the Protestants were free to continue their services, and she would have her Mass. The only member of her nobility to object to the latter part of the proclamation was the Earl of Arran. Perhaps in consultation with Knox, he issued his own proclamation at Edinburgh's market cross, demanding the death sentence for any of Mary's servants who celebrated or attended her Catholic services.

The Sunday after Mary's first Mass at Holyrood, Knox preached vehemently against Catholicism to a large congregation in St Giles. One Mass was more fearful to him than an invasion by a foreign army of ten thousand with the aim of suppressing the whole religion, he said. God would help believers to resist armed forces, but, if the Scots condoned idolatry as they were doing by allowing Mary her Roman Catholic services, He would desert them and then what would they do? Some of the courtiers in the congregation mocked what Knox said, but Lord James and his friends were seriously annoyed. Publicly condemning her Mass was not way to guide Mary towards Protestantism.[9]

Two days after Knox's sermon, the Queen made her formal entry into Edinburgh. She dined at the Castle and then moved in procession down the Royal Mile to Holyroodhouse, a gold-fringed purple canopy of state held above her head, and 50 young men disguised as Moors, in black masks and yellow taffeta suits, capering along in front of her. The fountain at the market cross flowed with wine and there were pageants, with local girls in diaphanous dresses posing as mythological figures. When Mary reached the Butter

Tron, a child came down from a painted cloud and presented her not only with the keys of Edinburgh but with two books in rich purple velvet covers. She opened them to find that one was a copy of the Bible in English instead of Latin, and the other was the Psalm Book, unmistakable symbols of the Reformed religion. The Roman Catholic Earl of Huntly later reported that he had stopped some people at the Salt Tron who were about to burn an effigy of a priest.[10]

To Mary it seemed obvious that one man in particular was responsible for these unseemly acts. She summoned John Knox to appear before her and so it was that he marched determinedly down to the Palace of Holyroodhouse on 4 September 1561. Knox's confrontations with Mary did not change the course of history, but descriptions of their arguments have had an enormous influence on the public perception of both Queen and reformer. Their encounters are crucial to an understanding of Knox's character and it is therefore worth examining the record of their discussions in some detail. What really passed between them when they met face to face? We only have Knox's side of the story, of course, set down in his *History of the Reformation*, but, even in this subjective account, it is possible to catch echoes of what was really said.[11]

They had heard so much about each other already that they met with deep feelings of suspicion, and the encounter reassured neither of them. The Queen spoke first, making four accusations against Knox. He had raised a number of her subjects against her mother, Mary of Guise, and against herself, she said. He had written a book against her just authority (meaning *The First Blast*), he had caused great sedition and slaughter in England, and she had heard that he had done all this by means of necromancy.

Knox listened quietly, and then he gave his answer, at some length. He had taught people only the truth, he said. He was hardly to be blamed if that caused them to question their obligation to obey their princes. He readily admitted having written *The First*

Blast, and if anyone could disprove the arguments in it, then he would willingly confess his error.

'Ye think, then, that I have no just authority?' Mary demanded. If the realm found no inconvenience from the rule of a woman, Knox replied, then he would be 'as well content to live under your Grace as Paul was to live under Nero'. Provided she did not persecute Protestants, then neither he nor *The First Blast* would do her authority any harm. He also pointed out that it had not really been written with her or her mother in mind. It had been aimed specifically at 'that wicked Jezebel of England', Mary I.

'But ye speak of women in general', Mary objected. That was true, said Knox, but if he had intended to make trouble in Scotland because she was a woman, he would surely have done it before her return. As to her other two accusations, he had certainly not stirred up sedition in England. Berwick had never been so peaceful as it was during his stay there, and those who accused him of dabbling in the black arts were slandering him, as anyone who had heard him preach could testify.

'But yet,' Mary persisted, 'ye have taught the people to receive another religion than their princes can allow. And how can that doctrine be of God, seeing that God commands subjects to obey their princes?'

Princes, said Knox, were often the most ignorant of all about the true religion, and he quoted various Old Testament examples to prove his point, arguing that subjects are not bound to the religion of their princes even though they are commanded to obey them.

'Yea, but none of those men raised the sword against their princes,' Mary objected.

That was because God had not given them the power to do so, said Knox.

'Think ye that subjects having the power may resist their princes?' Mary asked.

There was no doubt about it, Knox replied. Just as children would be justified in binding and imprisoning their father if he tried to kill them, so were subjects justified in restraining and incarcerating a prince who sought to murder the children of God.

At these words, the Queen stood as if amazed, for more than a quarter of an hour, until Lord James came over to her in concern to see what was the matter.

'Well then,' she said at last to Knox, 'I perceive that my subjects shall obey you and not me, and shall do what they list [please] and not what I command, and so must I be subject to them and not they to me.'

'God forbid', Knox retorted, 'that ever I take upon me to command any to obey me, or yet to set subjects at liberty to do what pleaseth them.' His object was that both princes and subjects should obey God, who commanded kings to be foster fathers of his church and queens to be nurses of the people. Submission to divine authority brought no humiliation to a monarch. On the contrary, it was a source of great dignity. By submitting to the will of God and His church, they would gain everlasting glory.

'Yea,' said Mary, 'but ye are not the kirk that I will nourish. I will defend the kirk of Rome for I think it is the true kirk of God'.

'Your will, Madam, is no reason,' Knox responded, 'neither doth your thought make that Roman harlot to be the true and immaculate spouse of Jesus Christ', and he offered to prove that the Jews who crucified Christ were not so degenerate as the Roman Catholic churchmen of their own day.

'My conscience is not so,' said Mary.

'Conscience, Madam, requires knowledge,' he replied, 'and I fear that right knowledge ye have none.'

'But I have both heard and read!' Mary protested.

So had the Jews who crucified Christ, said Knox. She had presumably heard only doctrines permitted by the Pope and cardinals, and they were hardly likely to allow criticism of their own church.

'Ye interpret the scriptures in one manner and they interpret in another,' Mary exclaimed. 'Whom shall I believe? And who shall be judge?'

She should believe the word of God, Knox said, and he went on to explain that the reformers condemned the Mass because it was the invention of man and nothing to do with the scriptures.

'Ye are oure sair [too difficult] for me,' sighed Mary when he had finished, and she wished aloud that some of the Roman Catholic clergy she had heard were present, for they would have been able to answer him.

Indeed, said Knox, he too wished that 'the learnedest papist in Europe' were there, for at the end of their discussion she would realise the vanity of her religion. However, the learned and crafty papist would never come and dispute in her presence, he added, for Roman Catholics knew that they could not win an argument unless 'fire and sword and their own laws be judges'.

The interview ended soon after that, when an attendant came to summon Mary to dinner.

'I pray God, Madam,' said Knox, 'that ye may be as blessed within the Commonwealth of Scotland, if it be the pleasure of God, as ever Deborah was in the Commonwealth of Israel,' and he left.

His friends were waiting outside. What did he think of the Queen, they asked eagerly.

'If there be not in her a proud mind, a crafty wit and an indurate heart against God and His truth, my judgment faileth me,' was his grim response.

Mary's recollection of their exchanges would no doubt have been different in emphasis, but Knox's version reads convincingly as a conversation between an experienced, authoritative man well used to theological argument and a young girl baffled by a view of religion and society which she had not encountered before. Of the two, Mary was possibly the more open to conviction. Although she had been brought up in the Roman Catholic Church, she was curious about Protestantism, she was intelligent and Lord James and Maitland may have been right in thinking that they could have guided her gradually towards a greater understanding of those she had been taught to regard as heretics. Knox, however, had come to

Holyrood already convinced of Mary's evil intentions, and nothing was going to alter his opinion.

According to Throckmorton, everyone in Scotland so far had been very favourably impressed by the Queen, 'saving John Knox, that thundereth out of the pulpit' and the ambassador feared 'nothing so much that one day he will mar all. He ruleth the roost and of him all men stand in fear.' Thomas Randolph thought so too. 'Mr Knox cannot be otherwise persuaded but that many men are deceived in this woman,' he wrote, and a few weeks later he was confiding to Cecil, 'You know the vehemence of Mr Knox's spirit, which cannot be bridled, and that doth sometimes utter such sentences as cannot easily be digested by a weak stomach. I would wish he should deal with her [Mary] more gently, being a young princess unpersuaded.' Knox's attitude was all the more regrettable, Randolph thought, because he exercised such influence in Scotland. 'The voice of one man is able, in one hour,' Randolph told Cecil, 'to put more life in us than 500 trumpets continually blustering in our ears.'[12]

Knox remained deaf to all their arguments. A few weeks after his audience with the Queen, he repeated his verdict on her in a letter to William Cecil. 'In communication with her I espied such craft as I have not found in such age,' he wrote.[13] His conclusions about Mary's character and intentions gave him no pleasure, and while she set off on a progress to Linlithgow, Perth, through Fife and back to Edinburgh again, he remained at home, deeply disturbed at the willingness of Lord James and the other nobles to allow her to have her Mass. He could only see the Scottish situation in terms of what had happened in England and he was convinced that the country was on the edge of disaster.

As the first anniversary of his wife's death approached, Knox was deeply depressed. 'Remedy there appeareth none, unless we would arm the hands of the people in whom abideth yet some sparks of God's fear,' he told Anna Locke on 2 October 1561,[14] but he had no real intention of stirring up 'the rascal multitude' and he added that he longed for death. He was eventually roused from his melancholy when he heard that Mary was consulting eminent scholars in various different countries in an attempt to find conclusive arguments against his views on government by women.

He well knew how Elizabeth I regarded his opinions on that particular topic, but he wrote to her all the same. 'It were but foolishness in me to prescribe unto Your Majesty what is to be done in anything,' he began, but he felt that he had to point out that the Queen of Scots was trying to persuade the English to condemn him as a common enemy of women and their rule. Not only that, but she was really 'shooting at another mark', in other words, plotting to gain Elizabeth's own throne. He also turned for advice to Calvin. 'I am a continual trouble to you,' he admitted, 'but I have no other to whom I can confide my anxiety,' and he went on to describe how wounded he was by the attitude of the Scottish nobility.[15]

It was not in his nature to sit still and do nothing, and so in early November, a meeting was held in the house of Sir James McGill, the Lord Clerk Register, to discuss the problem of Mary's Mass. Lord James, Maitland of Lethington, the Earl of Morton and Knox were there. Knox and some of the other preachers who were present put forward the view that subjects were entitled to 'suppress the idolatry of their prince' but the majority were of the opinion that no one could lawfully forbid the Queen to have her Roman Catholic services. Someone suggested that Calvin should be consulted and Knox offered to write to Geneva. At that, Maitland of Lethington swiftly intervened to say suavely that he would do it. Knox did not mention the fact that he had already written.[16]

The following month, some provision was at last made for the Protestant ministers. The Archbishop of St Andrews and three of the Roman Catholic bishops had offered to give the Queen a quarter of their revenues for one year. On 15 February 1562, the Privy Council issued an act stating that a third of all the ecclesiastical revenues were to be surrendered to the crown. Half would be used for the Protestant preachers' salaries, and Mary would keep the other half for her own household expenditure. 'I see two parts fully given to the devil and the third must be divided betwixt God and the devil,' Knox fulminated from the pulpit, while Maitland of Lethington observed wryly that if the ministers were given as much as they wanted, the Queen would not even be able to afford to buy herself a pair of shoes from the remainder. In practice, Lord James and many of the leading nobles were allowed to keep all their ecclesiastical revenues for themselves, and the sum collected was not nearly enough to fund all the Protestant pastors.[17]

Lord James received a further reward for his services to the Queen on 30 January 1562 when she made him Earl of Moray. His new title had to be kept secret, because the Earl of Huntly already held that earldom, and so on 7 February Mary also gave Lord James the title of Earl of Mar. This was a marriage gift, for on the following day he married Lady Agnes Keith, daughter of William, 4th Earl Marischal. Knox conducted the wedding service in St Giles and preached the sermon, warning Moray apparently in all seriousness that, if he did not continue his efforts on behalf of the kirk, people would blame his wife for changing his nature. Afterwards, Knox was highly critical of the lavish masques and celebrations at the wedding banquet at Holyroodhouse.[18]

13

Confrontation

UNDER THE INFLUENCE OF Moray and Maitland, Mary, Queen of Scots was by now working hard to reach an understanding with Elizabeth I, writing her long letters and plying her with gifts. As Mary herself remarked, 'We are both in one isle, both of one language, both the nearest kinswoman that each other hath, and both Queens.'[1] Surely past differences could be forgotten. By the New Year she and Elizabeth were actually thinking of meeting each other in York, but all chance of that vanished when Mary's uncle, the Duke of Guise, ordered his men to open fire on Protestants holding a prayer meeting at Vassy in Champagne, and 40 people were killed. Civil war broke out in France, and Elizabeth I immediately cancelled the plans for York.

Bitterly disappointed, Mary decided to make a progress to the north of Scotland where Moray encouraged her to turn on his rival, George, 4th Earl of Huntly, Scotland's most powerful Roman Catholic nobleman. When she summoned Huntly he defied her. Moray and Maitland then marched with a force against him, and defeated him at Corrichie, where he suffered a fatal stroke. His body was taken to Edinburgh, propped up in its coffin and 'tried' for treason. Knowing that Mary had proceeded against such a powerful

Roman Catholic did nothing to reassure Knox. He was convinced that, if the Duke of Guise and the Catholics triumphed in France, Mary would surely move against the Scottish Protestants.[2]

In the meantime, he was doing battle with Ninian Winzet, the master of Linlithgow Grammar School, who had been the Queen's confessor when she first came to Scotland. Winzet had written to Knox asking by what authority he preached. Unwilling to provide his critic with a forum for expressing his views, Knox ignored his repeated requests for a public disputation and preached against him. Winzet planned to retaliate by publishing a pamphlet, which he called *The Last Blast of the Trumpet of God's Word against the Usurped Authority of John Knox and his Calvinian Brethren Intruded Preachers* but Knox got to hear of it and Edinburgh Town Council seized and destroyed it at the printer's. Winzet was subsequently dismissed and banished.[3]

Winzet's challenge was an irritation, but much more serious was another piece of news which reached Knox that summer. He learned that a papal nuncio, Nicholas of Gouda, had arrived secretly in Scotland with a fellow Jesuit, Edmund Hay. Travelling in disguise, Gouda had come to ask Mary, Queen of Scots to send her bishops to the final session of the Roman Catholic Council of Trent. Knox immediately revealed Gouda's presence in his next sermon, raging against the pope as antichrist and characterising the nuncio as the emissary of Satan. In spite of this very public disclosure of his presence, Gouda was able to visit the Queen one day when Moray and the rest of her Privy Council were attending Knox's sermon in St Giles. Mary explained to him that, in the present situation, it was impossible for her to send representatives to the council but she assured the nuncio that she would never abandon her Roman Catholic faith. Shortly afterwards, Gouda managed to slip out of the country, disguised as a sailor, on a Flemish ship.[4]

Preoccupied with the political as well as the religious situation, Knox was finding it difficult to give enough time to his two young sons. Elizabeth Bowes seems to have returned south after Marjorie's death, but he really needed her to help with the boys. It was not satisfactory to leave them in the hands of servants, however reliable, and he had to make himself available to people at all hours. He therefore decided to ask Elizabeth to come back to Edinburgh. She agreed, and when she sought the necessary licence to leave England she was told that she could do so, taking all her own money with her provided it did not exceed £100 sterling.[5]

Knox then set off to preach in Ayrshire, and he took the opportunity of criticising a sermon delivered a few days earlier by Quintin Kennedy, Abbot of Crossraguel. The Abbot responded by challenging Knox to a public disputation about the Mass. Feelings were running so high that both men were in danger from each other's supporters, but it was agreed that the debate should take place in Maybole, two miles from Crossraguel, and both Knox and the Abbot would be allowed to bring along forty sympathisers.

The argument began on 28 September and centred on an episode in the Book of Genesis in the Old Testament when Melchisedek sacrificed bread and wine to God, thereby establishing, according to the Abbot, the origins of the Mass. Knox said that the bread and wine had merely been provisions for Abraham's army. The Abbot, a younger son of the 2nd Earl of Cassillis, had been educated in St Andrews and Paris and was an able and scholarly opponent. The debate lasted for three days, before a very large audience, and ended inconclusively. The following year, Knox published the text of the disputation as a pamphlet entitled *The Reasoning which was betwixt the Abbot of Crossraguel and John Knox in Maybole concerning the Mass.*[6]

Back in Edinburgh again, Knox kept a close watch on everything Mary, Queen of Scots was doing, and in December he heard that, on receiving news of a Roman Catholic victory in France, she danced for joy until after midnight. This was a false rumour. Far from being elated about her uncle's campaign she had, according to Randolph, regretted the Duke of Guise's ill-advised actions at Vassy, and was afraid that he would be overthrown. Knox believed otherwise however, and on 13 December 1562 he preached a sermon against the ignorance and vanity of princes, criticising in particular Mary's fondness for dancing. As soon as she heard about it, she sent for him, and, on Tuesday 15 December 1562 he made his way down to Holyroodhouse for his second audience with her.[7]

This time he found her in her bedchamber, with Moray, Maitland, the Earl of Morton, some of her ladies and attendants, and several of her guard. At their first encounter, their argument had been to a large extent impersonal. They had clashed over their different religions. Now, Mary was indignant, and she immediately embarked upon a long speech, accusing Knox of having spoken of her irreverently, of trying to make her subjects hate and despise her, and of going far beyond the bounds of the text from which he was supposed to have been preaching.

Knox replied that people who stubbornly refused to listen to God were often punished by having to hear false rumours. Troublemakers had quoted him out of context. 'If there be into you any sparkle of the spirit of God, yea, of honesty or wisdom, ye could not justly have been offended with anything that I spake,' he observed, and he went on to summarise what he had actually said. Having reminded people of the obedience due to kings and rulers, who were God's lieutenants, he had asked what was to be done when murderers oppressed 'the poor saints of God', while princes were spending their time 'in fiddling and flinging' and listening to flatterers more than they did to men of wisdom and gravity. As for dancing, although he found no praise of it in the scriptures, and, although the writers of classical times had termed it the activity of madmen rather than of sober people, he did not utterly damn it, providing religious observance was not neglected in its favour and as long as it was not an expression of triumph over God's people.

'If any man, Madam, will say that I spake more,' he concluded, 'let him presently accuse me,' and many of those present agreed that this was indeed what he had said.

The Queen could see that he was speaking the truth. Casting a significant glance at some of the guard who had given her the false reports, she turned back again to Knox to say,

'Your words are sharp enough as ye have spoken them, but yet they were told to me in another manner,' and she went on to comment,

'I know that my uncles and ye are not of one religion and therefore I cannot blame you, albeit you have no good opinion of them. But if ye hear anything of myself that mislikes you [that you dislike], come to myself and tell me, and I shall hear you.'

If she intended this as a conciliatory gesture, she was disappointed. As far as Knox was concerned, her uncles were enemies to God, ready to spill the blood of innocents for their own pomp and worldly glory. As for coming to tell her about her faults, 'I am called, Madam, to a public function within the Kirk of God, and am appointed by God to rebuke the sins and vices of all. I am not appointed to come to every man in particular to show him his offence, for that labour were infinite.'

The Queen could attend his public sermons, or she could arrange a time with him when he would come and repeat to her what he had preached, 'but to wait upon your chamber door, or elsewhere, and then to have no further liberty but to whisper my mind in your Grace's ear, or to tell to you what others think and speak of you, neither will my conscience nor the vocation whereto God has called me suffer it.'

Even as they spoke, people were probably criticising him for being at Court instead of at his book.

Losing her patience, Mary exclaimed, 'You will not always be at your book,' and turned her back on him. The audience was at an end.

As Knox left the palace, he passed some Catholic courtiers who, seeing his cheerful expression, asked him why he was not afraid. 'Why should the pleasing face of a gentlewoman effray [frighten] me?' he retorted. 'I have looked in the faces of many angry men and yet have not been afraid above measure.'

He was so suspicious of Mary that he never could give her the benefit of the doubt. As Randolph commented two days after that second confrontation, Knox 'hath no hope (to use his own terms) that she will ever come to God or do good in the commonwealth. He is so full of mistrust in all her doings, words and sayings, as though he were either of God's Privy Council . . . or . . . knew the secrets of her heart so well that neither she did or could have for ever one good thought of God or of His true religion . . . ' Knox, he said, was convinced that Mary was planning to bring in an army of French troops to re-establish Roman Catholicism in Scotland, and although Randolph himself did not think that this was likely, he did respect Knox's opinions.

The situation was made doubly difficult by the question of Mary's marriage. Here she was, twenty years old, tall, healthy, extremely eligible and a widow. It was time that she took another husband and had sons, to secure the Scottish succession. The problem lay in finding a suitable candidate. Women might gossip about a handsome husband for their Queen, but that was foolish talk. No one from the propertied classes, let alone royalty, married for romance. Marriages were arranged to make political alliances or to increase wealth and influence. If mutual affection followed so much the better, but it was never regarded as a prerequisite for matrimony.

For Knox, Mary's eligibility was simply another fault. It gave a foreign, Roman Catholic prince the opening to come and rule Scotland. Any hope of marrying her to a Scottish Protestant had all but vanished when the Earl of Arran suffered a mental breakdown and had to be confined in Edinburgh Castle. It was unlikely that the Queen would have considered him in any event, for although he was obsessed with her, she did not care for him and she seems to have regarded him as being far beneath her in status. In the spring of 1563, the Duke of Guise was assassinated by a French Protestant and shortly afterwards the Queen tried to revive her plan to marry Don Carlos, persuading a significant number of her Protestant Lords to favour the idea. No doubt on her orders, the scheme was kept from Knox.[8]

That Easter, various priests in the west of Scotland were arrested by the local Protestant lairds for saying Mass. Mary was staying at Lochleven when she heard about it, and she sent for Knox at once.[9] When he arrived, she spent two hours before she went to supper trying to get him to promise to persuade the gentlemen of the west not to punish anyone for their religious observances. Deciding that she was attempting to trap him into some damaging concession, he replied tersely that he could promise that there would be quietness throughout the country if she punished wrongdoers according to the law. If she did not do so, he feared that there were those who would take the law into their own hands.

'Will ye allow that they shall take my sword in their hand?' Mary demanded indignantly.

'The Sword of Justice, Madam, is God's,' said Knox, 'and is given to princes and rulers for one end.' If they failed in their duty and spared the wicked, then those who intervened and dealt out the requisite punishment would not offend God. Nor were those who restrained kings from striking innocent men committing any sin, as numerous Biblical examples demonstrated.

In Scotland, judges were empowered by Act of Parliament to seek out and punish those who celebrated Mass and, he told her, it was her duty to support them. She should therefore consider what it was that her subjects expected from her, 'and what it is that ye ought to do unto them by mutual contract. They are bound to obey you and that not but in God. Ye are bound to keep laws unto them. Ye crave of them service: they crave of you protection and defence against wicked doers. Now, Madam, if ye shall deny your duty unto them . . . think ye to receive full obedience of them? I fear, Madam, ye shall not.'

At that Mary, 'somewhat offended', went to supper and Knox hurried away to give the Earl of Moray an account of their latest interview. By that time it was too late for him to return to Edinburgh, and so he spent the night at Lochleven. When he rose next morning, he was surprised to receive a message from the Queen, telling him to meet her later in the day near Kinross, where she would be out with her hawks. He found her in an unexpectedly conciliatory mood. She seemed to have forgotten her anger of the previous day either, he thought, because of her night's sleep or because of 'a deep dissimulation locked in her breast'. A more likely reason does not seem to have occurred to him. The Earl of Moray had obviously spoken to her and urged her to placate him.

At any rate, she said no more about the Protestants in the west, and broached a different matter altogether. She had heard that Knox was going to Dumfries for the election of a Superintendent, and she warned against one of the candidates, Alexander Gordon, Bishop of Galloway. 'If ye knew him as well as I do,' she said, 'ye would never promote him to that office, nor yet to any other within your kirk.' Knox was doubtful, for Gordon was a friend of his and a frequent visitor to his house. However, he found out later that she was right. Gordon had been using bribery to try to have himself elected, and so Knox postponed the election and left it to his colleagues to examine Gordon as to his doctrine.

Having given him this friendly advice, Mary enlisted his help over a confidential family matter. Her half-sister, Jane Stewart, Countess of Argyll, one of her father's illegitimate daughters, was unhappy in her marriage and indeed she and the Earl later divorced. At this stage she had left her husband to live permanently at Court. Argyll was, of course, one of the leading Protestant Lords and the Queen knew that Knox had intervened once before to try to improve the relationship between husband and wife. She urged him to speak to Argyll again, saying that she was very fond of the Earl. Knox was not to reveal the fact that the Queen had spoken to him about the problem, and she added that if the Countess 'behave not herself so as she ought to do, she shall find no favours of me'.

The conversation was almost amicable, and just before they parted she suddenly referred to their argument of the previous evening, saying, 'And now, touching our reasoning yesternight, I promise to do as ye required. I shall cause summon all offenders, and ye shall know that I shall minister justice.'

No doubt suspicious, Knox replied, 'I am assured then that ye shall please God, and enjoy rest and tranquillity within your realm, which to Your Majesty is more profitable than all the Pope's power can be.'

Mary was, of course, trying to smooth the way for her Spanish marriage, and while Knox went to Dumfries and then on to Glasgow, she had the Archbishop of St Andrews and several of his colleagues arrested and imprisoned on 19 May 1563 for saying Mass. However, when her first Parliament since her return to Scotland met at the end of the month, nothing was done either to ratify the legislation establishing Protestantism in Scotland or the Treaty of Edinburgh. Mary had often declared that the acts of the 1560 Parliament were illegal and, with marriage to a Roman Catholic prince in prospect, she was not about to change her mind. She had accordingly persuaded Moray not to raise the question of religion in Parliament, and instead the Protestant Lords humbly begged her to grant an act of oblivion to all who had been involved in the recent civil war. This she did.[10]

Knox was furious. The Queen had promised to settle the religious situation when Parliament met, and, although she would obviously have been unwilling, it had been the responsibility of the Protestant Lords to make sure that the treaty and the acts were ratified. They had deliberately let the opportunity pass them by, and he was bitterly angry with them all, especially Moray. Knox felt betrayed. Moray, a man he had long admired and trusted, had succumbed to Mary's blandishments just like all the other courtiers. Knox lost no time in warning the Lords of the dangers which would ensue if they continued to do nothing.

They defended themselves by saying that the Queen would never have agreed to let Parliament meet at all if they had insisted on her ratifying the previous legislation. They even said that the omission of any ratification did not matter, because it seemed that Mary would marry very soon and then she would grant them everything they wanted. Knox thought that this was nonsense. They had fallen victim to the Queen's manipulation, and he told them so.

He and Moray quarrelled fiercely and afterwards he wrote the Earl an angry letter accusing him being more interested in his own advancement than in God. 'I praise my God I this day leave you victor of your enemies, promoted to great honours, and in credit and authority with your Sovereign,' he said with savage irony. 'If so ye long continue, none within the realm shall be more glad than I shall be; but if after this ye shall decay (as I fear that ye shall), then call to mind by what means God exalted you, which was neither by bearing with impiety, neither yet by maintaining of pestilent papists.' The two men did not speak to each other for the next 18 months.[11]

Before Parliament was dissolved, Knox preached to a large congregation, reminding them of God's past mercy to Scotland and criticising their ingratitude. He himself had been with them during all their most dangerous days, in Perth, in Cupar and most of all on 'that dark and dolorous night' when the Protestants had withdrawn from Edinburgh and retreated to Stirling in a state of shame and fear. In spite of these traumas they had survived, and he demanded, 'Shall this be the thankfulness that ye shall render unto your God? To betray his cause, when ye have it in your hands to establish it as you please?'

He then turned to the rumours about the Queen's marriage. By this time he knew all about her plans. She had many suitors, he said, Dukes, the brothers of Emperors, Kings, all striving for the best prize, but, if the Lords consented to her marriage with an infidel, 'and all papists are infidels', then they would be banishing Christ Jesus from the realm. By so doing 'ye bring God's vengeance upon the country, a plague upon yourself, and perchance ye shall do small comfort to your Sovereign'.[12] His sermons always angered the Roman Catholics, but this time he offended many of the Protestant courtiers too. Even his closest friends condemned him for having the temerity to speak against the Queen's marriage plans and she herself was bitterly upset. Once more, he was summoned to appear before her.[13]

Lord Ochiltree and various other loyal supporters accompanied him to Holyroodhouse, but only John Erskine of Dun went with him up to the Queen's private cabinet, where they found her waiting for them, in a state of nervous agitation. As soon as she saw Knox, she exclaimed that never had a prince been treated as she was.

'I have borne with you in all your rigorous manner of speaking,' she told him, 'both against myself and against my uncles; yea I have sought your favours by all possible means. I offered unto you presence and audience whensoever it pleased you to admonish me; and yet I cannot be quit of you. I avow to God, I shall be once revenged,' and with that she burst into hysterical tears, weeping so much that her page boy ran away to fetch more handkerchiefs for her so that she could dry her eyes.

Knox stood and waited somewhat uncomfortably until she had calmed down a little, and then he observed carefully that it was true that he and she had often argued in the past, but he had never noticed that she was offended by him. Moreover, once God had delivered her from the error of her ways, she would find nothing offensive about what he said. He believed he could say that, outside the preaching place, few had reason to take offence at him. In the pulpit it was a different matter, of course, for there, 'I am not master of myself, but must obey Him who commands me to speak plain and to flatter no flesh upon the face of the earth'. It was as close as he could come to an apology for his brusque manner and his freedom of speech.

'But what', Mary burst out, 'have ye to do with my marriage?'

At first he gave an evasive reply, saying that God had not sent him to wait upon the Courts of princesses nor the chambers of ladies. He was sent to preach the word of God and since the nobles were so desperate for her favour that they neglected their duties, then he had to speak out. Mary brushed this aside.

'What have ye to do,' she asked again, 'with my marriage? Or what are ye within this commonwealth?'

Knox's dignified reply has become famous. 'A subject born within the same, Madam,' he said. 'And albeit I neither be Earl, Lord nor Baron within it, yet has God made me (however abject that ever I be in your eyes) a profitable member within the same.'

It was his duty to warn of anything which he thought might hurt the commonwealth, and so he would repeat to her what he had said from his pulpit. Were the Scottish nobility to consent that she should be subject to an ungodly husband, they would be renouncing Christ, banishing his truth, betraying the freedom of the realm and in the end perhaps not even doing any good to the Queen herself. There were rumours, he went on, that the Queen would make a Spanish alliance. If this happened without tight restrictions being placed on her and her husband to make sure that they could not harm either nation nor kirk, then he would have no hesitation in denouncing as troublemakers and enemies to God those nobles who had agreed to the marriage.

At this, Mary broke into violent sobbing again. The gentlemanly Erskine of Dun came over to try to comfort her, praising her beauty and her excellence, and telling her that all the princes of Europe would be glad to seek her favours, but that only seemed to make matters worse. Knox stood waiting impassively for what seemed to him 'a long season', until in the end even he was forced to say, 'Madam, in God's presence I speak. I never delighted in the weeping of any of God's creatures, yea I can scarcely well abide the tears of my own boys whom my own hand corrects, much less can I rejoice in Your Majesty's weeping.'

He had given her no reason to take offence, he said, and had spoken only the truth, as his vocation compelled him to do. He would, therefore, have to endure her tears, however unwillingly, rather than hurt his conscience or betray his commonwealth by keeping silent.

At this, Mary was even more offended, and she ordered him to leave the cabinet and wait outside. Erskine of Dun stayed with her, and one of her half brothers, Lord John Stewart, went in to help to comfort her while Knox stood uneasily in the outer chamber. Knowing that the Queen was furious with him, the courtiers in the room ignored him, and only Lord Ochiltree stood with him and kept him company. Time passed, and after nearly an hour Knox turned to a group of fashionably clad ladies sitting nearby. In a determined effort to break the silence, he said, 'O fair Ladies, how pleasing were this life of yours if it should ever abide and then in the end that we might pass to heaven with all this gay gear. But fie upon that knave Death, that will come whether we will or not!' When that happened, 'the foul worms will be busy with this flesh, be it never so fair and so tender', and they would be unable to take with them their gold, their trimmings, their tassels, their pearls and their precious stones. That got their attention, and their no doubt indignant replies kept him entertained until Erskine of Dun came and told him to go home. The Queen would have liked to punish him for speaking to her in such a way, but, although she was dissuaded from doing so, their relationship had taken on a new bitterness and Mary never sent for Knox again to come to a private audience.

When they next met, it was before the entire Privy Council. In August, while the Queen was in Stirling, those of her retinue left behind at Holyroodhouse had celebrated Mass, whereupon a band of Protestants burst into the Chapel Royal and threatened the priest. The Protestant authorities prosecuted 22 Roman Catholics for attending the Mass, and, when she returned to Edinburgh the Queen retaliated by ordering the arrest of Patrick Cranstoun and Andrew Armstrong, the two ringleaders of the Protestant disturbance in her chapel. Their trial was fixed for 24 October 1563 and Knox called on the people throughout the country to come and protect them that day. No one did come in response to his summons but, probably to avoid civil disorder, the trial was adjourned. It seems that no further proceedings were taken against the two men. However, Knox himself was called before the Queen and her Privy Council.[14]

Shortly after receiving the summons, he was visited secretly by John Spens of Condie, the Queen's advocate, who warned him that he was in grave danger of being charged with treason. He should apologise to her. That had no effect, and so the Master of Maxwell came and threatened to end their long friendship if Knox did not ask Mary's pardon for his offence. Knox said that he had done nothing wrong. Maxwell pointed out that the situation had changed dramatically in recent months. The Queen was home now in her own country and 'Ye will find that men will not bear with you in times to come as they have done in times bypast'. Knox remained unrepentant, and on the appointed evening he went down to Holyroodhouse accompanied by a large group of supporters.[15]

14

The Fall of the Queen

I T WAS BETWEEN SIX and seven o'clock in the evening when Knox was shown into the council chamber.[1] The Queen and her councillors had already met but, unable to reach any conclusion, they had adjourned, Mary retiring to her apartments. The others were grouped around, chatting to each other as they waited for proceedings to begin again. When Knox appeared, they resumed their places. The Queen would, of course, sit at the head of the table, with the Duke of Châtelherault to her right and the Earl of Argyll opposite him. Five other council members would be seated at the table, the rest standing behind. Knox stood waiting, bareheaded, at the far end. When they were all ready, the door to Mary's cabinet opened and she came in, ceremoniously escorted by Maitland of Lethington and the Master of Maxwell.

The Queen sat down, looked at Knox and laughed exultantly. The courtiers joined in, obsequiously, he thought.

'This is a good beginning,' said Mary. 'But know ye whereat I laugh? Yon man gart me greit and grat never tear himself. I will see if I can gar him greit.' ['That man made me weep and wept never a tear himself. I will see if I can make him weep!']

After a whispered conference with Maitland, she passed him a letter and he turned to Knox. The document, he said, was proof that Knox had been trying to raise rebellion against the Queen. It was the letter he had written on 8 October 1563, urging his fellow Protestants to come to Edinburgh to defend Patrick Cranstoun and Andrew Armstrong against the terrible summons they had received. Knox freely admitted that he had dictated and signed letters of that description, but he added that he had also given his secretaries various blank letters which he had signed.

'Ye have done more than I would have done,' said Maitland, meaning that Knox had been very trusting.

'Charity', replied Knox, 'is not suspicious.'

At that, Mary ordered him to read his letter aloud, which he did.

'Heard ye ever, my Lords, a more despiteful and treasonable letter?' the Queen demanded, looking round the table, but no one answered.

Maitland asked him if he was not heartily sorry. Did he not repent writing as he had done?

'My Lord Secretary', said Knox, 'before I repent I must be taught my offence,' and he went on to argue that he had a perfect right to protect his poor flock when it was in danger.

The Queen broke in to ask who had given Knox any authority to gather her subjects together. Surely what he had done was treason?

Before he could reply, Lord Ruthven spoke for him and said that it was not, for Knox gathered people together almost every day to hear his prayers and sermons. Regardless of what the Queen and others thought about that, it was no treason.

'Hold your peace!' Mary interrupted. 'And let him make answer for himself.' She would say nothing about his religion or about his gathering people together to hear his sermons, but she wanted to know what authority he had to convene her subjects without her command.

In reply, Knox denied that he had ever convened people. Following the instructions of the Church he had given various notifications, and great crowds had gathered, but that was no treason.

'Ye shall not escape so,' said Mary. 'Is it not treason, my Lords, to accuse a prince of cruelty? I think there be Acts of Parliament against such whisperers.'

There was a murmur of agreement from the councillors.

'But wherein,' Knox persisted, 'can I be accused?'

At that, she read out part of the letter he had written, where he had referred to the 'fearful' summons and had said that it was a prelude to the execution of cruelty upon a greater number. Knox stood his ground. 'The obstinate Papists' were the deadly enemies of true believers. He had done nothing to offend against the Acts of Parliament, and in his letter he did not accuse the Queen or say that she had been cruel. However, it was clear to him that the arrest of Cranstoun and Armstrong was the start of a campaign of bloody persecution of Scottish Protestants, and the pestilent Papists who had inflamed her against these poor men were the sons of the devil.

'Ye forget yourself,' one of the councillors exclaimed, shocked. 'Ye are not now in the pulpit.'

'I am in the place where I am demanded of conscience to speak the truth,' Knox retorted. The Queen was surrounded by corrupt flatterers and deadly enemies of Christ. These men were dangerous, as her own mother had found.

Maitland hastily leaned over and whispered something to the Queen, to avert her anger. She composed her features and told Knox that he spoke fairly enough in the presence of her Lords, but the last time they had met privately he had made her weep many salt tears, and he had not cared.

Repeating much of what he had said to her on that occasion, Knox reminded her that he had told her that he hated to see anyone cry, even his own children, but that he was compelled to speak the truth. Those were the most extreme words he had spoken to her that day.

After another whispered conference with the Queen, Maitland turned to Knox and said, 'Mr Knox. Ye may return to your house for this night.'

'I thank God and the Queen's Majesty,' said Knox, 'and, Madam,

I pray God to purge your heart from papistry and to preserve you from the counsel of flatterers . . . .'

That was the last time he ever appeared before Mary, Queen of Scots.

When he had gone, a vote was taken, the Lords found unanimously that he had committed no offence and the Queen went back to her cabinet. Some of those present were angry, especially Maitland, who brought her back so that the vote could be taken over again. Resenting Maitland's high-handed intervention, the Lords all voted in Knox's favour once more. When she saw how things had gone, Mary reproached one of the councillors, Henry Sinclair, Bishop of Ross, for supporting 'the old fool' Knox. The Bishop answered coldly, 'Your Grace may consider that it is neither affection to the man nor yet love to his profession that moved me to absolve him, but the simple truth . . . .'

Nearing the age of fifty, Knox was certainly old by sixteenth-century standards, and in the spring of 1564 his friends and enemies alike were startled when he married again. There was nothing unusual about a widower with young children taking a wife, but his choice caused a scandal. There had earlier been talk of him being interested in Châtelherault's daughter, Lady Fleming, and his enemies had sneered at him for social climbing. Lady Fleming rejected him, so it was said, but by early 1563 he had compounded the fault. Thomas Randolph told Cecil incredulously, 'Mr Knox shall marry a very near kinswoman of the Duke's, a lord's daughter, a young lass not above 16 years of age.' The girl in question was Margaret Stewart, daughter of Knox's old friend, Lord Ochiltree, and she was Châtelherault's great-niece. Knox had known her since she was a small child. No wedding took place that year, but on Sunday 25 March 1564, Knox married Margaret, now seventeen.[2]

Mary, Queen of Scots was reportedly furious that he had dared to marry someone of her own family, the royal house of Stewart, and she was apparently threatening again to drive him out of

Scotland. Roman Catholic propagandists produced all sorts of lurid stories, alleging that he had used the black arts to ensnare Margaret, and even today people are apt to snigger when his name is mentioned and refer to his alleged fondness for young girls. Be that as it may, this was probably yet another marriage of convenience. He and Lord Ochiltree both presumably decided that this was the long-term solution to Knox's domestic problems. Elizabeth Bowes was elderly now and she could not be expected to run his household forever. After the wedding, Knox decided to send his two sons to the safety of England, to be educated under the supervision of their Bowes relatives, and Elizabeth probably went with them.[3]

Two months after Knox's second marriage, the General Assembly met in Edinburgh and the courtiers, led by Châtelherault, Moray and Maitland, decided to ask for a public debate with leading members of the Assembly. They hoped that, by allowing the Church to air its grievances in public, they could force Knox to stop his perpetual preaching against the Queen. His never-ending criticism was upsetting her, and that was liable to have dangerous repercussions on the delicate relationship with England which they were so anxious to cultivate. The Assembly agreed, and a dozen representatives were chosen to put the case for each side. Châtelherault, Moray, Maitland and Argyll were to lead the courtiers, while the Church would be represented by Knox, Erskine of Dun and several other superintendents and ministers.[4]

In the event, Maitland and Knox dominated the debate. Maitland opened the proceedings by praising God, by whose providence they had freedom to worship as they chose, despite the fact that their Queen was not of the same religion. Emphasising the need for the Reformed Church to be seen to be supporting Mary, he complained about Knox's violent criticism of her. 'Your extremity against her Mass, in particular, passes measure,' said Maitland. 'Ye call her a slave to Satan, ye affirm that God's vengeance hangs over the realm by reason of her impiety, and what is this else but to rouse up the hearts of the people against her Majesty, and against them that serve her?'

His colleagues murmured their assent, and the Master of Maxwell commented bluntly, 'If I were in the Queen's Majesty's place, I would not suffer such things as I hear.' Knox was unperturbed. If the words of the preachers were always twisted and people took the worst possible interpretation out of them, he remarked, it would be hard for them to say anything at all.

Maitland then asked Knox to change the way that he was in the habit of praying for Mary. Knox usually said, 'O Lord, if Thy pleasure be, purge the heart of the Queen's Majesty from the venom of idolatry, and deliver her from the bondage and thraldom of Satan, in the which she has been brought up, and yet remains for the lack of true doctrine . . . .'

According to Maitland, by using the phrase 'if Thy pleasure be', Knox was putting doubts into people's heads as to whether Mary ever would convert to Protestantism. Since they were all relying on that happening, to suggest otherwise was to stir up dangerous trouble. Maitland added urbanely that he was implying no criticism of Knox himself. He simply feared that others might imitate Knox's example, while lacking his modesty and foresight.

Knox brushed that aside and answered in his downright way that any such doubts about the Queen arose from her own obstinate rebellion and nothing else. When questioned as to what he meant, he said that she rebelled against God 'in all the actions of her life', but particularly in refusing to hear the true preaching and in maintaining the idolatrous Mass.

'She thinks not that rebellion,' said Maitland, 'but good religion.'

She refused all godly admonitions, said Knox, and despised all threatenings.

'Why say ye that she refuses admonition? She will gladly hear any man!' Maitland protested.

For all that was spoken to her, Knox retorted, she showed no obedience to God, and when was she going to attend a public preaching?

'I think never, so long as she is thus entreated,' Maitland replied wryly.

Invited to provide an example of a godly nation punished by God because of its prince's iniquity, Knox produced a stream of biblical comparisons, citing the stories of tyrants such as Jezebel. On and on he went, until Maitland leant against the Master of Maxwell in an exaggerated show of exhaustion, sighing that he wished that someone else would take up the argument so that they could get to the real point.

The Lord Chancellor, James, 4th Earl of Morton, intervened to ask Mr George Hay, one of the ministers, to argue against Knox, but Hay declined and Maitland entered the fray once more, taking Knox up on the previous day's sermon in which he had said that people need not obey magistrates and princes if they were told do something against God's ordinances.

That indeed had long been his judgment, said Knox. God's ordinance was holy, just and perpetual. Men in authority were usually profane and unjust, changeable and subject to corruption, and he expounded this belief at considerable length.

'I understand sufficiently what you mean,' Maitland broke in, impatiently, and approached the question from a different direction. If the Queen ordered him to slay John Knox because Knox had offended her, he would refuse. On the other hand, if Knox were condemned by some legal process, Maitland was not sure that he would then defend him. Knox had an answer to that, too. If Maitland knew him to be innocent and allowed him to die, then Maitland would be guilty of his death.

'Prove that, and win the play!' Maitland exclaimed.

They argued on until Maitland demanded, as Mary herself had done, 'Then will ye make subjects to control their princes and rulers?'

All this reasoning was to no purpose, for the Queen was never going to become an enemy to the Protestant religion and persecute people. The question at issue was whether or not she should be allowed to have her Mass.

'The idolater ought to die the death,' said Knox.

'I know,' said Maitland, 'that the idolater is commanded to die the death, but by whom?'

'By the people of God,' said Knox. Kings were just as liable to God's punishment as anybody else.

That might be so, said Maitland, but the people did not have the power to judge or punish their king.

Maitland only said so because he was more afraid of offending princes than he was of offending God, Knox remarked.

'Why say ye so?' Maitland asked angrily, 'I have the judgements of the most famous men within Europe and of such as ye yourself will confess both godly and learned,' and with that he produced and read from the writings of Luther, Melancthon, Calvin and other Protestant authorities, all advising how Christians should behave in time of persecution, but none expressing similar views to Knox. Gathering all these writings had taken him more work than he had had reading legal commentaries these seven years past, Maitland observed.

'The more pity,' said Knox dryly, and remained unmoved, piling biblical example upon biblical example to demonstrate that subjects had always been able to defy ungodly princes and that God had upon occasion armed subjects against their kings and ordered them to take vengeance upon them.

'Well,' said Maitland, 'I think ye shall not have many learned men of your opinion.'

The truth, replied Knox, remained the truth, whether or not men contradicted it, and he held up a copy of the *Apology of Madgeburg*, produced by the Protestants of that city when they had stood against the Holy Roman Emperor 30 years earlier. Handing the document to Maitland, Knox told him to read the long list of names of ministers who had signed it. Maitland did so and then said mockingly in Latin, 'Men of no importance.' 'Yet servants of God,' said Knox, also in Latin.

With that, Maitland called upon the assembled company to vote on whether the Queen should be allowed her Mass.

As the leaders began to give their votes, Knox objected. The Lords had promised that the whole General Assembly should decide the matter, he said, and he refused to vote until the Assembly had heard all the arguments from both sides. Others who were present joined in, some speaking for the Mass, others voting against it. In the end, Knox was instructed to write to Calvin and to various prominent Protestants on the continent to seek their opinion, but he refused. They had already given him their opinions, and they would think him ignorant, forgetful or inconstant if he asked again. The meeting broke up in disarray, with nothing gained.

That summer, the Queen went to Perthshire for the hunting, while her marriage remained a matter of concern and political machination at the highest level. Knox was not alone in seeing the prospect of the Spanish marriage as a dire threat. The English were greatly concerned. Queen Elizabeth herself had come up with a novel plan to distract Mary's attention, offering her Lord Robert Dudley as a husband instead. That astonished everyone, for Dudley was generally believed to be Elizabeth's lover, and his wife had died in highly suspicious circumstances.[5]

In the end, however, the Spanish match fell through when, on 6 August 1564, Philip II announced that his negotiations with the Scots were at an end. There were reasons of diplomacy, of course, but it had also become clear that Don Carlos was in no fit state to marry anyone, let alone a reigning queen. While pursing a serving woman he had fallen downstairs and suffered serious brain damage. Mary was greatly disappointed. To prevent her from finding another foreign Roman Catholic suitor, Elizabeth moved to make Lord Robert Dudley more acceptable and created him Earl of Leicester. At the same time, she produced an alternative candidate Mary could not ignore – Henry Stewart, Lord Darnley.

The elder son of Matthew, 4th Earl of Lennox and his wife Lady Margaret Douglas, Darnley was dynastically important. His father was, like his rival the Duke of Châtelherault, a descendant of King James I of Scotland and, even more importantly, his mother was the niece of Henry VIII of England. As a result, he and Mary were cousins, and if she were to marry him, her claim to the English throne would be considerably strengthened. Lady Lennox, a devout Roman Catholic, had long envisaged a magnificent future for her adored son, and, ever since the death of François II, she had been plotting to marry him to Mary. Elizabeth I correctly surmised that Darnley would be a distraction Mary would be unable to resist.[6]

Lennox, who had lost all his Scottish estates and been banished, was a naturalised Englishman who had lived in the south for the past 19 years, but in September 1564 Elizabeth set her plan in motion by giving him permission to return to Scotland. Mary, Queen of Scots welcomed him back, Parliament restored him to his extensive estates in the west of Scotland and there was a public reconciliation with the Hamiltons who were, of course, furious at their great rival's return. Everyone then waited to see if his son would follow him north. Sure enough, on 10 February 1565, Lord Darnley crossed the border and rode to Wemyss Castle in Fife, where the Court were staying.

Darnley was now 19 years old, tall, fair-haired and athletic. The following day, he renewed his acquaintance with Mary, whom he had met twice before, in France. Sir James Melville was at Wemyss and he later commented that the Queen was taken with Darnley, 'and said that he was the lustiest and best-proportioned long man that she had seen, for he was of high stature, long and small [meaning small-boned], even and erect, from his youth well instructed in all honest and comely exercises'. Not everyone was impressed with him, it was true. Melville himself had told Elizabeth I that 'no woman of spirit would make choice of such a man, that was more like a woman than a man', while Mary's uncle the Cardinal of Lorraine, who had met him in France, dismissed him as 'a girlish nincompoop'. Even so, Darnley was soon a valued member of Mary's inner circle of friends, their relationship progressed rapidly and by the summer they were betrothed.[7]

Throughout that spring, Mary had remained deeply suspicious of Knox, and a hitherto unpublished letter to the Lord Advocate, John Spens of Condie dated 9 April 1565, bears a postscript in her own handwriting. She had, she said, 'heard some rumour of certain secret meetings which will take place this evening at Knox's house, where Kellounin [Gavin Hamilton, Commendator of Kilwinning] is. I pray you to endeavour to learn something of what is done or said and inform me thereof, using all the diligence you can, but take good care that no one knows that I have written anything to you on this matter.' She evidently suspected Knox of plotting with the Hamiltons to oppose the marriage.[8]

There was, of course, another much more powerful opponent of the plan. Queen Elizabeth had never intended that Mary should actually marry this Tudor relative, and she was furious. She recalled Lennox and his son at once, but they refused to return south and on 29 July 1565, Mary and Darnley were married. The Roman Catholic ceremony was held at six o'clock in the morning in the Queen's private chapel at Holyrood. Because Darnley claimed to be a Protestant, despite his Roman Catholic background, he did not attend the nuptial Mass.[9]

Angry and hurt at being edged out of the Queen's innermost circle of advisers by this arrogant young man, the Earl of Moray was said to be plotting to kidnap Darnley and Lennox and send them back to England. He refused to appear when Mary summoned him to Court, gathered a force and was joined by Châtelherault, the Earl of Glencairn, Kirkcaldy of Grange and Knox's father-in-law, Lord Ochiltree. Moray was denounced as a rebel on 6 August and the Queen prepared to ride out with an army against him. Anxious not to lose any more support, Mary issued a proclamation promising to preserve the Protestant religion and the privileges of the Reformed Church and, on Sunday 19 August 1565, she even sent Darnley to St Giles to listen to Knox's sermon.

Darnley sat on a throne specially installed for him, but the occasion was not a success. As usual, Knox spoke out against wicked princes, saying at one point that God punished sinful people by putting boys and women to rule over them. Not surprisingly, Darnley took umbrage, nor was he mollified when Knox referred to 'that harlot Jezebel'. Knox's sermon lasted for an hour longer than usual, by which time Darnley was so furious that he refused to eat his dinner afterwards and rushed off to calm himself with an afternoon's falconry.[10]

Inevitably, Knox was summoned yet again by the Privy Council, who confronted him in Maitland's chamber, but the Queen herself was not there. He was told that the King was offended at part of his sermon, and he was forbidden to preach for fifteen or twenty days. His colleague John Craig would take his place. Knox maintained that he had in no way departed from his biblical text, but he said that whenever the Church ordered him to preach or not to preach, he would obey. The town council protested against his suspension, asserting that he could preach whenever he wished, but before they could get the order rescinded, the Queen rode out of Edinburgh in pursuit of Moray, Darnley at her side in a fine suit of gilded armour.

In the aptly named Chaseabout Raid, they pursued Moray and his friends to the west and then back to Edinburgh again, through a raging storm and even Knox had to admit that that 'albeit the most part waxed weary, yet the Queen's courage increased man-like, so much that she was ever with the foremost'. Eventually, Moray and the others slipped over the border and rode south, hoping for Queen Elizabeth's support. She refused it, of course, for she was never going to be seen to be openly supporting another country's rebels, but she did send them some assistance privately afterwards. Mary, Queen of Scots was threatening to have them attainted for treason when Parliament met the following spring and, determined to prevent the hearing from taking place, they hatched a sinister plot.[11]

Conspiring with James, 4th Earl of Morton and other Protestant nobles in Scotland, they signed a bond pledging themselves to murder David Riccio, Mary's secretary, for her French correspondence.

Morton and his other Douglas relatives drew Darnley in by playing on his jealousy of Riccio and his desire to obtain the crown matrimonial, which Mary was refusing to grant him. Almost everyone at the Scottish Court was aware of what was happening, and by 25 February Randolph and the English knew too. The Queen chose to ignore warnings about the intentions of the banished Lords. She opened Parliament on 7 March 1566 and it was agreed that a bill of attainder against Moray and the other exiled Lords would be presented on 12 March. The Duke of Châtelherault was the only member of their group not included. The Queen had already pardoned him on condition that he go into exile for five years and he had withdrawn to France.[12]

On the evening of 9 March 1566, the conspirators struck. Darnley appeared unexpectedly in the Queen's small supper chamber and a few moments later Lord Ruthven, Morton's illegitimate brother George Douglas, Andrew Ker of Fawdonside, and a group of armed men burst in. While Ker seized the Queen, who was more than six months pregnant, and held a pistol to her stomach, the others dragged Riccio into the outer chamber where they stabbed him to death. The Earl of Moray, waiting in Newcastle, rode for Edinburgh as soon as he heard that the deed had been done.

Distraught though she was, the Queen managed to detach Darnley from the other assassins and they escaped together from the Palace. Realising that they had been out-manoeuvred, all the conspirators but Moray fled. He had not been in Edinburgh on the fatal night, and so he decided that it was safe enough for him to stay, despite the fact that many people knew that he had signed the bond for Riccio's murder. Morton, Lord Ruthven, Lord Lindsay and Andrew Ker of Fawdonside escaped to England. William Maitland had not been present in the supper chamber, but he thought it prudent to withdraw to Dunkeld, in Perthshire. John Knox travelled to Ayrshire.

What, then, had Knox been doing during those dramatic events? Despite his quarrel with Moray he had, since the Chaseabout Raid, been praying publicly for the exiled Lords and it is generally agreed that he must have known in advance about the Riccio murder plot. All his friends did. Indeed Mary and Riccio himself must have been almost the only two who had not realised what was going to happen. Knox took no part, but he certainly approved of the murder of the man he called 'that poltroon and vile knave'. He had never made any secret of his views and, had he stayed in Edinburgh, the Queen would almost certainly have had him prosecuted and condemned to death for treason.[13]

On 19 June 1566 Mary, Queen of Scots gave birth to a son, the future James VI. Knox was still in Kyle, where he seems to have stayed until September. In his absence, John Craig took the services in St Giles. Mary was now going out of her way to appease the Protestants, but Knox had no illusions about that. It is not known if he attended the December meeting of the General Assembly, but he certainly applied to the Assembly for leave of absence so that he could go to England to see his sons. The Assembly agreed, and he spent the next six months in the south.

Presumably he stayed with the Bowes family and the boys in the north of England. In allowing him to go, the Assembly had instructed him to take up the cause of a number of English clergymen who had been imprisoned or dismissed because they had broken the law by refusing to wear vestments. Knox looked into the matter and urged moderation, telling the English Puritans that they should not stay away from services simply because they did not like the attire of the clergymen. His attitude might seem surprising, considering the fire and fury with which he attacked Roman Catholics and their candles, their vestments and their incense. That was different, however, from a dispute among fellow Protestants. Unity mattered more than anything else and just as he had done everything in his power to try to settle the controversies in Frankfurt, he was once more acting as a peacemaker.[14]

While he pursued his earnest discussions with his English colleagues, the reign of Mary, Queen of Scots reached its dramatic conclusion. In December 1566 she pardoned the Riccio murderers. On 9 February 1567 Lord Darnley was assassinated at Kirk o' Field and, on 15 May, Mary married James, Earl of Bothwell, the man generally believed to be the principal murderer of her husband. It was a fatal mistake. Moray, Morton and the other Protestant Lords confronted her army with theirs at Carberry Hill, not far from Edinburgh, on 15 June. Ordering Bothwell to flee and find help, the Queen surrendered and was imprisoned in Lochleven Castle. By 25 June, Knox was back in Scotland, preaching vehemently against her and demanding that she be put to death for her crimes.[15]

Alarmed at what was happening to her fellow monarch, Queen Elizabeth sent Sir Nicholas Throckmorton to Scotland to protect Mary against her rebellious subjects. When Throckmorton heard Knox preach, he was appalled. He went to see him and tried to persuade him to moderate his language but Knox would not listen. His longstanding hostility to Mary had become an obsessive, vengeful hatred. People have long speculated about why he loathed her so much, suggesting, for example, that he was suppressing feelings of sexual attraction towards her. That theory is wide of the mark. From the beginning, he never could see the real woman standing before him. To him she was a second Mary Tudor – Bloody Mary – who had sent his Protestant friends to their deaths. Many years before, his own mentor, George Wishart, had died at the stake, and ever since he had been gripped by a horror of more persecution, more burnings.

Knox was unable, ever, to give Mary the benefit of the doubt, because, for him, she symbolised all the evils of the Roman Catholic Church and, as her situation in Scotland went from bad to worse, he had no thought of the human being caught in distressing circumstances. He simply saw her as another Jezebel, another evil queen like those he knew so well from the Old Testament. She had ruined everything. She had come back to a Scotland newly transformed into an officially Protestant country, and, instead of taking her realm forward to a peaceful, godly future, she had menaced it with the Mass. He had seen her duplicity from the start. Now, he believed, she had shown herself to be a murderer and an adulterer and he knew no pity.[16]

15

The Death of Knox

THROUGHOUT THE DRAMATIC EVENTS of the Queen's rush to destruction, Knox was living a settled and harmonious private life in the comfortable house in Trunk Close. He and Margaret Stewart appear to have been happy together. Marriage to her father's admired friend had brought her a prominent role in society as the wife of Edinburgh's leading minister. She seems to have been an energetic, sensible young woman, brought up in the Protestant faith and suitably devout. Like her predecessor Marjorie, she was well-educated and she was able to help Knox with his voluminous paperwork, although in the end he did employ a secretary. There was much to be done.

Certainly Knox spent long hours sitting at his big table, his books and papers spread out around him, but the atmosphere was far from one of perpetual gloom. People were constantly coming to the house to seek his advice and he liked to entertain. All the leading Protestant notabilities came to supper at one time or another and there was laughter as the wine was brought out and they joked with each other, as well as anxiously discussing the serious issues of the day. Moreover, although he loved his sons deeply and must have missed them very much, he went on to have a second family with Margaret. Towards the end of 1565 she had their first child, a daughter. Knox had never followed tradition and named his children after their grandparents. He had looked to the Scriptures when he called Nathaniel and Eleazer after Old Testament figures, and he now named his new baby Martha, after the practical, housewife who was a sister of Jesus's friend Lazarus. With the birth of a second daughter about the time of the Queen's captivity in Lochleven, he departed from his usual practice and christened her Margaret, as a tribute to his wife.[1]

Mary, Queen of Scots was also pregnant in 1567, but on 24 July she miscarried twins, the children of Bothwell. As she lay recovering, weak from loss of blood, Lord Lindsay came in and forced her to sign a document saying that she abdicated in favour of her little son. The Earl of Moray would rule as Regent. Ten days later, the thirteen-month-old James was crowned King of Scots in Stirling Parish Church. Knox had at last made up his quarrel with Moray and he preached the sermon. Afterwards, he returned to Edinburgh.[2]

He preached at the opening of Parliament in December 1567 and watched with grim approval when the members ratified all the 1560 acts in favour of the Reformed Church, confirmed Mary's abdication and accused her of being implicated in the murder of Lord Darnley. All the same, he lived in dread of Mary somehow regaining her throne, and he spoke against her whenever he preached, usually five times a week. The following spring, it seemed that his fears were justified. On 2 May 1568, Mary escaped from Lochleven Castle, rode west to Hamilton to gather her supporters, and marched against the Regent Moray. Their armies met at the village of Langside, near Glasgow. Moray's army was smaller but he had experienced commanders like Morton and Kirkcaldy of Grange. The Queen's disorganised forces were quickly routed. Convinced that Elizabeth would support her against her rebellious subjects, she fled to England.[3]

Knox's *History* ends with the proclamation of the Earl of Moray as Regent the previous year, and so we do not have his comments on Mary's defeat. Triumphant as he may have felt, her departure did not quieten his fears, for there remained the danger that her powerful friends might restore her to Scotland. The Duke of Châtelherault, for instance, was still living in France. The French had, in fact, already rejected his urgings that they should help Mary, but, on 10 September 1568, Knox was warning John Wood, a friend in England, 'We look daily for the arrival of the Duke and his Frenchmen, sent to restore Satan to his kingdom in the person of his dearest lieutenant,' meaning Mary, Queen of Scots. England must beware 'for assuredly their neighbours' houses are on fire.'[4]

Knox wanted Queen Elizabeth to send financial help to Moray and the Scottish Protestants, for he had heard rumours that Mary's friends meant to murder both Moray and the little King, but the English attitude to the whole dilemma was disappointing. Their investigation into Mary's alleged crimes began at York that autumn and was moved to London, but its findings were inconclusive. Moray was unable to show that she had been involved in her husband's death, while Mary's representatives failed to prove that her subjects had rebelled against her. Elizabeth obviously had no intention of executing her royal prisoner for murder and adultery.[5]

In the summer of 1569, there were widespread rumours that Elizabeth would solve the problem of what to do with Mary by providing her with a reliable Protestant husband and then restoring her to the throne of Scotland. Thomas, Duke of Norfolk was the possible bridegroom, but all thoughts of the marriage were set aside when the Roman Catholic Earls Northumberland and Westmorland raised a rebellion against Elizabeth. The Earls were defeated, but their plot had made everyone very conscious of the dangers of Roman Catholic support for the Queen of Scots.[6]

On 2 January 1570, Knox warned Cecil, 'If ye strike not at the roots, the branches that appear to be broken will bud again (and that more quickly than men can believe) with greater force than we would wish.' In a mood of gloomy foreboding, he signed himself,

'John Knox, with his one foot in the grave'.[7] There were those who thought his fears exaggerated, but he was still hearing reports of a plot to murder Moray. He sent Moray a series of urgent messages, warning him of the danger if he rode through Linlithgow, but Moray ignored his advice. Just three weeks later, the Regent was assassinated as he left Linlithgow. The man who shot him was James Hamilton of Bothwellhaugh, probably acting at the instigation of Archbishop Hamilton.[8]

Even the Regent's enemies were shocked by his murder, and his friends were left desolate. Despite their lengthy quarrel, Knox had been close to Moray for many years and the next day he praised the Regent warmly from the pulpit, saying that his death punished the Scots for the sins and ingratitude of those who had not appreciated him. 'He is at rest, O Lord,' Knox concluded, 'We are left in extreme misery.' When she heard the news, Elizabeth I wept, saying that she had lost her best and most useful friend in all the world, but Mary, Queen of Scots rejoiced. She had long been convinced that her half-brother wanted her throne for himself. As a token of gratitude, she granted Hamilton of Bothwellhaugh a pension.

Moray's body was taken to lie in Holyroodhouse, and, on Tuesday 14 February, his coffin was carried in procession to St Giles, where Knox conducted the funeral service. More than 3,000 people crowded into the church that day. Taking as his text 'Blessed are they that die in the Lord', Knox reduced his congregation to tears with his description of the Regent's virtues. Moray was then buried in the south aisle of the church.[9] Meanwhile, James VI's supporters had sent a message to Queen Elizabeth, consulting her as to who should succeed as Regent. She suggested Darnley's father, Matthew, Earl of Lennox and he was duly chosen, but by this time the struggle between James VI's supporters and those of Mary, Queen of Scots had degenerated into open civil war, with the King's Party fighting the Queen's Party.[10]

Knox was in his mid-fifties now, and the long years of stress had taken their toll on his health. In the autumn he suffered a stroke and for a few days he lost the power of speech. His enemies declared with satisfaction that God had struck him dumb as a punishment for his past sins, but within weeks he was back preaching in St Giles. Even so, he was never the same again. He was later to say that he had been half-dead ever since the illness, and it is possible that he suffered partial paralysis or at least permanent weakness on one side.[11]

Apart from struggling with ill-health, Knox was living in increasingly dangerous circumstances. During his regency, the Earl of Moray had appointed William Kirkcaldy of Grange to be Captain of Edinburgh Castle, and Kirkcaldy was holding the stronghold for the King's Party. At the end of the year, however, Knox heard that Kirkcaldy had changed sides. Mary, Queen of Scots had surrendered to Kirkcaldy at Carberry and, feeling responsible for her, he had not approved of her imprisonment and her forced abdication. When Maitland of Lethington was arrested in September 1569 on a charge of complicity in Darnley's murder and imprisoned in Edinburgh Castle, the two men had long discussions. Maitland was seriously ill, but his intellect was as sharp as ever and he was a member of the Queen's Party. As a direct result of his influence, Kirkcaldy declared for Mary.

Knox was appalled. He and Kirkcaldy had been friends and allies ever since those long-past days when Beaton had been murdered in St Andrews Castle and they had both been taken as prisoners to France. 'To see stars fall from heaven and a man of knowledge to commit so manifest a treason,' Knox exclaimed, 'what godly heart cannot but lament, tremble and fear?' Kirkcaldy brushed aside his remonstrations, and the castle garrison named one of their guns 'Knox', because it made so much noise. When it exploded shortly afterwards, killing some of the gunners, the King's Party immediately claimed that God had punished those who had dared to mock their famous preacher.[12]

The enemy cannon might be trained on the town, but Knox continued to preach against Mary, Queen of Scots, demanding her death. This infuriated her supporters and made him unpopular with more moderate Protestants who complained yet again that he was denying her the opportunity of repenting. Others accused him of being a traitor to his own country because he supported Elizabeth I. When the General Assembly met in Edinburgh in March 1571, papers were nailed to the door of St Giles criticising him for his outspoken opposition to the deposed Queen. The Assembly members had no desire to be drawn into the war between the King's Party and the Queen's Party, and so they tried to persuade Knox to ignore this provocation, but of course he refused.

One of the papers condemned Knox for openly criticising his sovereign lady. When he read it, he wrote angrily in the margin, 'No sovereign lady is she to me, nor yet to this realm, and so ye are traitors.' He then composed a lengthy response to all his critics. He denied that he had ever said that Mary would never repent, but 'That I have called her an obstinate idolatress, one that consented to the murder of her own husband, and one that has committed whoredom and villainous adultery, I gladly grant.' As to a claim that his actions in supporting the government of Queen Elizabeth in England were seditious, just because he prayed for a country did not imply that he agreed with everything done there. He had never sought the help of another nation against his own.[13]

Soon after the General Assembly had dispersed, the King's Party captured Dumbarton Castle, held by the Hamiltons for Mary, Queen of Scots. Archbishop Hamilton was inside, and his long career ended when he was taken out and hanged at Stirling on 7 April 1571. His relatives and supporters flocked to Edinburgh, eager for revenge, and joined Kirkcaldy in the castle. With so many of the enemy close at hand, Knox's friends feared for his life and a group of them stood guard outside his house at night. A few evenings later a shot was apparently fired at his window. Had he been in his usual place, reading or writing at the head of the table, he would have been killed. Providentially, he had been sitting at one side, and the shot hit the candelabrum above his head. [14]

On 30 April 1571, Kirkcaldy issued a proclamation ordering all the supporters of the Regent Lennox and the King's Party to leave

Edinburgh within six hours. Knox had already refused to go, but his colleague John Craig now came to him and urged him to withdraw to some place of safety. He was most unwilling, but, when Craig said that if he stayed he would be endangering the lives of those local people who would insist on guarding him, he gave way. His third daughter, Elizabeth, had been born the previous year and on 5 May he and his wife, their three small girls and his secretary Richard Bannatyne, left the house in Trunk Close, crossed the Forth and very slowly made their way to Abbotshall, near Kirkcaldy. Even as they left, some of Kirkcaldy of Grange's men were demolishing parts of St Giles so that it would not provide shelter for any of the Queen's Party and they placed their own cannon on the roof. When the Earl of Morton marched up from Leith with a band of soldiers, Kirkcaldy fired on them from the castle and many of the houses in the centre of the town were destroyed. Knox had left not a moment too soon.[15]

In July 1571 Knox travelled slowly to St Andrews, where he and his household lodged near St Leonard's College. His nephew Paul Knox, son of his brother William, was studying for the ministry at St Salvator's and must have been a frequent visitor. Knox was so frail now that he fully expected to die in St Andrews, where his career in the Protestant Church had begun. Even so, he preached whenever he could and James Melville, then a 15-year-old student, was to describe how he used to see Knox walking slowly to church each day wearing a long robe with furs round his neck, and leaning heavily on a stick with his right hand, while Bannatyne supported him on the left side with a hand under his armpit.

Once inside, the faithful secretary and other friends had to lift Knox up into the pulpit. Leaning on it for support he preached from the Book of Daniel. He would speak quietly for the first hour, analysing his text, but when he moved on to draw comparisons with contemporary events, all his old fire returned as he denounced Mary, Queen of Scots, his former friend Kirkcaldy of Grange and the Hamiltons. Young Melville, sitting taking notes, found himself trembling so much as he listened that the pen dropped from his hand. It seemed to him that Knox would shatter the pulpit as he thumped it vigorously for effect, and, indeed, Melville half expected to see him fly out of it at any moment. On one particularly sombre occasion, a woman convicted of witchcraft was brought in and chained to a pillar opposite the pulpit so that Knox could denounce her before she was taken out and executed.

On good days, Knox would go and sit in the gardens of St Leonard's College, sometimes calling students over to give them his blessing. However alarming he might be in the pulpit, Melville decided that the greatest benefit he himself derived from his university days was the opportunity of seeing 'that extraordinary man of God, Mr John Knox', whom he described as the 'prophet and apostle of our nation'. In July 1571, Knox was well enough to attend the wedding of Mr John Colville, minister of East Kilbride. The celebrations included a play about the hoped-for storming and capture of Edinburgh Castle by the King's Party. The action culminated in a scene where Kirkcaldy of Grange and two others were hanged in effigy. Knox presumably watched with approval, for he had long been predicting that Kirkcaldy would be hanged 'in the face of the sun'.[16]

For the time being, Kirkcaldy was unassailable in Edinburgh Castle, but the violence continued elsewhere and, that autumn, the Regent Lennox was shot and killed in a skirmish at Stirling. John, 1st Earl of Mar replaced him briefly as regent, but real power lay with the Earl of Morton. Meanwhile, in England, the scheme to marry Mary, Queen of Scots to the Duke of Norfolk was revived by Roman Catholic plotters in the Ridolfi conspiracy, but Elizabeth I's intelligence system soon discovered what was happening, Ridolfi was arrested and Norfolk too was tried for treason and beheaded. The House of Commons urged Elizabeth to execute the Queen of Scots as well but she refused. However, there was no more talk of restoring Mary to the Scottish throne.[17]

As well as continuing to call for Mary's death whenever he preached, Knox was also concerned about another long-standing issue, the financing and structure of the Church of Scotland. It had been agreed that the lesser ecclesiastics would gradually be replaced with well-qualified Protestant ministers, and, in January 1572, an extraordinary meeting of the General Assembly at Leith decided at last that bishops would definitely be retained. When archbishoprics and bishoprics fell vacant, suitably qualified men aged at least 30 would be nominated within a year and a day and, once appointed, these Protestant bishops and archbishops would exercise exactly the same power as superintendents. Most importantly, they were all to be subject to the Church and the General Assembly in spiritual matters, just as they were subject to the crown in temporal affairs.

The most obvious problem with the arrangement was that the nobles went on nominating the candidates for the vacancies, and all too often they chose someone with whom they had made a private financial arrangement. Now that Archbishop Hamilton was dead, his Archbishopric of St Andrews was vacant. The Earl of Morton was given the right to select the next incumbent, and chose his kinsman John Douglas, Rector of St Andrews University. The two men had come to a private agreement whereby Morton instead of Douglas would receive the teinds from the Archbishopric.

Knox refused to inaugurate Douglas as Archbishop, although he was a friend, for he disapproved of the General Assembly's insistence that the new Archbishop must continue to hold his university appointments. However, as always, he was anxious to preserve unity and so he did not make a public issue of the matter and agreed to preach immediately before the service of inauguration. John Rutherford, the Principal of St Salvator's College, resented Knox's refusal to officiate and told people that Knox was jealous. Knox had wanted to be Archbishop himself, he claimed. When Knox heard the rumours, he dismissed them with dignity, reminding people that, many years earlier, when he was in England, he could have had a far wealthier bishopric than the see of St Andrews, had he so desired.[18]

He had long been disillusioned by the behaviour of the Protestant Lords, and he was sickened by the continuing civil war. 'Both the parties stand, as it were, fighting against God himself in justification of their wickedness,' he wrote to one of George Wishart's relatives on 19 July 1572. The murderers in Edinburgh Castle and their supporters insisted on justifying all they had done, and the other party cared no more than they did about the oppression of the Church. The Lords were concerned only with their own property, 'For if they can have the church lands to be annexed to their houses, they appear to take no more care of the instruction of the ignorant and of the feeding of the flock of Jesus Christ than ever did the papists, whom we have condemned, and yet are worse ourselves in that behalf'. Even the Roman Catholics in their blind zeal had spared no effort to uphold 'that which they took for God's service', whereas 'we, alas, in the midst of the light, forget the heaven and draw to the earth'.[19]

That same month, a deputation of university teachers and minis-ters came to complain to Knox about his sermons. A student named Archibald Hamilton was refusing to attend his services because Knox was always saying that the Hamiltons were murderers. Knox retorted angrily that neither they nor any other group of private people had the right to judge the Church and its representatives. Only God and the General Assembly could do that, and he sent them away. A fortnight later, he wrote to tell the General Assembly meeting in Perth, 'Albeit I have taken my leave not only of you, dear brethern, but also of the whole world and all worldly affairs, yet remaining in the flesh I could not nor cannot cease to admonish you of things which I know to be most prejudicial to the Church of Christ Jesus within this realm.' They must never allow the Church to become subject to the universities.[20]

Old and ill, Knox felt that he had lived on beyond his time. He was so weak now that he usually got up only once a week. Even so, he sat propped up in bed preparing for publication a final pamphlet entitled *An Answer to a Letter of a Jesuit named Tyrie*. He had written this tract six years earlier, refuting Tyrie's claims that the Roman Catholic Church was the true church. He now prefaced it with an address to his 'faithful reader' saying, 'I heartily salute and take my goodnight of all the faithful in both realms, earnestly desiring the assistance of their prayers that, without any notable slander to the Evangel of Jesus Christ, I may end my battle. For as the world is weary of me, so am I of it,' and he prayed God to be merciful to 'my desolate bedfellow [Margaret, his wife], the fruit of her bosom [their daughters] and my two dear children, Nathaniel and Eleazer. Now Lord, put end to my misery.' As he was finishing, he received the news that his old friend Elizabeth Bowes had died.

Knox decided that when his *Answer to a Letter of a Jesuit* was published, it should have as its appendix a letter he had written to Mrs Bowes in 1554. Possibly out of deference to her family, and probably thinking of his own reputation, he wanted to put an end once and for all to the malicious gossip about his relationship with Mrs Bowes. He knew very well that people had always said that they were too friendly, and he had resolved to 'declare to the world what was the cause of our great familiarity and long acquaintance, which was neither flesh nor blood, but a troubled conscience upon her part, which never suffered her to rest but when she was in the company of the faithful of whom, from the first hearing the Word at my mouth, she judged me to be one'.

He wrote this, he said, 'for the discharge of my conscience and the instruction of her children'. He had listened to the troubles of many in Scotland, England, France and Germany, but he had never met anyone else who had experienced quite the spiritual conflict endured by her, and he emphasised again, 'For her temptation was not in the flesh, nor for anything that appertained to the flesh (no, not when she was in greatest desolation) but it was in spirit, for Satan did continually buffet her.' She felt that her sins would never be forgiven because of her previous idolatry. With more truthfulness than gallantry, he went on, 'Her company to me was comfortable (yea, honourable and profitable, for she was to me and mine a mother), but yet it was not without some cross, for besides trouble and fasherie [tribulation] of body sustained for her, my mind was seldom quiet, for doing somewhat for the comfort of her troubled conscience.' Knox was an honest man, his words have the ring of truth and his surviving letters give us no reason to doubt this final verdict on their long friendship.[21]

On 31 July 1572, the King's Party and the Queen's Party at last signed a truce, and Knox received messages from some of the congregation of St Giles, urging him to come back to Edinburgh. The castle was still held by Kirkcaldy and there were fears that Spanish troops might land in Scotland to support the cause of Mary, Queen of Scots, but, in spite of these dangers and in spite of his frailty, Knox decided to go back. He and his family travelled to the south coast of Fife by easy stages, sailed across the Forth to Leith and, by the last week of August he was back in the capital.

It was obvious to all who saw Knox that the end could not be far off. He managed to preach in St Giles on 31 August, but his voice was so feeble that few of the congregation could hear what he said. It was therefore agreed that he should move to a much smaller space. In about 1566, the three western bays of the nave of St Giles had been partitioned off to form two storey premises known as the Outer Tolbooth. The lower room seems to have been given over to meetings of the town council, but the upper room was used for worship and Knox now preached there. When word reached Scotland that large numbers of Protestants had been killed in Paris in the Massacre of St Bartholomew on 24 August, he preached with something of his old vehemence, but he knew himself that he could not go on much longer.[22]

He sent his last greetings to William Cecil, telling him that, although he could have been a great bishop in England, having been the instrument to establish Christ's gospel in Scotland had given him even greater satisfaction. He also wrote to one of his colleagues, James Lawson in Aberdeen, asking him to come and see him, with the urgent postscript, 'Make haste, my brother, otherwise you will come too late.' He was going to resign, and he wanted Lawson to succeed him, for John Craig, with whom he had shared the ministry at St Giles, had made himself unpopular by trying to maintain a politically neutral stance and had now left the capital.[23]

Lawson came, preached several times in St Giles, was judged acceptable by the congregation, and on Sunday 9 November 1572 was inducted as minister. Knox delivered a sermon as usual at the Tolbooth that day, and then he addressed the new minister from the pulpit of St Giles, reminding him of his duties. That was the last time that he preached, or indeed left his house. He seems to have contracted a chest infection for, the following day, a doctor had to be called when he had a bad fit of coughing.[24]

He lay in bed, listening to his wife and his secretary read to him from the Bible and from some of Calvin's sermons. On Friday, Margaret found him trying to get up, for he thought that it was Sunday, and he had to go and preach. Next day he seemed a little better, and would not hear of his wife cancelling a small supper party which had been arranged for that evening. His visitors came, and he was well enough to join them. He even called for a new cask of wine to be opened, urging his guests to drink as much as they liked for, he said, he would not live long enough to finish it himself. The following week, a steady procession of old friends came to say goodbye to him. As the Earl of Morton sat by his bed, Knox asked him earnestly if he had been involved in Darnley's murder. Morton swore that he had known nothing about it. Possibly Knox did not believe him, for he warned Morton that, as he was about to be made Regent, he must use his advantages to better purpose than he had done in the past.

At the end of his second week of illness, Knox told his secretary to make sure that his coffin was ready. He could hardly speak now, but he received more visitors that Saturday, including James Lawson, his successor. He confided to him that he was deeply troubled about Kirkcaldy of Grange, and, in one last effort to save his old friend, he urged Lawson and David Lindsay to tell Kirkcaldy from him that, unless he repented of his recent actions, he would die miserably, 'for neither the craggy rock in which he miserably trusts, nor the carnal prudence of that man [Maitland] whom he looks upon as a demi-god, nor the assistance of foreigners, as he falsely flatters himself, shall deliver them'. Instead, Kirkcaldy would be 'disgracefully dragged from his nest to punishment, and hung on the gallows in the face of the sun'. 'The man's soul is dear to me', Knox said sadly, 'and I would not have it perish if I could save it.' Lawson and Lindsay did as he asked, but Kirkcaldy refused to take any advice.

On Monday 24 November 1572, Knox insisted on rising and getting dressed, but after only half an hour sitting in a chair he had to go back to bed again. It seems likely that he was suffering from pneumonia. When his old friend Robert Campbell of Kinzeancleuch came to see him, Knox asked him to look after his wife and children. At about midday Margaret read to him from the Bible, at his request, the 15th chapter of the First Epistle to the Corinthians with its famous verses, 'The trumpet shall sound and the dead shall be raised, incorruptible, and we shall be changed . . . O death, where is thy sting, O grave, where is thy victory?' He murmured faintly that he commended his soul, spirit and body to God.

At about five o'clock in the afternoon, he told Margaret, 'Go read where I cast my first anchor'. She knew what he meant, and turned to the 17th Chapter of St John, where Jesus told God how he had preached in the world and, although people had hated his words, He had prayed that God should keep them from evil so that they might all be united one day in glory. From time to time Knox was able to take a sip of a little weak ale, from a cup held by his wife, and then at about seven o'clock in the evening, he fell asleep. He seemed to stir a little around ten, when the usual evening prayers were said in his room. His doctor bent over him to ask if he could hear the prayers and he answered, 'I would to God that ye and all men heard them as I have heard them, and I praise God of that heavenly sound.' Richard Bannatyne and Campbell of Kinzeancleuch were sitting by his bed when he died about an hour later. Two days after that, his funeral took place in St Giles. The Earl of Morton gave the eulogy. 'There lies he,' the Earl declaimed, 'who never feared nor flattered any flesh.' After the service, Knox was buried in the cemetery just to the south of the church.

Conclusion

Knox had made his will almost six months earlier, when he was still in St Andrews.[1] Dated 13 May 1572, it began with characteristic directness, 'Lord Jesus, I commend my troubled spirit into Thy protection and defence, and Thy troubled Kirk to Thy mercy.' After a salutary reminder to his adversaries that, if they had listened to him and repented, they could have been saved, he observed that, throughout his life, he had shown the truth in all its simplicity. 'None have I corrupted, none have I defrauded.' He had preached the Word of God and beaten down the pride of the proud.

His flock would be without him now, but they must do their duty and remain faithful to God. They had often urged him to enter the struggle between the King's Party and the Queen's Party, but his vocation was to preach, not to embroil himself in political conflict. He did, however, predict that in the end Edinburgh Castle and its occupants would come to destruction, and he was right. Six months after his death the castle was captured with English help, the civil war ended and William Kirkcaldy of Grange was hanged. Maitland of Lethington died before he could be executed. Some said that he had taken poison. His enemies defeated, the Earl of

Morton as Regent governed Protestant Scotland with a firm hand until his own fall from power and subsequent execution in 1581.[2]

Having dealt with public concerns, Knox then turned to his own family and made various bequests. He left his sons that same blessing which their dearest mother had given them when she was dying. They were to inherit his two silver drinking cups which were both marked with the initials 'JKM' on one side and 'EBN' on the other, the 'B' presumably for Marjorie's maiden name of Bowes. The boys were to have Knox's two silver salts, eighteen silver spoons and some of his books, which were works of theology and the classics. He had already sent £600 to their uncle, Mr Robert Bowes, for them. A hundred pounds had come to them from their mother, but he had saved up the rest himself.

Eight days after his death, Knox's sons entered St John's College, Cambridge. Nathaniel graduated with the degree of Bachelor of Arts and became a Fellow of the College in 1577, but soon afterwards he contracted a violent fever and died a fortnight later. He was just 20. Two of his half-sisters named sons after him. His brother Eleazer entered the Church of England, became vicar of Clacton Magna, near Colchester, and died, unmarried, on 22 May 1591. He was buried in the chapel of St John's College. Knox left his nephew, Paul, £100 to help with his education. He became a Church of Scotland minister in the Borders.[3]

The total value of Knox's estate was £1,528 Scots, a sizeable sum. As well as his belongings, he died with £100 in his possession and he was owed £80 by his father-in-law and £10 by William Fiddes, baker, an advance payment for bread for Communion services. Knox himself owed no money at all. His widow and their daughters would be his executors, supervised by members of his congregation. Margaret already had 800 merks from the lands of Pennymoir, settled on her by her father, and she and the girls were to receive the residue of Knox's estate. Amongst his other possessions, she presumably inherited his papers, for it was she who owned the book containing the transcript of his letters to Elizabeth Bowes.[4]

Margaret was about 24 when Knox died and after being a widow for two years, she married again. Her second husband was another older man, a widower in his forties, Andrew Ker of Fawdonside. An energetic Protestant and cousin of Lord Ruthven, he had been the conspirator who threatened Mary, Queen of Scots and held a pistol to her stomach that night in the Palace of Holyroodhouse when David Riccio was murdered. Margaret went on to have a second family with Ker, including a son named John who became a well-known minister in the Church of Scotland.

Knox's three daughters were all under the age of eight when he died. Martha, the eldest, married Alexander Fairlie, the son of Knox's friend Robert Fairlie of Braid. She had three sons and a daughter before her early death at about the age of 27. Margaret and Elizabeth both married eminent Church of Scotland ministers, Zachary Pont and John Welsh. A fierce critic of James VI's ecclesiastical policies, Welsh spent 16 years in exile in France. According to tradition, his wife went on one occasion to the King to seek permission for him to return, and the daughter of John Knox confronted the son of Mary, Queen of Scots. Elizabeth explained her request, and James VI asked her the name of her father. She told him.

'Knox and Welsh!' the King exclaimed. 'The devil never made such a match as that!'

'It's right likely, Sire,' Elizabeth retorted, with all Knox's fearlessness and trenchant humour, 'for we never asked his advice.'[5]

It may seem perverse to end a biography of an austere man of God with a humorous and possibly apocryphal anecdote about his daughter, but the incident is a useful corrective for those who think of Knox only as a caricature of bigotry. He was no two-dimensional figure and those who read his *History of the Reformation in Scotland* find themselves in the presence of a strong and vibrant personality. Straightforward in many ways, complex in others, he knew that he was tactless and readily admitted to being churlish, yet he was an admired pastor, a patient counsellor and an affectionate husband, father and friend. He shrank from violence, but his moral courage never failed. The contrast between his sensitivity and his vehement denunciation of anyone of whom he disapproved may seem to us puzzling, until we realise that the prophets of the Old Testament harangued their contemporaries in exactly the same outspoken manner. As always, Knox took the Bible as his model. His searing honesty discomfited friends as well as enemies, but his unflinching faith in God earned him the respect not only of the leading reformers of the day but of the machinating politicians at the Scottish and English Courts.

It is true that his fundamentalist approach to religion finds little favour now and his *First Blast of the Trumpet* continues to bring him opprobrium. Moreover, his role in the Scottish Reformation has undoubtedly been exaggerated in the past, for he did not overthrow Roman Catholicism single-handed nor did he introduce a complete system of Calvinist church government. The nobility carried the Reformation through and Andrew Melville, who came back to Scotland from Switzerland in 1573, was the true founder of Scottish Presbyterianism. It was under Melville's leadership that presbyteries were set up, bishops abolished and the old ecclesiastical property was given to the Reformed Church.

Nevertheless, Knox's achievements were considerable. He travelled extensively, consulted all the leading Swiss reformers and lived and worked in Geneva. He was Calvin's follower and respected friend. When he died, Theodore Beza wrote, 'We have been afflicted beyond belief by the death of Mr Knox.'[6] He provided spiritual leadership at a time of great upheaval. His logic led him to develop a new theory of revolution. He was one of the first leaders of English Puritanism and he was responsible for the Church of Scotland's acceptance of Calvinism rather than Lutheranism. In short, John Knox's energy, eloquence, powerful convictions and moral certainty played a significant part in making Scotland and the Scots what they are today.

Note on Sources

IN WRITING THIS BOOK, I have tried to allow Knox to speak for himself, wherever possible, and I have modernised the spelling throughout. The principal sources for his writings are *The Works of John Knox* ed. David Laing, (1854) six volumes, and *John Knox's History of the Reformation in Scotland* ed. W. Croft Dickinson, (1949) two volumes. As his title indicates, Laing printed all Knox's writings, including his letters to Elizabeth Bowes and other relevant correspondence. Roger A. Mason's *On Rebellion* (Cambridge 1994) includes the full text of *The First Blast of the Trumpet* and several of Knox's shorter texts are to be found on the Internet.

The *History* is the source of the direct speech which I have quoted in, for instance, my account of Knox's various confrontations with Mary, Queen of Scots. Naturally, it does not record the speakers' words verbatim, for Knox was setting down conversations which had taken place several years before and he recorded them from his own particular viewpoint. It is, however, the nearest we can come to what was actually said. Dickinson's classic edition has comprehensive footnotes and a new edition of the *History* is presently being prepared for publication by James Kirk and Margaret Sanderson.

No portrait of Knox from the life has survived, if indeed any ever existed. When Calvin's friend and successor, Theodore Beza, was compiling his *Icones*, a set of essays on the lives of famous reformers, he looked in vain for a likeness of Knox in Switzerland and eventually wrote to Sir Peter Young, one of James VI's tutors, to see if he could help. Less than seven years had passed since Knox's death. Young replied on 12 November 1579 to say that no portrait existed, but that he had commissioned the Flemish artist, Adrian Vanson, to produce one. Vanson was living in Edinburgh and had probably seen Knox, even if he had not met him. Young sent this posthumous portrait to Beza, with his own verbal account of Knox's appearance. I have based my description of Knox on Young's recollection. The Vanson portrait has vanished, but it is known to us in the form of the woodcut used by Beza in the *Icones*, and it has since inspired a long series of paintings and statues. Other portraits reputedly representing Knox seem to be either later copies based on the woodcut, or portraits of sixteenth century men which have lost their true identity.

References

INTRODUCTION

1 John Knox, *History of the Reformation in Scotland* ed. W. C. Dickinson (Edinburgh 1949), i, p. 13 and for a full account of the interview see Chapter 12 of this present book. For Knox's appearance, see Knox, *History*, i, p. lxxxvii

2 Quoted in Gordon Donaldson, *John Knox* (Pitkin Pictorial, 1983), frontispiece

3 Thomas McCrie, *The Life of John Knox* (Edinburgh 1960 edn), p. 276

4 *The Works of John Knox* ed. D. Laing (1854), vi, p. lxxxvii

CHAPTER ONE: THE PRIEST

1 Laing, vi, pp. xiv–xviii; McCrie, p. 1; Roger Mason, *Kingship and the Commonweal* (1998), p. 140

2 Laing, vi, p. xix; Mason, *Kingship*, p. 140; McCrie, pp. 2–4

3 Gordon Donaldson, *The Scottish Reformation* (Cambridge 1960), pp. 29–50; Gordon Donaldson, *Scotland: James V to James VII* (Edinburgh and London 1965), pp. 132–45; Gordon Donaldson, *The Faith of the Scots* (London 1990), pp. 36–80; Ian B. Cowan, *The Medieval Church in Scotland* ed. James Kirk, *passim*; Alister E. McGrath, *Reformation Thought: An Introduction* (Oxford 1988), pp. 1–37

4 Ranald Nicholson, *Scotland: The Later Middle Ages* (Edinburgh 1974),

pp. 239–41, 561–2; Timothy George, *Theology of the Reformers* (British edn, Leicester 1989), pp. 35–7; *The Reformation* ed. Pierre Chaunu (British edn, Gloucester 1989), pp. 58–60

5 *Letters and Papers (Foreign and Domestic) of the Reign of King Henry VIII,* ed. J. Brewer and J. Gairdner (London 1862–1910, iv part ii, no 2903; Donaldson, *Scottish Reformation* (Cambridge 1960), p. 29; George, pp. 51–62, 82–99, 104; James K. Cameron, 'Aspects of the Lutheran Contribution to the Scottish Reformation' in *Records of the Scottish Church History Society,* xxii (1984), pp. 1–12

6 Knox, *History,* i, pp. 11–15; Donaldson, *James V to James VII,* pp. 22, 139; Gordon Donaldson and R. S. Morpeth, *Who's Who in Scottish History* (London 1973), pp. 58–9

7 Laing, vi, xx–xxi; Knox, *History,* i, pp. xxxi–xxxii; Mason, *Kingship, passim; Who's Who in Scottish History,* p. 59; I am grateful to Professor Alexander Broadie of Glasgow University for confirming that it is almost beyond doubt that Knox was taught by Mair

8 Donaldson, *James V to James VII,* pp. 132–8

9 Laing, vi, p. lxxxiii

10 J. H. Burns, 'Knox: Scholastic and Canonistic Echoes' in *British Reformations* ed. Roger Mason (Aldershot 1998), pp. 121–3; John Durkan, 'The Early Scottish Notary' in *The Renaissance and Reformation in Scotland: Essays in Honour of Gordon Donaldson* (Edinburgh 1983), pp. 28–9; Knox, *History,* i, p. xxxii

11 Laing, vi, p. xxi; McCrie, 21

12 J. Cameron, *James V: The Personal Rule 1528–1542* (East Linton 1998), pp. 177–327; Donaldson, *James V to James VII,* pp. 54–9

13 Laing, vi, pp. xxii–xxiii; Knox, *History,* i, p. 42; David Calderwood, *The History of the Kirk of Scotland* (Edinburgh 1842–9), i, pp. 155–6

14 Knox, *History,* i, pp. 60–7; Donaldson, *James V to James VII,* p. 74; *Who's Who in Scottish History,* pp. 67–8; Jasper Ridley, *John Knox,* (Oxford 1968), pp. 37–8

15 Rosalind K. Marshall, *Mary of Guise* (London 1977), pp. 108–67; Donaldson, *James V to James VII,* pp. 69–72

16 Knox, *History,* i, pp. 67–72; Foxe's text reprinted in Knox, *History,* ii, pp. 233–45

17 Knox, *History,* i, pp. 67–8; Donaldson, *James V to James VII,* pp. 74–5; Margaret Sanderson, *Cardinal of Scotland: David Beaton c. 1494–1546* (Edinburgh 1986)

CHAPTER TWO: THE GALLEY SLAVE

1 Knox, *History*, i, pp. 79–82; Donaldson, *James V to James VII*, pp. 74–5

2 John Guy, *Tudor England* (Oxford 1988), pp. 197–203; A. G. Dickens, *The English Reformation* (London 1964), pp. 279–80; *Calendar of Letters, Documents and State Papers relating to the Negotiations between England and Spain in Simancas and elsewhere, 1485–1558*, ed. P. de Goyangos *et al* (London 1862–1954, hereafter cited as *CDSP Spanish*), ix (1547–9), pp. 6–7, 18–22, 52, 88ff.

3 Knox, *History*, i, pp. 82–3; Mason, *Kingship*, pp. 140–1

4 Knox, *History*, i, pp. 83–4

5 Knox, *History*, i, pp. 84–94; Carol Edington, 'John Knox and the Castilians: A Crucible of Reforming Opinion?' in *British Reformations*, pp. 29–50

6 Knox, *History*, i, pp. 94–5

7 Knox, *History*, i, p. 96; Ridley, pp. 60–4

8 Knox, *History*, i, pp. 96–8; *A Diurnal of Remarkable Occurrents* (Edinburgh 1833), p. 44

9 Knox, *History*, i, p. 96

10 H. Decaëns and P. Bérenger, *Rouen* (Rennes 1996); A. M. Carment-Lanfry, *The Cathedral Notre Dame de Rouen* (Rouen n.d.)

11 Knox, *History*, i, p. 97; Ridley, pp. 69–70; Gordon Donaldson, 'Knox the Man' in *John Knox, A Quatercentenary Reappraisal* ed. Duncan Shaw (Edinburgh 1975), p. 20

12 Knox, *History*, i, pp. 108–9

13 R. Lindesay of Pitscottie, *The Historie and Cronicles of Scotland* (Scottish Text Society 1899–1911), ii, pp. 96–102; John Lesley, *The History of Scotland* (Bannatyne Club 1830), ii, pp. 42, 297–301; *Diurnal of Occurrents*, p. 45; Marshall, *Mary of Guise*, pp. 162–75

14 Knox, *History*, i, pp. 108–9; Gordon Donaldson, *Scottish Historical Documents* (Edinburgh 1970), pp. 113–4 (text of the Treaty of Haddington)

15 Laing, iii, 4ff.

16 Knox, *History*, i, pp. xxxiv, 92 n.2; E. G. Rupp, 'The Europe of John Knox' in Knox, *Reappraisal* ed. Shaw, pp. 7–8

17 Knox, *History*, i, p. xxxiv, 110

CHAPTER THREE: THE ENGLISH YEARS

1 Peter Lorimer, *John Knox and the Church of England* (London 1875), p. 15; McCrie, pp. 43–4; Dickens, pp. 273–313
2 Ridley, pp. 84–5; Dickens, pp. 301–7
3 Lorimer, p. 18
4 Ridley, pp. 86–100; Berwick, *A Short History and Guide* (Morpeth 1987). The church where Knox preached no longer exists
5 Miri Rubin, *Corpus Christi: The Eucharist in Late Medieval Culture* (Cambridge University Press, 1991), *passim*; McGrath, pp. 161–4
6 McGrath, pp. 165–80; George, pp. 144–58; John Stephenson, 'Martin Luther and the Eucharist' in *Scottish Journal of Theology* (1983), xxxvi, pp. 447–61; Chaunu, p. 94
7 Laing, iii, pp. 33–70; Ridley, pp. 94–7
8 Lorimer, p. 76; McCrie, p. 43; Ridley, pp. 91–104
9 David Mathew, *Lady Jane Grey: The Setting of the Reign* (London 1972) *passim*; Lorimer, pp. 77–8; Dickens, pp. 314–27
10 W. K. Jordan, *Edward VI: The Young King* (1968) and *Edward VI: The Threshold of Power* (1970), *passim*
11 *CDSP Spanish*, x, p. 593; Lorimer pp. 98–99; Ridley, pp. 106–9
12 Lorimer, pp. 98, 102–36, 261; Diarmaid MacCulloch, *Thomas Cranmer: A Life* (London 1996), pp. 527–30; Guy, pp. 206–7; Dickens, pp. 261–2, 339–43; Patrick Collinson, 'John Knox, the Church of England and the Women of England' in *British Reformations*, p. 89
13 Lorimer, pp. 149–50
14 Laing, iii, pp. 81–6; Lorimer, pp. 150–62
15 Lorimer, p. 163
16 Lorimer, p. 162–9; Ridley, pp. 120–9; Laing, iii, p. 357
17 Laing, iii, p. 364

CHAPTER FOUR: ELIZABETH BOWES

1 Laing, iii, p. 333; vi, p. xxxiii; Christine M. Newman, 'The Reformation and Elizabeth Bowes: a study of a sixteenth-century northern gentlewoman' in *Women in the Church* ed. W. J. Shiels and Diana Wood (Oxford 1990), 325–7
2 For the doctrine of predestination and its implications, see George, pp. 36–7, 73–9, 123–6; McGrath, pp. 120–33; Donaldson, *Faith of the Scots*, pp. 63–4
3 Laing, iii, p. 335
4 The following paragraphs are based on a detailed analysis of Knox's

letters to Elizabeth Bowes, printed in Laing, iii, pp. 337ff.

5 *c.f.* Patrick Collinson, 'John Knox, the Church of England and the Women of England' in *British Reformations*, pp. 74–98; Patrick Collinson, 'Not Sexual in the Ordinary Sense: Women, Men and Religious Transactions' in his *Elizabethan Essays* (London 1994), pp. 119–50; Robert Louis Stevenson, 'John Knox and his Relations to Women' in his *Familiar Studies of Men and Books* (London 1895), pp. 331–40; A. Daniel Frankforter, 'Elizabeth Bowes and John Knox: A Woman and Reformation Theology' in *Church History* (1987), pp. 56, 333–47

6 Rosalind K. Marshall, *Virgins and Viragos: A History of Women in Scotland from 1080–1980* (London 1983), pp. 18–27

7 Lorimer, pp. 171–3

8 Lorimer, pp. 174–5

9 Laing, iii, pp. 337–40

CHAPTER FIVE: CALVIN

1 Mathew, *Lady Jane Grey, passim*; David Loades, *Mary Tudor: A Life* (Oxford 1989), pp. 171–3; Rosalind K. Marshall, *Mary I* (London 1993), pp. 61–3; Jordan, *Threshold of Power*, p. 510

2 Lorimer, pp. 178–83; Ridley, pp. 146–50

3 René de Vertot, *Ambassades de MM de Noailles en Angleterre* (London 1763), ii, pp. 52–107; Loades, *Mary I*, pp. 181–8; Guy, pp. 226–9; Marshall, *Mary I*, pp. 69–70

4 Lorimer, pp. 185–7; Laing, iii, pp. 374–6

5 Laing, iii, pp. 376–8

6 David Loades, *The Reign of Mary Tudor* (London 1991), pp. 104–6

7 Laing, iii, pp. 369–71; Ridley, pp. 160–1

8 Laing, iii, p. 353

9 Laing, iii, pp. 369–71

10 Laing, iii, p. 118ff.; Lorimer, pp. 190–4; McCrie, pp. 65–8

11 Laing, iii, pp. 184ff.

12 Loades, *Reign*, pp. 204–15

13 Mason, *Kingship*, p. 156; Oliver K. Olson, 'Theology of Revolution: Magdeburg 1550–1661, in *Sixteenth Century Journal 3* (1972), pp. 56–79

14 For Calvin's career, see Alister E. McGrath, *A Life of John Calvin* (Oxford 1990); T. H. L. Parker, *Calvin's Preaching* (Edinburgh 1992); Alexander Ganoczy, *The Young Calvin*, transl. D. Foxgrover and W. Pravo (Edinburgh edn 1988); Chanou, pp. 120–36; George,

pp. 163–251; McGrath, pp. 188–201

15 C. Bonnet, O. Fatio and J-E. Genequand, *Saint-Pierre: The Cathedral of Geneva* (Geneva 1984); E. W. Monter, *Calvin's Geneva* (London 1967), pp. 12–15, 144–65

16 Laing, iii, pp. 221–6; McCrie, pp. 69–70; Ridley, pp. 178–81

CHAPTER SIX: FRANKFURT

1 Laing, iii, p. 347

2 Loades, *Reign*, pp. 212–5; Guy, pp. 229–32

3 Marshall, *Mary of Guise*, pp. 195–8

4 Laing, iii, pp. 231–6, 244–7

5 Laing, iii, pp. 184–94, 202, 208, 293–5; Ridley, pp. 180–1

6 Laing, iii, pp. 370–2

7 McCrie, pp. 76–7; Euan Cameron, 'Frankfurt and Geneva: The European Context of John Knox's Reformation' in *British Reformations*, pp. 51–61; Ridley, pp. 188–94

8 See Plate 7

9 The following paragraphs are based on *Narrative of the Proceedings and Troubles of the English Congregation at Frankfurt on the Maine*, arguably attributed to Knox, in Laing iv, p. 9ff; see also, Dickens, pp. 394–400 and Ridley, pp. 189–214

10 John Calvin, *Calvini Opera* ed. C. G. Bretschgneider and H. F. Bindseil (Brunswick and Berlin 1863–1900), pp. xv, 628–9 where, as Ridley points out, the letter is wrongly dated 12 June (Ridley, p. 212)

CHAPTER SEVEN: BACK TO SCOTLAND

1 Marshall, *Mary of Guise*, pp. 199–203; Donaldson, *James V to James VII*, pp. 85–7; Ridley pp. 220–223

2 Laing, iv, pp. 217–8

3 Knox, *History*, i, pp. 118–121; Laing, iv, pp. 217–8

4 Knox, *History*, i, pp. 78n, 121; Ridley, p. 115, n1

5 Knox, *History*, i, p. 121

6 Knox, *History*, i, pp. 122–3

7 Laing, iv, p. 423–60

8 Knox, *History*, i, p. 123; Laing, vi, pp. xxxiii–xxxiv

9 Knox, *History*, i, pp. 123–4

10 Laing, iv, pp. 133–40

11 Ridley, pp. 242–3; *Livre des Anglois à Genève* ed J. S. Burns (1831), p. 12

12 *Livre des Anglois* p. 12
13 C. Martin, *Les Protestants Anglais réfugiés à Genève au temps de Calvin* (Geneva 1915), p. 45–73; M. Roset, *Les Chroniques de Genève* (Geneva 1894); E. Doumergue, *Jean Calvin* (Lausanne 1905); E. Doumergue *Geneva Past and Present* (Geneva? 1909); E. Choisy, *La théocratie à Genève au temps de Calvin* (Geneva 1896); B. Croce, *Vite di avventure di fede e di passione* (Bari 1936), pp. 202–8. I am grateful to Angus Armstrong for a translation of the relevant passages from Croce's work; Alain Dufour, 'Le Mythe de Genève au temps de Calvin' in his *Histoire Politique et Psychologie Historique* (Geneva 1966), pp. 63–96; Monter, *Calvin's Geneva*, pp. 144–65
14 Laing, iv, pp. 237–41
15 *Livre des Anglois*, p. 14
16 Laing, iv, pp. 219–22; Collinson, 'Knox, the Church and the Women of England', pp. 82–6; Ridley, pp. 247–8
17 Knox, *History*, i, pp. 132–3
18 Knox, *History*, i, pp. xxxvii–xxxviii, 133–6; Ridley, p. 249

CHAPTER EIGHT: *THE FIRST BLAST OF THE TRUMPET*

1 Knox, *History*, i, pp. 133–6
2 Laing, iv, pp. 276–86
3 J. Row, *History of the Kirk of Scotland* (Edinburgh 1842), pp. 8–9; Laing iv, p. 245
4 Laing, iv, pp. 363–420; the most recent edition of *The First Blast* is to be found in Roger Mason, *John Knox: On Rebellion* (Cambridge 1994), pp. 3–47
5 Marshall, *Virgins and Viragos*, pp. 17–86
6 Amanda Shephard, *Gender and Authority in 16th Century England* (Keele 1994), *passim*; Roger Mason, 'Knox on Rebellion' in *British Reformations*; Mason, *On Rebellion*, pp. viii–xxiv
7 Laing, iv, pp. 429–60; Mason, *On Rebellion*, pp. 48–71
8 Laing, iv, pp. 465–520; Mason, *On Rebellion*, pp. 72–114
9 Laing, iv, pp. 523–38; Jane Dawson, 'Two John Knoxes: England, Scotland and the 1558 Tracts' in *Journal of Ecclesiastical History*, p. xlii (1991), pp. 556–76; Jane Dawson, 'Trumpeting Resistance: Christopher Goodman and John Knox' in *British Reformations*, pp. 131–53; Mason, *On Rebellion*, pp. 115–27
10 Laing, iv, pp. 558–60
11 Laing, iv, pp. 539–40; Mason, *On Rebellion*, pp. 128–9

CHAPTER NINE: THE SERMON AT PERTH

1 Dickens, pp. 384–5; Ridley, p. 280
2 Laing, v, p. 5
3 Matthew Parker, *Correspondence of Matthew Parker* (Cambridge 1853), pp. 60–1
4 *Livre des Anglois* p. 5; *Registre du Conseil* in *Calvini Opera* p. xvii, p. 491
5 Zürich Letters (Cambridge 1852–5), i, p. 77
6 Shephard, pp. 26–7, 116–8
7 Marshall, *Mary I*, pp. 135–45
8 Laing, v, pp. 473–94
9 Laing, v, pp. 501–36
10 Laing, v, pp. 21–468
11 Knox, *History*, i, p. 137
12 Knox, *History*, i, p. 190 and note 1; Marshall, *Mary of Guise* pp. 215–7
13 Knox, *History*, i, pp. 127–8; Marshall, *Mary of Guise*, pp. 217–9
14 *Livre des Anglois* p. 13; Dickens, p. 186
15 *Livre des Anglois*, p. 15
16 Ridley, p. 307
17 Laing, vi, p. 11
18 Laing, vi, p. 15; Knox, *History*, i, pp. 282–7
19 Laing, vi, p. 890
20 Knox, *History*, i, pp. 152–60; ii, pp. 255–6; Donaldson, *Scottish Historical Documents*, pp. 117–18; Donaldson, *James V to James VII*, pp. 91–2
21 Knox, *History*, i, pp. 153–9; Donaldson, *James V to James VII*, pp. 92–3; Ridley, pp. 315–6
22 Knox, *History*, i, pp. 161–2
23 Laing, vi, p. 23
24 Knox, *History*, i, pp. 163–80; Laing, vi, p. 24; Marshall, *Mary of Guise*, pp. 221–4
25 Knox, *History*, i, p. 181; Marshall, *Mary of Guise*, p. 224

CHAPTER TEN: NEGOTIATIONS WITH ENGLAND

1 Knox, *History*, i, p. 181
2 Knox, *History*, i, pp. 181–2; Ridley, pp. 324–6
3 Laing, vi, pp. 21–7
4 Ridley, p. 350
5 Marshall, *Mary of Guise*, pp. 226–7; Pitscottie, ii, pp. 152–9

6 Knox, *History*, i, pp. 187–92; *Calendar of State Papers (Foreign Series) of the reign of Elizabeth 1558–89* ed. J. Stevenson *et al* (London 1863–1950, hereafter cited as *CSP Foreign*), 344; Marshall, *Mary of Guise* pp. 227–8, 344; Michael Lynch, 'John Knox, Minister of Edinburgh and Commissioner of the Kirk' in *British Reformations*, pp. 242–63

7 *CSP Foreign*, i, p. 973

8 Laing, vi, pp. 45–7

9 Laing, vi, pp. 47–50

10 Laing, vi, p. 55

11 Knox, *History*, i, pp. 196–204

12 Laing, vi, pp. 56–8

13 Laing, vi, p. 61

14 Laing, vi, pp. 59–61; Knox, *History*, i, p. 295; McCrie, pp. 141–2

15 A. Teulet, *Papiers d'Etat, Pièces et Documents relatifs à l'Histoire de l'Ecosse au XVIe siècle* (Paris 1851–60), i, p. 333; Knox, *History*, i, pp. xliv, 198 and 198 n2

16 *CSP Foreign 1558–9*, p. 509; Ministère des Affaires Etrangères, Paris, Angl. Reg. xv, pp. 40–1

17 *CSP Foreign 1559–60*, p. 36

18 Laing, vi, p. 74

19 Knox, *History*, i, pp. lxxxviii–cix

20 Knox, *History*, i, pp. 249–55; *Calendar of Scottish State Papers relating to Mary, Queen of Scots* ed. J. Bain *et al.* (Edinburgh 1898–1952, hereafter cited as *CSP Scottish*), i, p. 255; *CSP Foreign 1559–60* pp. 46–7; Donaldson, *James V to James VII*, p. 97

21 Laing, vi, pp. 89–94

22 *The State Papers and Letters of Sir Ralph Sadler* ed. A. Clifford (Edinburgh 1809), ii, p. 70

CHAPTER ELEVEN: THE SCOTTISH REFORMATION

1 Knox, *History*, i, pp. 260–5; Donaldson, *James V to James VII*, pp. 98–9; Ridley, pp. 355–8

2 Knox, *History*, i, pp. 265–71

3 Laing, vi, p. 85

4 Laing, vi, pp. 87, 105–6

5 *Register of the Kirk Session of St Andrews* (Scottish History Society 1889–90), pp. 1–18; Knox, *History*, i, pp. 277–8; Donaldson, *Scottish Reformation*, pp. 29–50; Ridley, pp. 366–72

6 Knox, *History*, i, pp. 277–8

7 Laing, vi, p. 27
8 Knox, *History*, i, pp. 280–1; *CSP Foreign 1559–60*, pp. 295, 313; *Diurnal of Occurrents*, p. 55; Marshall, *Mary of Guise* pp. 242–4
9 Knox, *History*, i, pp. 301–8; Donaldson, *Scottish Historical Documents* pp. 119–20; Maryshall, *Mary of Guise*, pp. 245–6, 256; Jasper Ridley, *Elizabeth I* (London 1987), pp. 102–4; J. E. Neale, *Queen Elizabeth* (London 1934), pp. 91–110
10 Knox, *History*, i, pp. 312–3; *CSP Foreign 1558–9*, ii, pp. 105, 1088; iii, pp. 44–164; *CSP Scottish*, i, pp. 737 ff.
11 Knox, *History*, i, p. 319; *CSP Foreign 1558–9*, pp. 604–5; Marshall, *Mary of Guise*, pp. 239–41, 249–54
12 *Two Missions of Jacques de la Brosse* ed. Gladys Dickinson (Scottish History Society 1942), pp. 105–6; Marshall, *Mary of Guise*, p. 258
13 *Diurnal of Occurrents*, p. 277; Ministère des Affaires Etrangères, Angl. Reg. xv, pp. 112–4; Pitscottie, ii, p. 171; *CSP Foreign 1560–1*, pp. 116–26; Marshall, *Mary of Guise*, pp. 259–66
14 Donaldson, *Scottish Historical Documents*, pp. 120–3
15 Knox, *History*, i, p. 335
16 Donaldson, *Scottish Historical Documents*, pp. 124–6
17 Knox, *History*, ii, pp. 280–35; i, pp. 343, 351–2; Donaldson, *Scottish Historical Documents*, pp. 126–34; Donaldson, *Scottish Reformation*, pp. 58–63, 78–97, 111–6
18 Donaldson, *Scottish Reformation*, pp. 63–4, 75; Marshall, *Virgins and Viragos*, pp. 124–41
19 Knox, *History*, i, pp. 351–2; Donaldson, *James V to James VII*, pp. 141–3
20 *Extracts from the Records of the Burgh of Edinburgh 1403–1589* (Edinburgh 1869–82), iii, pp. 63–76, 87–99, 104–36, 154–78, 210–60; Ridley, pp. 380–1
21 Knox, *History*, i, p. 351
22 Laing, vi, pp. lxiii, 124–5; *Calvini Opera*, xviii, pp. 434–6
23 Knox, *History*, i, p. 351; Antonia Fraser, *Mary, Queen of Scots* (London 1969), pp. 106–7

CHAPTER TWELVE: THE RETURN OF
MARY, QUEEN OF SCOTS

1 Knox, *History*, i, p. 351; Fraser, pp. 116–7
2 J. A. Froude, *History of England from the fall of Wolsey to the Defeat of the Spanish Armada* (London 1862), vi, p. 443; *CSP Foreign 1560–1*, p. 472; Fraser, pp. 111–2; Rosalind K. Marshall, *Queen of*

Scots (Edinburgh 1986), pp. 46–55

3 R. K. Hannay, 'The Earl of Arran and Queen Mary' in *Scottish Historical Review*, xviii (1920), pp. 258–76; J. Durkan, 'James, third Earl of Arran: The Hidden Years' in *Scottish Historical Review*, lxv (1986), pp. 154–66; Knox, *History*, i, pp. 351–2

4 Knox, *History*, i, pp. 354–5; Maurice Lee, *James Stewart, Earl of Moray* (New York 1953), pp. 73–9

5 *CSP Scottish*, i, p. 983

6 Knox, *History*, ii, pp. 7–8

7 David Hay Fleming, *Mary, Queen of Scots*, (London 1898), pp. 46–7, 257; Knox, *History*, ii, p. 8; Fraser, pp. 135–9; Marshall, *Queen of Scots*, pp. 59–60

8 Knox, *History*, ii, p. 9

9 Knox, *History*, ii, pp. 9–13; Ridley, p. 391

10 Knox, *History*, ii, p. 21; *Diurnal of Occurrents*, pp. 67–9

11 Knox, *History*, ii, pp. 13–20

12 Laing, vi, pp. 127–9, 136–7

13 Laing, vi, p. 131

14 Laing, vi, pp. 129–39

15 Laing, vi, pp. 126, 133–5

16 Knox, *History*, ii, pp. 23–4

17 Donaldson, *Scottish Reformation*, pp. 69–71; Knox, *History*, ii, pp. 28–9; Gordon Donaldson, *Accounts of the Collectors of Thirds of Benefices* (Scottish History Society 1949), pp. x–xxxv

18 Knox, *History*, ii, pp. 32–3; Lee, *Moray*, p. 97; *CSP Scottish*, i, pp. 561–4, 602–3

CHAPTER THIRTEEN: CONFRONTATION

1 *CSP Foreign*, iv, p. 278; Fraser, pp. 152–66

2 Knox, *History*, ii, pp. 58–63; Donaldson, *James V to James VII*, pp. 108–112; Lee, *Moray*, pp. 105–8

3 N. Winzet, *Certain Tractates together with the Book of Four Score Three Questions* ed J. Harrison (Edinburgh and London 1888); Ridley, pp. 408–11; McCrie, pp. 191–2

4 J. H. Pollen, *Papal Negotiations with Mary, Queen of Scots* (Edinburgh 1901), pp. 72–5, 103–4, 113–39, 144–8

5 Ridley, p. 384

6 Knox, *History*, ii, p. 57; Laing, vi, pp. 176–84, 216

7 Knox, *History*, ii, pp. 43–6

8 Fraser, p. 169; Ridley, p. 425

9 Knox, *History*, ii, pp. 71–4
10 Knox, *History*, ii, pp. 76–8; Lee, *Moray*, p. 117; Ridley, pp. 425–6
11 Knox, *History*, ii, pp. 79–80, 85
12 Knox, *History*, ii, p. 80
13 Knox, *History*, ii, pp. 82–4
14 Knox, *History*, ii, pp. 88–92; R. Pitcairn, *Criminal Trials in Scotland* (Edinburgh 1883), i, pp. 434–5
15 Knox, *History*, ii, pp. 92–3

CHAPTER FOURTEEN: THE FALL OF THE QUEEN

1 Knox, *History*, ii, pp. 91–100
2 Laing, vi, p. lxv; *CSP Scottish*, i, p. 1163
3 *CSP Scottish*, ii, p. 67; Laing, vi, p. lxiv; Ridley, pp. 432–3
4 Knox, *History*, ii, pp. 107–34
5 Sir James Melville of Halhill, *Memoirs*, ed. F. Steuart (Edinburgh 1929), p. 92
6 Melville, *Memoirs*, p. 82; Simon Adams, 'The Release of Lord Darnley and the Failure of Amity' in *Mary Stewart, Queen in Three Kingdoms* (Glasgow 1987), pp. 122–9
7 Adams, pp. 129–44; Jane Dawson, 'Mary, Queen of Scots, Lord Darnley and Anglo-Scots relations in 1565' in *International History Review*, viii (1986), pp. 1–24; Caroline Bingham, *Darnley* (London 1995), pp. 65–87
8 National Archives of Scotland, SP13/88
9 Knox, *History*, ii, pp. 156–8; Bingham, pp. 102–8; Fraser, pp. 230–2
10 Knox, *History*, ii, pp. 159–60; Bingham, pp. 113–4
11 Knox, *History*, ii, pp. 156–73; Lee, *Moray*, pp. 135–52; Donaldson, *James V to James VII*, pp. 118–9; Bingham, pp. 114–5
12 Claude Nau, *The History of Mary Stewart* ed. J. Stevenson (Edinburgh 1883), pp. 3–16; Fraser, pp. 247–8, 258, 260; Ridley, pp. 446–7; Lee, *Moray*, p. 162; Hay Fleming, pp. 380–1
13 Knox, *History*, i, p. 44, 112; *Diurnal of Occurrents*, pp. 89–98; Melville, *Memoirs*, pp. 60–1; Laing, vi, pp. 437–40, 483–4; Ridley, pp. 447–50; Fraser, pp. 249–58
14 Laing, vi, pp. 437–40; Ridley, pp. 460–4
15 Knox, *History*, ii, pp. 193–212; Bingham, pp. 145–201; Fraser, pp. 259–333; Donaldson, *Mary, Queen of Scots* (London 1974), pp. 91–120; Laing, vi, p. 552
16 J. Stevenson, *Selections from unpublished manuscripts . . . illustrating the reign of Mary, Queen of Scots* (Glasgow 1837), pp. 219–23; R. Keith,

History of the Affairs of Church and State in Scotland (Edinburgh 1844–50), ii, pp. 684–94; Ridley pp. 470–1

CHAPTER FIFTEEN: THE DEATH OF KNOX

1 Laing, vi, p. lxvii
2 Knox, *History*, ii, p. 216; Keith, ii, pp. 706–12; Fraser, pp. 344–7; Lee, *Moray*, pp. 201–6
3 Ridley, pp. 474–82; Fraser, pp. 363–8
4 Laing, vi, p. 561
5 Gordon Donaldson, *The First Trial of Mary, Queen of Scots* (London 1969), pp. 106–230; Lee, *Moray*, pp. 235–52
6 Neville Williams, *A Tudor Tragedy: Thomas Howard, Fourth Duke of Norfolk* (London 1964), pp. 126–88; Fraser, pp. 409–31; Donaldson, *First Trial*, pp. 162–6
7 Laing, vi, p. 568
8 Lee, *Moray*, pp. 273–4; George Buchanan, *History of Scotland* (Edinburgh 1751), ii, pp. 570–2
9 Ridley, p. 485; *Lettres, Instructions et Mémoires de Marie Stuart, Reine d'Ecosse* ed. A. Labanoff (London 1844), iii, p. 354; R. Bannatyne, *Memorials of Transactions in Scotland 1569–1573* (Edinburgh 1836), p. 289–90; Laing, vi, 570–1
10 Gordon Donaldson, *All the Queen's Men* (London 1983), pp. 83–116; Ridley pp. 490–4
11 Laing, vi, p. 568; Bannatyne, 62
12 *CSP Scottish*, iii, pp. 183–213; Bannatyne, 70–81; Ridley, pp. 494–6; *Diurnal of Occurrents*, 197
13 Bannatyne, 91–100; *Diurnal of Occurrents*, p. 201
14 Bannatyne, p. 111; Ridley, p. 498–9
15 Bannatyne, pp. 113–9
16 J. Melville, *The Autobiography and Diary of Mr James Melville, Minister of Kilrenny in Fife* ed. R. Pitcairn (Edinburgh 1842), pp. 26–58; Bannatyne, p. 255
17 Williams, pp. 195–205; Fraser, pp. 424–9; P.J. Holmes, 'Mary Stewart in England' in *Queen in Three Kingdoms*, pp. 202–5
18 *Thirds of Benefices*, pp. xxxii–xxxiii; Melville, *Diary*, pp. 31–2; Bannatyne, pp. 222–3
19 Laing, vi, p. 617
20 Laing, vi, pp. 619–20
21 Laing, vi, pp. 479–520, 617–8
22 Bannatyne, p. 263; Laing, vi, p. 633; J. Cameron Lees, *St Giles*,

Edinburgh (Edinburgh 1889), p. 157; A. I. Dunlop, *The Churches of Edinburgh* (Scottish Record Society 1988), p. 15

23 Laing, vi, p. 632; Bannatyne, p. 264
24 For Knox's last days, Bannatyne, pp. 279–81; Laing, vi, pp. 653–4; John Wilkinson, 'The Medical History of John Knox' in *Proceedings of the Royal College of Physicians of Edinburgh*, xxviii, no 1 (January 1998), pp. 81–110

CONCLUSION

1 Laing, vi, pp. liii–lvii
2 Donaldson, *All the Queen's Men*, pp. 121–31; *CSP Scottish*, iv, p. 666 ff
3 Laing, vi, pp. lxiii–lxxv
4 Laing, iii, p. 325; Ridley, pp. 538–47
5 Laing, vi, pp. lxix–lxxiii; McCrie, pp. 285–7
6 Laing, vi, p. lxxxiii

Index